For Greg, Stephanie, Marisa, and Corinne Stubbs

Carson-Iceberg

Wilderness

Jeffrey P. Schaffer

Wilderness Press
Berkeley

Acknowledgments

Foremost, I would like to thank Jim Ryan, a former associate fishery biologist with the Department of Fish and Game, for his very significant contributions to this book both in the original edition and in this new edition. With his imput, this book now has first-rate coverage of the area's trout—where they are, how they are managed, and how you catch them.

Steve Felte, General Manager of the Calaveras County Water District, answered all my questions about the North Fork Stanislaus River Hydroelectric Development Project.

Gladys Smith, an outstanding Sierra botanist with a guide to vegetation of the Lake Tahoe area, identified one perplexing, though fairly common, plant in the Carson-Iceberg Wilderness, the western mugwort.

Peter Browning gave his expertise on the origin of Sierra Nevada place names.

For the first edition the following people reviewed part or all of the manuscript: Bruce Ungari (Calaveras Ranger District), Steve Brougher and Bob Riede (Summit R.D.), Jack Carlson and Neil Botts (Carson R.D.), and Jim White (Calif. Dept. of Fish & Game).

During the summers of 1990 and '91, when I worked on the glacial history of the Stanislaus River drainage, I extracted cores from a series of lakes, ponds and bogs to determine when they came into being. Aiding me in this strenuous task were Eric Edlund, Eddie Matzger, Ken Ng and Rudy Goldstein. During this research, Greg and Stephanie Stubbs allowed me unrestricted use of their mountain home as a base camp, which made the physical hardships of my daily work far more bearable.

Hiking alone in the wilderness can be lonely and at times dangerous, and I thank those who've at times accompanied me, particularly on summit ascents: Ken Ng, Steve Rieser, John Mills and Rudy Goldstein.

Finally, this book project and my two-summer glacial research have been very stressful, as most mountain field work tends to be, and I thank my wife, Bonnie, and my daughter, Mary Anne, who endured my long absences from home.

First edition August, 1987
SECOND EDITION May, 1992
Copyright © 1987, 1992 by Jeffrey P. Schaffer

Chapter 5 (Fish) by James H. Ryan; fish data in Chapters 7-18 also by James Ryan

Photographs by the author
Topographic map (in pocket) revised and updated by the author, based on U.S. Geological Survey maps

Library of Congress Card Catalog Number 92-10046
International Standard Book Number 0-89997-135-0

Manufactured in the United States of America

Published by Wilderness Press
2440 Bancroft Way
Berkeley, CA 94704
(510) 843-8080

Write for free catalog

Cover: **Bull Run Peak above Sword Lake**
Title page: **The Iceberg (left) and the East Carson canyon, viewed from the summit of Stanislaus Peak**

Library of Congress Cataloging-in-Publication Data

Schaffer, Jeffrey P.
    Carson-Iceberg Wilderness / Jeffrey P. Schaffer. — 2nd ed.
        p.   cm.
    Includes bibliographical references and index.
    ISBN 0-89997-135-0
    1. Hiking—California—Carson-Iceberg Wilderness—Guidebooks.
    2. Natural history—California—Carson-Iceberg Wilderness-
    -Guidebooks. 3. Trails—California—Carson-Iceberg Wilderness-
    -Guidebooks. 4. Fishing—California—Carson-Iceberg Wilderness-
    -Guidebooks. 5. Carson-Iceberg Wilderness (Calif.)—Guidebooks.
    I. Title.
    GV199.42.C22C377 1992
    917.94'4—dc20   92-10046
                                               CIP

Contents

Part One
Introductory Chapters

Carson Falls

Chapter 1   Introducing Carson-Iceberg Wilderness

The Wilderness and its Adjacent Lands

Writing about the Sierra Nevada in *My First Summer in the Sierra,* John Muir stated, "Probably more free sunshine falls on this majestic range than on any other in the world I've ever seen or heard of. It has the brightest weather, brightest glacier-polished rocks, the greatest abundance of irised spray from its glorious waterfalls, the brightest forests of silver firs and silver pines, more starshine, moonshine, and perhaps more crystal-shine than any other mountain chain, and its countless mirror lakes, having more light poured into them, glow and spangle most. . . . Well may the Sierra be named, not the Snowy Range, but the Range of Light."

While most of the Sierra, particularly the High Sierra, fits this description, the area covered by Carson-Iceberg Wilderness does not. This wilderness is a relatively dark spot in an otherwise lake-blessed range of light-colored granitic rock. There are few lakes to reflect the strong light of the mostly sunny summer days, and much of the granite that is here is buried under dark volcanic peaks and ridges. If that's a drawback, there's also some good news: although the wilderness lies between the Sierra's two most heavily visited recreation lands, Yosemite National Park and the Lake Tahoe basin, Carson-Iceberg Wilderness and its adjacent lands see relatively few visitors.

Most of the visitors to the high-mountain lands between Highways 4 and 108 congregate in campgrounds at three readily accessible reservoirs near the wilderness: Lake Alpine and Spicer Meadow Reservoir, reached via Highway 4, and Pinecrest Lake, reached via Highway 108. Another magnet for anglers, who probably make up the bulk of the users outside the wilderness, is the canyon of the Clark Fork of the Stanislaus River, just off Highway 108.

This moderate-size Federal wilderness is about 251 square miles (160,871 acres) in size, but not all the area is equally used. On a given summer night, most of the campers will occupy small areas of the wilderness not amounting to more than 2 square miles—mostly at campsites bordering Sword, Lost, Rock, Bull Run, Heiser and Asa lakes and campsites around Soda Springs Guard Station, deep in the canyon of East Fork Carson River. Moderately used campsites exist at a few other places, particularly Bull, Poison and Tamarack lakes, Commissioners Camp, Connells Cow Camp, and Hiram and Clark Fork meadows. That leaves most of the wilderness—about 98% of it—for seekers of solitude. If you haven't found the peaceful High Sierra solitude John Muir so reveled in over a century ago, perhaps you've been visiting the wrong parks and wildernesses of the Sierra Nevada; try the canyons and valleys of Carson-Iceberg Wilderness.

Four Guidebooks in One

This guidebook can be thought of as four guidebooks. First and foremost, it is a guide to every mappable trail in and around Carson-Iceberg Wilderness. Most of these are official, maintained trails, but a few are *de facto* or rarely maintained at best. The book is also a guide to many cross-country routes, some so popular that they have become almost like trails.

This book is also as an outdoor course in the natural history of the area. Learning natural history increases one's awareness and understanding of the terrain one travels through. Many hikers and equestrians come to the High Sierra year after year without learning more natural history than the identification of a few prominent tree species. I've provided general introductions to the area's geology (Chapter 3) and to its plants and animals (Chapter 4), which serve as a foundation for comprehending and treasuring the natural history described in some detail along the routes.

Third, this is a fishing guide, for Sierra trout are the primary lure for many visitors. Not being a fisherman, I gave the task of writing Chapter 5 to a person highly qualified to do so, Jim Ryan, of the California Department of Fish and Game. He not only gives practical advice about fishing the Carson-Iceberg country, he also gives a sound appreciation for the natural history of its fish. Ryan has also added many notes about fish in Chapters 7–18.

Fourth, this is a climbing and mountaineering guide. Along the routes, I mention some Class 5 (difficult, roped) climbing routes. However, far more people are interested in finding the easiest route up a peak than are interested in finding the hardest route up a cliff. For them, I offer dozens of suggestions, since perhaps nowhere else in the Sierra is there an area of comparable size that has so many readily attainable summits as Carson-Iceberg Wilderness.

Using This Guidebook

The "meat" of this guidebook is Part Two, twelve chapters that cover the area's trails and cross-country routes. I refer to each hike (or ride, if you're on horseback) as a "route." Not all the routes are along trails. For example, Chapter 12's Route WC-4 contains segments of road, trail and cross-country travel.

Each chapter is centered around a trailhead or a group of close-together trailheads.

Most visitors stay for just a short while, usually at just one campground, and if they're interested in hiking or riding, they'll want to know all the routes available in their vicinity.

Each route has a two-letter code that is the same for all the routes in a given chapter. These two letters refer to a main feature near the trailhead. For example, the code in Chapter 7 is **SM**, for **S**picer **M**eadows Road/Reservoir, and the code in Chapter 8 is **LA**, for **L**ake **A**lpine. The routes shown on this book's topographic map have these markings, which permit you to immediately determine what chapter and route number describe any stretch of trail or cross-country route appearing on the map.

This topographic map shows both distances between points along a route and elevations at those points. Hence you can calculate the length of the route you want to do as well as estimate the amount of ascending and descending encountered along it. At the start of each route, I list the mileages to all the major points on it. The topographic map is a composite of several U.S. Geological Survey 15' topographic maps, corrected and updated after very extensive observations in the field.

The Twelve Route Chapters

If you're new to the area, you may not know what part to visit first. The following synopses of the twelve route chapters should give you an idea of what to expect.

Chapter 7: Spicer Meadow The primary interests in this area are the reservoirs, not the trails. Anglers predominate. The newer Spicer Meadow Reservoir was opened to the public in 1991, and it could become a popular fishing area for those with small motor boats. Route SM-4 provides a relatively easy way in to the reservoir's east end, which unfortunately can be a mud flat in August or later. The most popular hike is Route SM-3, to Rock Lake. It's heavily overfished, but is great for swimming.

Chapter 8: Lake Alpine The Lake Alpine Recreation Area has the most campgrounds of any area in this book. Still, they are not enough, for the area is very popular. Fortunately, there's an overflow campground. Most folks seem content to fish, swim, boat or sunbathe around the lake. Short trails to Osborne Point and Inspiration Point offer fine views of the local area. Route LA-6 provides a

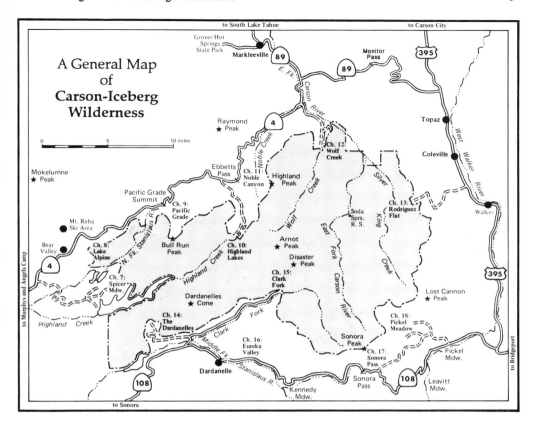

A General Map
of
**Carson-Iceberg
Wilderness**

0   5   10 miles

to South Lake Tahoe

to Carson City

Grover Hot
Springs
State Park

Markleeville 89

Monitor
Pass

395

89

E. Fk.

Carson River

Raymond
★ Peak

4

Topaz

West Walker River

Ch. 12:
Wolf
Creek

Noble Creek

Coleville

Mokelumne
★ Peak

Ebbetts
Pass

Ch. 11:
Noble
Canyon

Highland
★ Peak

Silver Creek

Pacific Grade
Summit

Ch. 9:
Pacific
Grade

Ch. 13:
Rodriguez
Flat

Walker

Mt. Reba
Ski Area

Soda
Sprs.
R. S.

King Creek

Bear
Valley

Ch. 8:
Lake
Alpine

N. Fk. Stanislaus R.

Bull Run
Peak

Ch. 10:
Highland
Lakes

Arnot
★ Peak

East Fork

4

to Murphys and Angels Camp

Wolf Creek

Disaster
★ Peak

395

Ch. 7:
Spicer
Mdw.

Highland Creek

Ch. 15:
Clark
Fork

Lost Cannon
★ Peak

Dardanelles
★ Cone

Fork

Carson River

Ch. 18:
Pickel
Meadow

Highland   Creek

Ch. 14:
The
Dardanelles

Clark Fork

Ch. 16:
Eureka
Valley

Sonora
Peak

Pickel
Mdw.

to Bridgeport

Middle Fk.

Ch. 17:
Sonora
Pass

Dardanelle

Stanislaus R.

108

Kennedy
Mdw.

Sonora
Pass

108

Leavitt
Mdw.

to Sonora

Road 7N17 descending Slide Rock

long way in to Rock Lake and the east end of Spicer Meadow Reservoir, but these are more easily reached along Chapter 7 routes.

Chapter 9: Pacific Grade Bull Run and Heiser lakes are two justifiably popular, easily reached goals in this lake-deficient landscape between Highways 4 and 108. Expect a lot of company on summer weekends. In Pacific Valley most of the campers seem content to fish the adjacent creek, so trails receive only light use. The Bull Run Creek, Milk Ranch and Weiser trails pass through generally viewless canyons, but they offer you ready access to three peaks with exceptional views: Bull Run, Lookout and Peep Sight.

Chapter 10: Highland Lakes These popular fishing lakes lie on a picturesque subalpine flat between Hiram and Folger peaks. For day hikers, this is perhaps the best area to visit. I describe 10 routes, more than in any other chapter, and most can be done as day hikes. Popular though unofficial routes ascend Hiram and Folger peaks, Hiram offering premier summit views. Asa and Bull lakes, reached from other trailheads also, offer lakeside backcountry camping. Backpackers can descend the canyons of Highland, Arnot and Disaster creeks, or tackle the relatively isolated central and upper reaches of the giant East Fork Carson River canyon.

Chapter 11: Noble Canyon This short chapter describes access to Noble Lake via the Pacific Crest and Noble Canyon trails. This windswept lake, lying just outside the wilderness, is used more than it deserves to be, for the lake is not handsome and camping space by it is limited. Still, the lake serves as a base for side trips to Asa and Bull lakes and to Highland and Silver peaks—all worthy goals.

Route NC-3's Peak 10,824

Route RF-1's Silver King Creek

Chapter 12: Wolf Creek The most popular route to attractive Bull Lake is from the southern Wolf Creek Meadows trailhead. This lake is a good goal for backpackers, particularly during the week, when trail use is generally light. The four remaining routes, equally suited for hikers and equestrians, visit the lower and middle sections of the East Fork Carson River canyon, the Sierra Nevada's largest east-side canyon. The middle and upper parts of the canyon contain some of the most dramatic and most isolated scenery to be found in the wilderness.

Chapter 13: Rodriguez Flat The only pack station serving the eastern part of wilderness, Little Antelope Pack Station, operates from this high-elevation flat. The trails radiating from the flat are used mostly by equestrians. Still, this is one of my favorite areas. It has

plenty of creekside campsites, three inviting lakes, and the two best technical-climbing spots in the wilderness. Route RF-6 takes you to Whitecliff Lake, the most remote lake in the wilderness. Poison and Tamarack lakes receive more use, and both can accommodate quite a few people. You might see a large group at either lake. More likely, particularly on weekdays, you'll have the lake to yourself. This high-elevation sagebrush country is prime summer-grazing land, so expect to see lots of cattle, particularly down in the valleys.

Chapter 14: The Dardanelles The foremost attractions in this area are Sword and Lost lakes, which for most hikers are an easy hour's walk. No wonder they get dozens of visitors on sunny summer weekends. Fishing there is poor, but diving, swimming and sunbathing are excellent. The same holds true for lightly visited Twin Meadows and Burgson lakes, which require cross-country skills to reach. The Dardanelles, Dardanelles Butte and Dardanelles Cone offer some intimidating and some not-so-intimidating climbing routes. The Dardanelles give you a matchless view of the low, granitic, glacier-scoured lands containing this area's western reservoirs (the Chapter 7 area).

Chapter 15: Clark Fork Due to the presence of summer camps in the area, the heaviest trail users here are children, some on foot, some on horseback. This area is well suited for equestrians, since all trails lead up deep, forested canyons to distant crests. Views are generally few and far between, though you can make fairly strenuous cross-country excursions to the summits of Dardanelles Cone, Arnot Peak and Disaster Peak. The area has only one real lake, Boulder Lake, which is rather small and mostly shallow, but nevertheless is fine goal for a day hike.

Chapter 16: Eureka Valley The short nature trail to Columns of the Giants offers a diversion for folks camped in this area. However, the abundance of campgrounds and campers attests to the popularity of fishing in adjacent Middle Fork Stanislaus River, and hiking definitely takes a back seat.

Chapter 17: Sonora Pass This high pass provides access to the highest peaks in and near Carson-Iceberg Wilderness. Sonora Peak is the most accessible and also offers the best views. Generally, this area is too high and too windswept to have good camping potential. The area's only lake, Wolf Creek Lake, is fishless and too cold for swimming. The Pacific Crest Trail, both north and south from the pass, can be treacherous, so check with the Forest Service before you start hiking along it. I definitely discourage equestrians there. Finally, short trails to Sardine and Leavitt falls are suited more for the sightseer than the avid hiker.

Chapter 18: Pickel Meadow This is an area for the pathfinder, since trail tread is not always present. The route up Wolf Creek

Route PM-1's Chango Lake

canyon offers relatively easy access to the upper, subalpine end of the great East Fork Carson River canyon. The route up Silver Creek canyon offers a side trip to pleasant Chango Lake. Onward, you can enter the upper Silver King drainage for superb solitary camping.

The Climate

As John Muir noted in his first summer in the Sierra, the weather is quite nice indeed. From late June through mid-September it is *usually* not too hot or too cold, the days typically warming to the mid-70s to low 80s, the nights typically cooling to the 40s. At the lower elevations, the temperature may actually soar into the 90s, but this is uncommon. At the higher elevations, mainly above 9000 feet, the temperature may rise only into the 60s. However, with increasing elevation, the temperature usually seems warmer than it actually is. From late August on, expect some nights to drop to about the freezing level.

Most days are dry, but there can be isolated thunderstorms, most likely near the Sierra crest or well east of it. Such storms can cause a brief afternoon downpour. Also, you can get a week of stormy weather. Especially if you are backpacking, be prepared for bad weather, although chances are you won't have it. Major snow storms usually occur before late June and after mid-September and are very unlikely during the summer.

Extent of Hiking/Riding Season

Road Conditions

Highway 4 is kept open year-round as far east as Route 207, which lies between Lake Alpine and the ski-oriented community of Bear Valley. This short paved road climbs up to a popular ski area, Mt. Reba. Highway 108 is kept open year-round to the Cow Creek winter-sports staging area, above the settlement of Strawberry. On Highway 4, there is also a winter-sports staging area just east of the Mt. Reba Ski Area road. Snowmobiles are allowed on both highways, to the regret of cross-country skiers.

In years of light snowfall, such as 1977 and '87, Highways 4 and 108 open over the Sierra crest passes as early as May 1. However, in a typical year, CALTRANS usually has to fight to clear a snow-free path over Ebbetts and Sonora passes in time for Memorial Day, and in years of heavy snowfall the passes may not open until late June.

Other roads open at variable times. Paved, relatively low Clark Fork Road is usually open in time for Memorial Day, as is Spicer Meadow Road. Until the new Spicer Meadow Reservoir is ready for public use—about 1990—the last part of this road will stay closed. After construction in the area is done, the entire road will be paved and then it will re-open. In contrast to these two roads, unpaved Highland Lakes Road, climbing steep, north-facing slopes between 8100 and 8700 feet, is the last to open. Don't expect to get through before mid-July. All the other unpaved roads typically open by the Fourth of July.

Towns and Resorts

This book is aimed primarily at hikers and secondarily at equestrians who visit this area in late spring, summer, or early fall. Both groups typically stay in campgrounds rather than resorts or motels. Still, if you've decided not to rough it, you ought to know what's available. If you head east up Highway 4, you'll find lodging and vacation rentals in Angels Camp, Murphys, Arnold, and Dorrington. These, however, are relatively distant from the wilderness. Closer to it is Bear Valley Road, which leads into the ski village of Bear Valley. Year-round you can rent a condo or home or can stay at Bear Valley Lodge (toll-free number: 800-794-3866). Bear Valley Lodge is a fairly large complex with a restaurant, deli, sports shop and other facilities. Also here is Red Dog Lodge (209-753-2344), which is open most of the year except from about May through mid-June and mid-September through October. For more rustic accommodations close to the wilderness during the "summer" season, try a cabin at Lake Alpine Lodge (209-753-6358), which stands just above the lakeshore. These three lodges are suited for those hiking from Spicer Meadow

Road, Lake Alpine or Pacific Grade (Chapters 7 through 9).

The Highland Lakes area, covered in Chapter 10, is quite remote from any place of lodging, but if you're willing to drive for at least ½ hour, you could stay at the preceding places or at East Fork Resort, mentioned next.

For Ebbetts Pass, Noble Canyon or Wolf Creek Meadows (Chapters 11 and 12), your nearest accommodations are at East Fork Resort (916-694-2229), which has cabins, a trailer park, and a small store. This resort is located 2½ miles north of the Highway 4/89 junction and 2¼ miles south of Markleeville. For Rodriguez Flat (Chapter 13), you'll find several motels, none fancy, in Walker.

The lower part of Highway 108, like the lower part of Highway 4, abounds in motels and lodges, though after Mi-Wuk Village they're rather sporadic up to Pinecrest and Strawberry. Beyond Strawberry you drive about 18 miles to a junction with the Clark Fork Road (Chapters 14 and 15). The road could use a nearby resort. The closest one, which caters to anglers in campgrounds along Highway 108 (Chapter 16), is Dardanelles Resort (209-965-4355). It has cabins, a motel unit, a grocery store, fishing supplies (including licenses), gasoline pumps, and a restaurant and bar. Another option, at least for those who want to stay along the Middle Fork (Chapter 16) as opposed to the Clark Fork, is Kennedy Meadows Resort (209-965-3900). You reach it by driving 5 miles past Dardanelles Resort, then branching right on a spur road and driving one mile to road's end. It is equipped much like Dardanelles Resort, but it also has a pack station. Most pack trips go into adjacent Emigrant Wilderness, south of Highway 108, but arrangements can be made for pack trips into Carson-Iceberg Wilderness.

For hikers in the Sonora Pass area (Chapter 17), Kennedy Meadows Resort is the nearest choice. In former years one could drive about 7¾ miles east down to Leavitt Meadows Lodge (no phone), which had a few cabins, a store and a cafe. This lodge also served folks in the Pickel Meadow area (Chapter 18). Perhaps some day this lodge may once again open.

Campgrounds

On many summer weekends most of the campgrounds are likely to be full, so if possible, avoid the Friday afternoon to Sunday afternoon crowds. You are most likely to find a desirable site by arriving Sunday through Wednesday. Campgrounds range in size from a few campsites to about 100 campsites, and differ in degree of development (and in daily fee—most about $10; undeveloped camping areas are free). All campgrounds have outhouses. Those listed as developed also have trash pickup plus numbered campsites with tables and fireplace grills. The sites are relatively small, more suited for tent camping than for large RVs. Nevertheless, RVs abound. Note that none of the Forest Service campgrounds have RV hookups and that only one has an RV dump station. The nearest dump station on Highway 4 is at Calaveras Big Trees State Park (see first two entries, below), west of this book's area of coverage. You must pay a nominal day-use fee to enter the park in order to use the dump station. The best dump station on Highway 108 is ⅓ mile west of the Pinecrest Lake road, at the county refuse site. Also, there is an RV dump station at the Clark Fork Campground, where a nominal fee is charged. The following is a list of the area's campgrounds, compiled in the same order as the book's Chapters 7 through 18.

Highway 4

North Grove Campground Developed, 74 sites, at about 4680'. In Calaveras Big Trees State Park, whose entrance is along Hwy. 4 about 3 miles above Arnold. Campground is near highway, which has noisy logging-truck traffic beginning very early in the morning. Reservations are recommended. Phone MISTIX at 800-444-7275.

Oak Hollow Campground Developed, 55 sites, at about 4400'. In Calaveras Big Trees State Park (see above), about 4 miles along park road. Reservations are recommended. There are 129 family sites in these two state park campgrounds, plus one isolated group site.

Golden Torch RV Park Private, 117 sites, with RV hookups, dump station, pool, at about 4970'. Along Hwy. 4 at a pass 2.0 miles past the Calaveras Big Trees State Park entrance and 0.6 mile before Dorrington. Phone 209-795-2820.

Big Meadow Campground Developed, 68 sites, at about 6550'. Along Hwy. 4 just 0.2 mile west of Road 7N02. There is also an adjacent group campground with one site.

Stanislaus River Campground 6220'. Developed, 25 sites, at about 6210'. Along Spicer Meadow Road 7N01, 3.0 miles from Hwy. 4.

Union Reservoir Undeveloped camping area (no tap water), at about 6860'. Along Road 7N75 by reservoir's south shore.

Utica Reservoir Undeveloped camping area (no tap water), at about 6830'. Along Road 7N17 by reservoir's southwest shore.

Spicer Reservoir Campground Developed, 60 sites, at about 6670'. Near end of Spicer Meadow Reservoir Road 7N75. Also a nearby group campground along road to the dam.

Lodgepole Overflow Campground Semi-developed, about 30 sites (no official spaces), at about 7350'. Along Hwy. 4 about 1½ miles east of Bear Valley.

Silvertip Campground Developed, 23 sites, at about 7580'. At a pass along Hwy. 4 about 1 mile west of Lake Alpine.

Lake Alpine Campground Developed, 27 sites, at about 7380'. Along Hwy. 4 above west shore of Lake Alpine.

Lake Alpine Backpackers Campground Developed, 5 sites, at about 7330'. Along lake's east-shore road, about 0.2 mile from Hwy. 4. No parking for vehicles. Essentially for those hiking on the Tahoe-Yosemite Trail.

Pine Marten Campground Developed, about 33 sites, at 7340'. Along Lake Alpine's east-shore road, about ¼ mile from Hwy. 4.

Silver Valley Campground Developed, 25 sites, at 7380'. Along Lake Alpine's east-shore road, about 0.4 mile from Hwy. 4.

Mosquito Lakes Campground Semideveloped (no tap water), several sites, at about 8050'. Just west of Pacific Grade Summit at the upper Mosquito Lake.

Pacific Valley Campground Semideveloped (no tap water), about a dozen sites, at about 7540'. Spread along Pacific Valley spur road, which leaves Hwy. 4 just 1 mile beyond Pacific Grade Summit.

Hermit Valley Campground Semideveloped (no tap water), several sites, at about 7140'. Along Hwy. 4 about 1 mile east of the Mokelumne River bridge.

Bloomfield Campground Developed, 10 sites, at about 7800'. About 1 mile along Highland Lakes Road 8N01.

Highland Lakes Campground Developed, about 3 dozen sites, at about 8640'. Two areas, both near the upper Highland Lake, near the end of Road 8N01.

Silver Creek Campground Developed, 23 sites, at about 6800'. Along both sides of Hwy. 4 about 5.6 miles east of Ebbetts Pass and about 5.0 miles above the Wolf Creek Road junction.

Centerville Flat Undeveloped Camping Area Undeveloped (no tap water), about 2 dozen sites, at about 5920'. Along Hwy. 4 immediately north of and below the Wolf Creek Road junction.

Wolf Creek Meadows Undeveloped Camping Area Undeveloped (no tap water), several sites, at about 6520'. At end of Wolf Creek Road.

Markleeville Campground Developed, 10 sites, at about 5460'. Along Hwy. 89 about 0.7 mile east of Markleeville.

Highway 395

Shingle Mill Flat Campground Developed, 90 sites, at about 6030'. Along Hwy. 395 about 6 miles south of Walker.

Bootleg Campground Developed, 63 sites, at about 6440'. Along Hwy. 395 about 8⅓ miles south of Walker and 5 miles north of junction with Hwy. 108.

Chris Flat Campground Developed, 15 sites, at about 6550'. Along Hwy. 395 about 3½ miles north of junction with Hwy. 108.

Highway 108

Pinecrest Campground Developed, about 200 sites, at about 5620'. About 30 miles above Sonora. Take the Pinecrest Lake turnoff. Campground is just before the lake. Reservations are recommended! Phone MISTIX at 800-283-2267.

Meadowview Campground Developed, about 100 sites, at about 5580'. As above, take the Pinecrest Lake turnoff. Entrance is on Dodge Ridge Road, which branches right in 0.4 mile.

Pioneer Trail Group Campground Developed, 3 sites, at about 5850'. See above. Entrance is about 1¼ miles up Dodge Ridge Road.

Cascade Creek Campground Undeveloped (no tap water), 7 sites, at about 6060'. Just west of Hwy. 108. Road junction is about 10 miles beyond the Pinecrest Lake junction and about 9 miles before the Clark Fork junction.

Mill Creek Campground Semideveloped (no tap water), 17 sites, at about 6270'. Just ⅓ mile east of Hwy. 108. Road junction is about 12½ miles east of the Pinecrest Lake junction and about 6½ miles west of the Clark Fork junction.

Niagara Creek Campground Semideveloped (no tap water), several sites, at about 6560'. East of Hwy. 108. Road junction is

about 14 miles beyond the Pinecrest junction and about 5 miles before the Clark Fork junction. Go ⅓ mile east on Road 5N01, then keep left at junction, taking Road 6N24 ⅓ mile to the campground.

Fence Creek Campground Undeveloped (no tap water), 20 sites, at about 5610'. About 0.2 mile west on Road 6N06, which branches left from Clark Fork Road just 0.9 mile from Hwy. 108.

Clark Fork Campground Developed, 88 sites, at about 6090'. About 5¾ miles along the Clark Fork Road. Clark Fork Horse Campground, with 15 sites, is nearby.

Sand Flat Campground Developed, 53 sites, at about 6160'. About 6¾ miles along the Clark Fork Road.

Boulder Flat Campground Developed, 21 sites, at about 5660'. Along Hwy. 108 about 0.9 mile east of the Clark Fork Road junction.

Brightman Flat Campground Developed, 30 sites, at about 5700'. Along Hwy. 108 about 1.7 miles east of the Clark Fork Road junction.

Dardanelle Campground Developed, 28 sites, at about 5760'. Along Hwy. 108 about 2.8 miles east of the Clark Fork Road junction and across from Dardanelles Resort.

Dardanelles Resort Private resort with RV park, at about 5770'. About 0.4 mile before Stanislaus River bridge.

Pigeon Flat Walk-in Campground Semi-developed, 6 sites, at about 5960'. Along Hwy. 108 about 4.4 miles east of the Clark Fork Road junction and 1.6 miles east of Dardanelles Resort.

Eureka Valley Campground Semideveloped, 28 sites, at about 6060'. Along Hwy. 108 about 2.3 miles east of Dardanelles Resort and 2.7 miles west of Kennedy Meadow Road junction.

Baker Campground Developed, 44 sites, at about 6250'. At start of Kennedy Meadow Road, this junction being 7.8 miles east of the Clark Fork Road junction.

Deadman Campground Developed, 17 sites, at about 6280'. Just 0.6 mile along Kennedy Meadow Road.

Leavitt Meadow Campground Developed, 16 sites, at about 7150'. Along Hwy. 108 about 7.8 miles east of Sonora Pass and 7.3 miles west of Hwy. 395.

Sonora Bridge Campground Developed, 23 sites, at about 6830'. Along Hwy. 108 about 1.4 miles west of Hwy. 395.

Chapter 2   Exploring Carson-Iceberg Wilderness on Foot or Horseback

Introduction

Most of this book is devoted to trails—where they go, what they are like, what lakes, peaks or views you'll see, and what significant plants, animals or geologic formations you're likely to encounter along the trails. Although this book is aimed mainly at hikers, it should be equally useful for equestrians. This chapter offers advice and covers rules that apply to all outdoor users, regardless of their mode of travel or time of year. The first thing you must know is that to enter Carson-Iceberg Wilderness, you may need a wilderness permit.

Wilderness Permits

If you are only day hiking in the wilderness, you don't even need a permit. You need a permit only if you camp overnight in the wilderness from about April through November.

The wilderness falls under the administration of three ranger districts, and each handles wilderness permits differently. The easiest district to deal with is the **Carson Ranger District** (Toiyabe National Forest), which includes all wilderness lands east of the Sierra crest. The office is at 1536 So. Carson St., Carson City, NV 89701 (phone: 702-882-2766). Their permits are self-service, so you can fill one out on any day at any hour. You can do so at the district office or, more conveniently, at any major Carson Ranger District trailhead—no need to go out of your way.

Most folk entering the wilderness do so from Highway 4 west of Ebbetts Pass. This area is in the domain of the **Calaveras Ranger District** (Stanislaus National Forest). The office is on Highway 4 (P.O. Box 500) at Hathaway Pines, CA 95233 (phone: 209-795-1381). They do not have self-service permits at trailheads. You can write or phone for a permit, but you have to pick it up in person. You can get a permit at the office during normal business hours or arrange to pick it up after hours (it will be posted just outside the office). You can also get a permit during the summer season at the Alpine Ranger Station, on Highway 4 between Bear Valley and Lake Alpine. Besides being open on weekdays, it is open on Saturday and Sunday, although because it is staffed by volunteers, it can be closed for brief times.

9

Hiking in the backcountry entails unavoidable risk that every hiker assumes and must be aware of and respect. The fact that a trail is described in this book is not a representation that it will be safe for you. Trails vary greatly in difficulty and in the degree of conditioning and agility one needs to enjoy them safely. On some hikes routes may have changed or conditions may have deteriorated since the descriptions were written. Also trail conditions can change even from day to day, owing to weather and other factors. A trail that is safe on a dry day or for a highly conditioned, agile, properly equipped hiker may be completely unsafe for someone else or unsafe under adverse weather conditions.

You can minimize your risks on the trail by being knowledgeable, prepared and alert. There is not space in this book for a general treatise on safety in the mountains, but there are a number of good books and public courses on the subject and you should take advantage of them to increase your knowledge. Just as important, you should always be aware of your own limitations and of conditions existing when and where you are hiking. If conditions are dangerous, or if you are not prepared to deal with them safely, choose a different hike! It's better to have wasted a drive than to be the subject of a mountain rescue.

These warnings are not intended to scare you off the trails. Millions of people have safe and enjoyable hikes every year. However, one element of the beauty, freedom and excitement of the wilderness is the presence of risks that do not confront us at home. When you hike you assume those risks. They can be met safely, but only if you exercise your own independent judgment and common sense.

If you enter the wilderness from Sonora Pass or any other Highway 108 trailhead west of the pass, you'll have to contact the **Summit Ranger District** (Stanislaus National Forest). The office is immediately past the Pinecrest Lake turnoff, some 30 miles above Sonora and about 19 miles before the Clark Fork Road junction, at No. 1 Pinecrest Lake Road, Pinecrest, CA 95364 (phone: 209-965-3434). You can mail in or phone in a permit request, but except in special circumstances you'll have to pick up the permit in person. Pick it up at the office during normal business hours or after hours, using their night pickup box. If you plan to use their night pickup box, be sure to tell them when you'll be passing through.

July than around Labor Day. For the unsuspecting, it can be a bad experience. Mosquitoes are far more prevalent about this time, and they typically remain in pesky numbers through much of July. Be sure you bring insect repellent, and a tent wouldn't hurt. Also, the days are long and the sun is high, so you can get a bad sunburn—bring sun screen and dress appropriately. This applies especially to mountaineers, for higher up they encounter increasingly harmful radiation, more snow to reflect it at them, and less shade to protect them from it. This radiation—ultraviolet in particular—can be very harmful to your eyes, so generally above 9000 feet wear dark glasses and a hat.

Traveling in Early Season

In any year, your first visit to the wilderness is more likely to be around the Fourth of

Backpacking and Day Hiking

General Most of the routes in this book can be done as day hikes rather than as overnight hikes, although you may want to take more than one day to do many of them. Most folks who backpack tend to do so on weekends—typically hiking two or three hours to a campsite on a Friday evening or Saturday morning, then hiking out on Sunday afternoon. If you're in decent shape, you can reach the heart of the wilderness in no more than a long day's hike. If you want to explore the heart of the wilderness, you ought to allow at least three days. Five days is better, for you can see more terrain and do so at a more leisurely pace. Novices to backpacking can begin to learn the art by reading Thomas Winnett's *Backpacking Basics*.

Because this guidebook has an accurate, up-to-date map that gives mileages between major points, these mileages usually aren't duplicated in the text. The map also gives elevations at the major points, so you can determine the *minimum* amount of elevation gained or lost between any two points. The total amount of elevation change will be substantially greater if there are a lot of "minor" ups and downs between the two points.

In the text there are numerous instances where vertical distance in feet and horizontal distance in yards are given. The first tells you how much you will have to climb in a particular (often strenuous) stretch. The second has a more practical reason: some trail junctions and other features can be missed, particularly in early season when snow lingers. Therefore, I often identify such features by their distance from some readily recognized entity. Yards are given because they approximately equal the length of long strides; the hiker can pace off the distance when in doubt.

Your progress along a trail is often measured with respect to a prominent feature in the landscape, such as a peak above you. On this guide's topographic map, many unnamed summits are identified by an **X**, which marks the point, and a number, which gives its elevation. This guide usually refers to these high points as peaks—for example, Peak 10,824.

Some trails in this guide have sections that are potentially hard to follow. Parts of others may have early-season snow patches hiding them. In both cases, your route can usually be followed by watching for blazes or ducks that mark the trail. A *blaze* is a place on a tree trunk where someone has carved away a patch or two of bark to leave a conspicuous scar. A *duck* is one or several small rocks placed on a larger rock in such a way that the placement is obviously unnatural.

Minimal-impact hiking If thousands of hikers and equestrians carelessly traverse a mountain landscape, with its fragile soils, they are almost bound to erode it. The following suggestions are offered in the hope they will reduce your imprint on the landscape, thus keeping it attractive for those who might follow.

First, if you're healthy enough to make an outdoor trip in a wilderness area, you ought to be in good enough condition to do so on foot. Leave the horses behind. (This is not practical for most deer hunters.) Particularly in early season, when trails—especially through meadows—may be soggy, one horse can do more damage than a dozen backpackers. Also, a horse will contribute at least as much excrement as all of them, and it will do so indiscriminately, sometimes in creeks or at lakeshores. (Dogs are equally indiscriminate; moreover, they often intimidate other people. *Please* leave them at home.) Finally, a horse will selectively graze the meadows, which can cause a change in the native flora (this is a minor complaint, since the previous hordes of cattle have already altered the distribution of native species, so horses will have a minimal impact). If you're still intent on riding in the wilderness, either on your own horse or on a packer's, see the following section, "Packing in on Horseback."

If at all possible, dayhike rather than backpack. You can, for example, make easy-to-moderate day hikes to every lake in the wilderness save Whitecliff and Tamarack lakes (and even these I visited, plus a side trip to the top of Whitecliff Peak, in a one-day hike). Of course, fishermen will object to day hiking, since the best times for fishing are early morning and evening. And no one wants to get up at three in the morning to fish a lake at dawn. For them, packing in is a must.

I recommend day hiking, because day hikers have the least impact on the environment. For one thing, they usually use toilets near trailheads rather than soil near creeks or lakes. In a typical summer season, backpackers can contribute about a ton or more of excrement to the wilderness, the bulk of it typically within 100 yards of a lake, stream or trail. Whereas horse and cattle excrement, lying on the ground, decomposes rather rapidly, buried human excrement takes longer, for in mountain soils subsurface decomposers such as bacteria and fungi are not abundant. At a popular lake, excrement can lead to deterioration of its water quality. Always relieve yourself *at least 50 yards away* from any lake or stream, and the Forest Service recommends you bury feces 6–8 inches deep. It appears that *Giardia,* a microorganism discussed at the end of this chapter, may be spreading in the Sierra Nevada in large part due to contaminated human feces getting into lakes and streams.

Packing in on Horseback

Pack Animals Unlike Desolation and Mokelumne wildernesses to the north and Emigrant Wilderness and Yosemite National Park to the south, Carson-Iceberg Wilderness has relatively abundant forage. Cattle have been grazing most of its land for over a century. Hence, there are usually no restrictions on grazing, though in early summer, such as before mid-July, you could be required to pack in all your feed. Common-sense rules apply to managing horses in the wilderness. Pasture or tether stock outside the campsite and at least 200 feet from lakeshores, creeks or springs. Use hobbles, hitchlines, natural barriers and stock-handling facilities where provided. Stock should not be picketed or tied to trees overnight, lest their shifting hoofs dig out stomp holes.

Pack Stations Three pack stations serve Carson-Iceberg Wilderness: Little Antelope, Wolf Creek Meadows and Kennedy Meadows. There is some overlap in their coverage, but generally each serves a particular part of the wilderness. A fourth pack station, Leavitt Meadows, along Highway 108 midway between Sonora Pass and the Highway 395 junction, offers pack trips into the upper West Walker River drainage, northern Yosemite National Park, and northeastern Emigrant Wilderness, but not Carson-Iceberg Wilderness.

Little Antelope Pack Station (address: P.O. Box 179, Coleville, CA 96107; phone: 916-495-2443 or 702-782-4960), stands high on Rodriguez Flat, west of Highway 395 (see Chapter 13's Route RF-1 trailhead for directions to it). This pack station serves most of the eastern wilderness lands: the Wolf Creek drainage, including Asa and Bull lakes; the lower and middle East Fork Carson River drainage, including Poison Lake, Soda

Springs, Murray Canyon and Golden Canyon; and the Silver King drainage, including Tamarack, Whitecliff and Hidden lakes plus Corral, Coyote and Fly valleys.

Wolf Creek Meadows Pack Station (address: P.O. Box 1041, Verdi, NV 89439; no phone) is a newcomer, not appearing on the scene until the late 1980s. It is located near the end of the Wolf Creek Road, which branches southeast from Highway 4. It serves the Wolf Creek drainage, which includes the Bull Lake and Asa Lake environs. It also serves the lower, northern part of the East Fork Carson River drainage.

Finally, those entering Carson-Iceberg Wilderness from Highway 108 can use **Kennedy Meadows Pack Station,** which is operated by the Kennedy Meadows Resort (address: P.O. Box 4010, Sonora, CA 95370; summer phone: 209-965-3900; winter phone: 209-532-9096). You reach it by driving almost 8 miles east past the Clark Fork Road junction, then branching right on a spur road and driving one mile to road's end. Pack trips mostly go into adjacent Emigrant Wilderness, south of Highway 108, but arrangements may be made for pack trips into Carson-Iceberg Wilderness. Generally, they start from the Clark Fork Road.

Advice for Backpackers and Equestrians

If, in order to have a satisfactory wilderness experience, you decide to backpack or ride a horse for several days, you might consider the following advice.

1. Before you build a campfire, determine whether you really need one. Campsites in Carson-Iceberg Wilderness generally have more wood and fewer people than those in most other parts of the Sierra Nevada, so wood is usually available. Packers in particular like to have campfires, since they can carry in all the pots, pans, grills, coffee pots, etc. to enjoy one. And many packer sites are in spots where wood is abundant. Backpackers, on the other hand, travel light, and typically carry a lightweight stove, so they really don't need a campfire. Theirs is a more ecologically sound approach. Also, if you use a stove, you won't have to carry a shovel, which is required if you build a fire.

Particularly around lakes, don't build a campfire. At them, wood is typically in short supply due to the nature of the vegetation and the heavy visitor use. Also, ashes from one season's worth of campfires can end up in the lake with the following spring's melting snow, thereby reducing the lake's purity. Campfires, though not prohibited, do use up wood that would otherwise serve as food and home to insects and other invertebrates. By denying these organisms a meal, you also deny a meal to the larger organisms, such as shrews, woodpeckers and bears, that partly depend on them. If you do build a campfire, use only *downed* wood. Cutting or defacing standing vegetation, whether living or dead, is strictly prohibited. If you build a campfire outside the wilderness, you'll need a campfire permit. One can be obtained at ranger stations.

2. If you don't build a campfire, pack out toilet paper. If you do build one, burn it. Toilet paper and tampons can take years to decompose, and some of the popular campsites, such as those around Sword Lake, have become littered and unsightly.

3. Don't wash clothes or dishes in lakes or streams, and don't throw fish guts into them. And don't lather up in them, even with biodegradable soap. *All* soaps pollute. Do your washing and pot scrubbing well away from lakes and streams, and bury fish entrails ashore.

4. Set up camp at least 100 feet from streams, lakeshores and trails. At some lakes this may be practically impossible. If so, you must be extremely careful not to degrade the environment. Always camp on mineral soil (or perhaps even on bedrock, if you've brought sufficient padding), but never in meadows or other soft, vegetated areas. Use a site already in existence rather than brush out a new campsite, making one more human mark upon the wilderness landscape.

5. Leave your campsite clean. Don't leave garbage behind, for it attracts mice, bears and other camp marauders. If you can carry it in, you can carry it out. After all, your pack is lighter on the way out and your route is likely to be mostly downhill.

6. Don't build structures. Rock walls, large fireplaces and bough beds were okay in the last century, but not today. There are just too many of us on this planet, and one goes up into the wilderness to get a bit of solitude and to escape the trappings of civilization, not to be reminded of it.

7. Noise and loud conversations, like motor vehicles, are inappropriate. Have some consideration for other campers nearby. Camp far enough from others to assure privacy for both them and you.

Advice for Everyone

Regardless of whether you are day hiking or staying overnight, you should observe the following advice.

1. The smaller your party, the better. *Groups in the wilderness are limited to a maximum of 15 people and 25 stock.* If your party is six or more, common courtesy dictates that you avoid the more popular areas, visit them on weekdays, or visit them on weekends out of season (before the Fourth of July or after Labor Day).

2. If you're 16 or older, you'll need a California fishing license if you want to fish. Licenses are usually available at sporting-goods stores and in the mountains at some resorts. Be aware that in the eastern part of the wilderness some streams and lakes are closed to fishing. You also need a license to hunt. When you get a hunting or a fishing license, you can pick up a copy of all the relevant rules and regulations.

3. Destruction, injury, defacement, removal or disturbance in any manner of public property or any natural feature, living or nonliving, is prohibited.

4. Smoking is not allowed while traveling through vegetated areas. You may stop and smoke in a safe place.

5. Pack and saddle animals have the right of way on trails. To avoid spooking the stock, hikers should get completely off the trail, on the side with the most room, and remain quiet.

6. Don't shortcut switchbacks. Additionally, help maintain trails. If you see a boulder or a branch across the trail, remove it. This doesn't take that much time. A few minutes' work by a lot of people goes a long way.

7. Be prepared for sudden, adverse weather (see next section, on hypothermia). It's good to carry a poncho or other raingear even on a day hike that starts out sunny. It can also double as a ground cloth or an emergency

shelter. A space blanket (2 oz. light) is also useful, and takes up no more room in your pack than an apple. Some day hikes accidentally turn into overnight trips, due to injury, getting lost or bad weather. Early-season and late-season hikers may encounter snow flurries or, rarely, full-fledged storms; and if they plan to camp out overnight, they should have a tent or at least a tube tent. Before you drive to your trailhead, find out what the weather is expected to be, but be prepared—I've known Sierra weather to go from a clear blue sky to an all-out thunderstorm in only an hour. Never climb to a mountaintop if threatening clouds are building above it, particularly if you hear thunder in the cloudy distance. If you see lightning, turn back.

8. The farther you are from your trailhead, the greater is the problem if you are injured. Rock climbers and mountaineers, who are in a higher-risk category, should bear this in mind. You shouldn't hike alone, since then you may have no one but yourself to rescue you in an emergency. In particular, crossing large streams—especially East Fork Carson River—in early season can be dangerous. Leave your trip itinerary with a friend or relative, so if your party runs into trouble and doesn't get back, they will know where to look for you.

9. No bicycles or motorized vehicles of any kind are allowed in the wilderness; check with Forest Service offices for non-wilderness routes.

Hypothermia

The number-one killer of outdoor recreationists is hypothermia, which is simply subnormal body temperature. It is caused by exposure to cold, and it is usually aggravated by wetness, wind and exhaustion. The moment your body begins to lose heat faster than it produces it, your body makes involuntary adjustments to preserve the normal temperature in its vital organs. Uncontrolled shivering is one way your body attempts to maintain its vital temperature. *If you've begun uncontrolled shivering, you have hypothermia and must act accordingly: seek shelter, insulation and warmth.* Slurred speech, drowsiness and coma may not be far behind. Unfortunately, almost everyone who starts developing symptoms denies he or she is in any danger, and it's that stubborn attitude that leads to death. I've hiked alone in hypothermia weather and know

how easy it is to rationalize away any danger.

What is hypothermia weather? It can be winter's subfreezing temperatures, but more often than not it's temperatures above freezing, even up into the 50s. *You can freeze to death at 50°!* If you think otherwise, try swimming in a cold lake for an hour. The cold that kills you is cold water running down your neck and legs, cold water held against your body by drenched clothes, cold water flushing body heat from the surfaces of the clothes.

Avoid even the risk of hypothermia by staying dry in the first place. Keep your clothes dry by having appropriate raingear. If clothes get wet, they can lose about 90% of their insulating value. Wool loses less; cotton and down lose more. Synthetics are best. I make sure that at *all* times I have a spare set of dry clothes and some foul-weather gear. If you're caught in bad weather, don't wait till you are soaking wet before taking action. If necessary, pitch a tent, get inside, and stay warm and dry, perhaps snuggled in your sleeping bag. Always make sure you carry your sleeping bag in a way that it won't get wet. If it does, you could be in *real* trouble.

If someone in your party does develop uncontrolled shivering and/or slurred speech, you must immediately try to warm him up. Get the person out of the bad weather and out of the wet clothes. The best way to warm up someone is to get in a dry down sleeping bag with him or her, both of you stripped naked. The heat from the warm person will quite rapidly transfer to the cold person. Clothes hamper this heat transfer. Modesty could cost you your life.

Animal Problems

Compared to the dangers of hypothermia, the dangers from animals are minor. Here is a list of animals and microorganisms, from large to small, and their potential danger to you.

Bears   Black bears aren't very common in and about Carson-Iceberg Wilderness, though they may become more widespread in future years. They are more likely to hang around campgrounds than wilderness campsites. In my many years of wilderness hiking, I've run into dozens of bears (almost literally at times), yet I've never felt threatened by one. However, if you're camping in the wilderness and a bear does get into your food supply, let it have the food. Once a bear has food, he thinks it is rightly his.

If a bear does become a problem in the wilderness, the rangers may tell you so when you apply for a wilderness permit. Some folks "bearbag" their food—suspend it from the ends of tree limbs—but smart bears can get virtually any bag of food regardless how it's suspended. If so, your trip may be prematurely ended by lost food, but not by injury. Fortunately, bears are more civilized than humans, and won't kill you to get your food. Supposedly, black bears have *never* made an unprovoked attack on humans. Humans have definitely provoked attacks, sometimes by getting between a sow and her cubs, but usually they just get chased or roughed up a bit.

Rattlesnakes   Unless you get off the trail at the lower elevations and scramble around rocks, brush and grass, your chances of meeting a rattlesnake are even slimmer than meeting a bear. I've met them in our area on only two occasions: in early summer at Wheats Meadow, and in midsummer among granitic slabs near Elephant Rock. In our area you're not likely to see one in any kind of vegetation above 8000 feet, or on the forest floor at lower elevations.

Some people's fear of rattlesnakes is almost rabid. Certainly, when one buzzes you unexpectedly on the trail, your adrenalin really shoots up. Still, dogs, cats and small children get bitten by rattlesnakes, and they *usually* live. If you're an adult in good health—particularly, no heart problems—then a snakebite probably won't kill you. Your chances of surviving are close to 100%. There are over a dozen variables affecting your body's reaction to the bite. One of them is that in about half the snakebite cases, the rattler injects little or no venom.

But if you feel severe, immediate pain, you've probably been envenomated. Then, the main thing to do is to keep calm. I met a man who had been bitten on two occasions (neither in California), and he survived without treatment both times. Small children have a much greater risk, and I would think twice about bringing them into any area inhabited by rattlers.

Rodents   Every now and then, one reads about rabid or plague-carrying rodents. The chance of actually meeting one is astronomically small, particularly in the wilderness. Your cat or dog may be more of a threat in this respect. Still, especially around campgrounds, avoid feeding or handling rodents, particularly if they appear lethargic or sick.

Mosquitoes   Almost surely you're going to be bitten by at least one mosquito. As with rodents, the chance that a mountain mosquito will transmit a disease is astronomically small. The main problem with mosquito bites is that they itch, and you can lose sleep over that. To minimize bites, you can do two things. First, visit the area *after* mid-July. By early August, the great majority of mosquitoes have died. The second thing you can do is use insect repellent. The strongest kinds, which work best, are unfortunately are almost nauseating, which is almost as bad as the bite itself. Therefore, use them sparingly, particularly on your face. When mosquitoes are really bad, as in wet meadows in June, you'll certainly want a tent if you're camping out.

Giardia lamblia   Some of our clear mountain lakes and streams may contain cystic forms of these microorganisms, which can give you a case of giardiasis (jee-ar-dye-a-sis). Although this disease can be incapacitating, it is not usually life-threatening. Symptoms usually include diarrhea, gas, appetite loss, abdominal cramps and bloating. Weight loss may occur from nausea and loss of appetite. These discomforts may last up to six weeks. Most people return home from vacation before the onset of symptoms. If not treated, the symptoms may disappear on their own, only to recur intermittently over a period of many months. Other diseases can have similar symptoms, but if you drank untreated water, you should suspect giardiasis and so inform your doctor. If properly diagnosed, the disease is curable with medication prescribed by a physician.

There are several ways to avoid risking giardiasis. The easiest is to day hike and carry water you know is safe. My rule of thumb is to take one quart for every 5 miles you hike. However, if you're going much farther, you won't want to take 1–1½ gallons (8–12 pounds), rather, you'll drink the mountain water. The traditional, most effective way to make the water safe is to boil it for 3 minutes (for 5 minutes at the highest elevations, where water boils at lower temperatures). The disadvantages are you have to carry a stove (a burden for day hikers but standard equipment

Two swimmers by a beaver lodge in Asa Lake. Is the lake's cold, clear water contaminated with *Giardia*?

for backpackers) and you'll have to wait for the water to heat up and cool down. You can avoid the wait if you carry two water bottles, so you can drink from one while you're boiling water to fill the other.

Chemical disinfectants, such as iodine and chlorine, are not as reliable as boiling unless you use them for a long time—say, an hour. But if you carry two water bottles, then while you're drinking from one, the second can be sitting in your pack, with the disinfectant working in it. The recommended dosages, *per quart,* for these substances are: 5 tablets of chlorine or 4 drops of household bleach or 2 tablets of iodine or 10 drops of 2% tincture of iodine.

Another option, which became readily available in the mid-'80s, is to carry a water filtration system. These cost about $40 and up (to over $700!), and most weigh under 2 pounds. With the less expensive ones, you'll have a quart of filtered mountain water in about 2 minutes.

How great is your risk of getting giardiasis? I've never gotten it despite 15 years of intensive hiking in the mountains. However, most of the time I carry my own water, since virtually all the work I do is as day hikes. But I did an "experiment" in the summers of 1985 and '86. I drank from both east- and west-side creeks in both years, but in '85 I used a First Need Water Purifier, and in '86 I drank the water untreated. After drinking untreated water from the East Fork Carson River, I was told by the Soda Springs ranger that it had giardia in it. Still, I didn't get sick.

So, to treat or not to treat the water, the choice is up to you. A 1986 U.S. Geological Survey study (Open-File Report 86-404) of 69 Sierra streams—none in Carson-Iceberg Wilderness—turned up only one stream with enough cysts to infect humans. However, some folks believe there may be a relationship between beavers and giardia (the disease is sometimes called "beaver fever"). And the *eastern* Carson-Iceberg Wilderness streams are beaver country; you can see their homes on Noble, Wolf and Silver King creeks and on the Carson River. Altogether, I think one ought to treat water east of the Sierra crest, but west of it the risk of infection is too small to worry about.

Chapter 3 Geology

Introduction

Carson-Iceberg Wilderness is a land born of "fire and ice." Volcanoes, while not actually fiery, may have appeared so as they erupted time and again during a period that lasted about 30 million years. During this time the pre-existing granitic landscape was buried under as much as 3000 feet of volcanic rocks in the form of lava flows, mudflows and volcanic sediments. As the volcanism came to an end, the Sierra Nevada began to rise, and with increasing height, snowfields began to enlarge. For about the last 2 million years, much of the wilderness has been repeatedly sculpted by the icy fingers of giant, advancing glaciers. The processes leading to the formation of these granitic rocks, volcanic rocks and glaciers are now quite well understood: they are the result of interactions between pieces of the earth's crust, known as plates.

The Earth's Restless Crust

By knowing how plates interact, you can understand the basic geologic processes and the origin of the rocks. One plate can dive under another and, with depth, melt. The lighter part of the melted material, known as *magma,* then rises and mixes with overlying continental rocks. The resulting product, if it cools and solidifies beneath the surface, is *granitic* rock. Each discrete mass of granitic rock derived from a unique source is known as a *pluton.* But if the magma breaks through the surface and erupts, the material cools and solidifies to form *volcanic* rock. Masses of volcanic rock can form an assortment of volcanoes, domes and flows. Granitic and volcanic rocks make up almost all of the Carson-Iceberg Wilderness landscape.

Plutonism and volcanism usually go hand in hand, so one can be reasonably sure that in a volcanic range, such as Oregon and Washington's Cascade Range, there are molten-magma chambers beneath "recently active" volcanoes. Over millions of years, eruptions can bury a landscape under several thousand feet of lava and other volcanic products, as happened in the Cascade Range.

That range grew to its present height—to over 14,000 feet for Mts. Rainier and Shasta—through the accumulation of products of volcanic eruption, not through uplift.

As a mountain range grows in height, erosion of it intensifies, and the weathered remnants of rocks are transported usually to the ocean or to a basin. Over typically tens of millions of years, these sediments harden sufficiently to form *sedimentary* rock. In and about Carson-Iceberg Wilderness, the sedimentary rocks one sees are simply eroded volcanic sediments that accumulated in former stream valleys. One can hardly call them rocks, for the sediments are still quite unconsolidated and are easily erodible.

Through the application of intense pressure and considerable heat, granitic, volcanic and sedimentary rocks can be transformed into *metamorphic* rocks. This transformation generally occurs on a large scale when lightweight rocks atop a diving plate fail to dive. Instead, they ram into the crust of the other plate, causing regional compression, which results in regional metamorphism. On a lesser scale, metamorphic rock can be created when rising magma deforms overlying rock—a process known as contact metamorphism. The oldest rocks in and about Carson-Iceberg Wilderness are metamorphic rock and were formed by these two processes.

Glossary of Selected Geological Terms

andesite A generally dark brown or dark gray volcanic rock, which is commonest kind of volcanic rock in our area. See **volcanic rocks.**

autobrecciated lava flow A lava flow that has broken into myriad blocks. The self-destruction occurs just as the lava is solidifying while the flow is still slowly moving.

basalt A dark volcanic rock usually erupted as a relatively fluid lava flow. See **volcanic rocks.**

bedrock Any solid rock—granitic, volcanic, metamorphic or sedimentary—as opposed to uncemented sediments such as glacial or stream deposits.

biotite A dark, usually shiny black mineral of the mica group that is commonly found in the Sierra Nevada's granitic rocks. See **granitic rocks.**

cirque A glacier-carved bowl, deep and steep-walled, at the head of a canyon.

conglomerate A sedimentary rock composed of compacted, cemented stream sediments (sand, gravel, pebbles, rocks, boulders). **dacite** A volcanic rock between andesite and rhyolite in composition. See **volcanic rocks.**

dike A flat, planar, often vertical body of solidified magma, which, when molten, had been forced into overlying bedrock.

erratic A boulder carried, pushed or dragged by a glacier from its original location to a new one.

fault A fracture in the earth's crust (or overlying sediments) along which there has been noticeable dislocation of the two opposing sides. Compare with **joint.**

feldspar A mineral, usually white, gray or pink in color, composed of silicon and oxygen combined usually with potassium, sodium or calcium. As a group, feldspars are the commonest minerals in the earth's crust.

glacier A thick mass of ice that slowly moved, typically down canyons in the Sierra Nevada.

gneiss A metamorphic rock, usually banded in appearance, and often the result of alteration of granitic rock.

granite A light-gray granitic rock rich in potassium feldspar. It also has some quartz and a little biotite. See **granitic rocks.**

granitic rocks Rocks formed from magma that solidified beneath the earth's surface. These are the commonest group of rocks in the Sierra Nevada. In our area, they range from granodiorite to quartz monzonite to granite. This order reflects decreasing density and decreasing dark minerals.

granodiorite A light-to-medium gray rock with potassium and sodium feldspars. It also has some quartz, biotite and hornblende. This is the commonest type of granitic rock in the Sierra Nevada. See **granitic rocks.**

grus The gravel-like detritus of weathered, eroded granitic rocks, composed mainly of quartz and feldspar minerals.

hornblende A type of dark mineral, usually forming elongate or prism-shaped crystals, which are common in granitic rocks ranging from diorite to quartz monzonite.

joint A fracture in the earth's crust where there has been no appreciable dislocation between the two opposing sides. Compare with fault. Large joints, which are typically several miles long, are called master joints.

lahar A landslide or mudflow of volcanic material. In our area, the latter was more common. Erupting volcanic material mixed with water, either from snowfields, glaciers or lakes, to form a muddy mass that rushed down canyons.

latite A volcanic rock with approximately equal amounts of potassium feldspar and plagioclase feldspar. See **volcanic rocks.**

lava Molten material, usually basalt or andesite, that flows from a volcano or a fissure in the earth's surface. The term also refers to the type of rock formed in a congealed, solid lava flow. Compare with **tuff.**

magma Molten material within the earth's crust. Magma solidifying in the crust forms granitic rocks. Magma breaking through the earth's crust forms volcanic rocks.

mass wasting A general term for a variety of processes by which large masses of earth material are moved by gravity either slowly or quickly from one place to another.

massif A mountainous mass.

metamorphic rocks   Rocks altered generally through heat and pressure.

migmatite   A composite rock that is part granitic, part gneiss.

monzonite   A granitic rock that lacks quartz but has approximately equal amounts of potassium feldspar and plagioclase feldspar, and has some dark minerals, usually biotite and hornblende. See **granitic rocks.**

moraine   A sedimentary deposit left by a glacier. Deposits left on a glacier's sides form a pair of lateral moraines; those left at its snout form a terminal moraine.

mudflow, volcanic   See **lahar.**

olivine   An olive-green mineral common in basalt.

pegmatite   A coarse-grained rock that typically makes up dikes intruding granitic rocks.

plagioclase   A mineral series of feldspars ranging in composition from sodium aluminum silicate to calcium aluminum silicate.

pluton   A body of magma, usually solidifying a couple of miles beneath the earth's surface, and usually ranging 1–10 miles across in size.

quartz   A glassy mineral, fairly common in all the granitic rocks in our area, composed of silicon dioxide.

quartz monzonite   A granitic rock that is similar to monzonite, but also has quartz. See **granitic rocks.**

rhyolite   A light-brown or light-gray volcanic rock that is rich in silicon dioxide and—usually—is erupted very violently. See **volcanic rocks.**

schist   A metamorphic rock that is rich in micas, which are arranged in parallel sheets.

sedimentary rocks   Rocks formed from compacted and cemented materials deposited by streams, glaciers and other agencies.

swale   A broad, shallow gully, usually with a marshy bottom.

trimline   A line running along a canyon wall that marks the greatest height of a glacier that occupied the canyon. Below this line, the canyon wall has been smoothed by the glacier, so the bedrock is quite smooth. Bedrock above this line has not been touched, so it is quite rough.

tuff   A volcanic rock, usually composed of rhyolite, which forms from settling, compacted fragments that were explosively erupted into the air. Compare with **lava.**

volcanic rocks   The solidified products of magma that was erupted onto the earth's surface or into the atmosphere. Volcanic rocks are similar to granitic rocks, since both are derived from magma, but gases and fluids escape from cooling, solidifying volcanic matter, whereas their molecules are incorporated into the crystals formed in the cooling, solidifying granitic matter. In our area the common volcanic rocks are basalt, andesite, dacite, latite and rhyolite. Their granitic equivalents are gabbro, diorite, quartz diorite, monzonite and granite.

The Metamorphic Rocks

There are only two small areas, each near the edge of the wilderness, where pre-granitic rocks can be seen. The area with the oldest rocks—perhaps about 200 million years old—is in the Rodriguez Flat area (Chapter 13). If one observes carefully, he or she will see metamorphosed rhyolite above the east side of the steep, north-climbing road to the flat. The flat itself, together with the nearby ridge between Snodgrass and Silver King creeks, is composed of metamorphosed volcanic sediments. These rocks are the result of regional metamorphism.

The second area is between Lake Alpine and Bull Run Lake. No trail traverses these metamorphic rocks, though when you drive up Highway 4 from Lake Alpine, you do pass through an assortment of them. Perhaps the most interesting formation is about 2¼ miles beyond the lake, where the road turns from east to north at what is called Cape Horn. Here, in addition to getting your first real good view of the western part of Carson-Iceberg Wilderness, you can investigate the local rock. It looks every bit like the granitic rock you saw lower down at Lake Alpine, and even as recently as 1981 it was classified as a *granodiorite,* which is the most common type of granitic rock found in the Sierra Nevada. Now, the rock is recognized as a granodiorite *gneiss,* which is a metamorphosed form of granitic rock. The contact metamorphism occurred about 98 million years ago, when rising magma intruded a slightly older, solidified mass of granodiorite.

The Granitic Rocks

In any mountain landscape, we notice the peaks and ridges that rise above the canyon floor we're treading upon. In Carson-Iceberg Wilderness, most of the high peaks and ridges are volcanic, therefore, we get the impression that the wilderness is mostly a volcanic landscape. Actually, it is mostly granitic, but in canyons and along the lower ridges, forests often obscure the granitic bedrock, so we don't notice it as much. Although the wilderness is mostly granitic, it is, nevertheless, more volcanic than any other part of the Sierra Nevada except for the range's north end, near the North Fork Feather River, where it grades into the volcanic Cascade Range.

As I said early in this chapter, plutonism and volcanism usually occur together, and in Carson-Iceberg Wilderness we certainly see granitic and volcanic rocks. However, here the volcanic rocks formed much later than the granitic ones. Granitic rocks originated during a period lasting from about 100 to 80 million years ago, a time when the area was intruded by rising magma about a dozen times. Each magma body slowly solidified, generally over millions of years, to become a pluton. The magma intruded the overlying bedrock, and where it broke through, eruptions ensued. Could we have visited this area back then, we'd have seen a volcanic landscape like today's Cascade Range, though the climate and vegetation would have been tropical.

Of the dozen or so plutons in the area, most are composed of *granodiorite,* which is easily the most common type of "granite" in the Sierra Nevada. The only true *granite* found in the area is a small body, at the base of Silver Peak opposite Highway 4's Silver Creek Campground. The youngest—and largest— granitic mass is the Topaz Lake pluton, which

Phenocrysts in Topaz Lake rock

is the northernmost of a lengthy stretch of chemically similar "Sierra crest" plutons extending south beyond Mt. Whitney. These plutons contain crystals of potassium feldspar that are up to 4 inches across. Climbers in Carson-Iceberg's high country can appreciate these large crystals, which make useful handholds and footholds. Granitic rocks with large crystals set in a matrix of smaller ones are said to have a *porphyritic* texture, and the large crystals are called *phenocrysts.* Such crystals are generally lacking in the plutons of the western part of the wilderness.

Uplift and Erosion

Early in the Sierra's history, magma was being generated through the diving of a former megaplate, the Farallon, which had been the source for magma generation in the Sierra Nevada since as early as 210 million years ago. A major mountain-building period known as the Nevadan orogeny occurred about 163–152 million years ago, but continued in a milder form until about 100 million years ago. During the orogeny a lofty range was created. Over time the diving Farallon plate steadily diminished and then, about 80 million years ago, it broke into three smaller plates. One plate, the remnant Farallon, shifted its angle of convergence with North America from oblique to head-on. Furthermore, it greatly increased its velocity and shallowed its angle of diving. The result of these changes is that the locus of magma generation shifted far east of the Sierra Nevada, creating the Laramide orogeny, a mountain-building episode in the Rocky Mountains.

In the Sierra Nevada, magma generation stopped, as did volcanic eruptions. The range now began a protracted period of erosion. First the volcanic landscape was eroded away, exposing the older, underlying metamorphic rocks. In time, this several-mile-thick layer was also eroded away, exposing the tops of some granitic plutons by about 60 million years ago. By about 50 million years ago, the Sierran landscape had become quite granitic in character, although it differed from today's in that it was covered with tropical or near-tropical vegetation. Mountain rivers transported granitic detritus westward toward an inland sea, whose swampy edge lay around the trace of today's Highway 99. The rivers' gradients decreased almost to zero as they approached this sea, and as their flow slowed, they dropped their heavier sediments. Specifically, the ancient, meandering Stanislaus River deposited extensive sediments around Vallecito, which is between Angels Camp and Murphys, and around Valley Springs, which is northwest of Angels Camp. These sediments proved to be rich in gold, and particularly around Vallecito they were hydraulically mined from the late 1850s through the 1880s. Using high-pressure water guns known as monitors, miners washed untold amounts of sediments downstream, which caused silting and flooding in the Central Valley.

For about 20 million years after the granitic rocks were first exposed, the Sierra Nevada continued to be eroded away. The Carson-Iceberg area, which once may have possessed some lofty volcanoes, was now reduced to a gently rolling landscape with a maximum elevation of perhaps 4000 feet in the area where today's crest stands. In this area, the highest summits stood about 1000 feet above the valleys. It is important to realize that the Sierra Nevada was broader back then, during the Eocene epoch. The range continued to slope eastward up into western Nevada, and it could have been 10,000 feet high or considerably more, judging from fossil evidence that indicates subalpine forests.

The Volcanic Rocks

At our latitude the Laramide orogeny came to an end about 40 million years ago as the Farallon plate slowed and steepened its dive. In response to this new motion, a wave of volcanism swept westward from the Rockies across the Great Basin, and the first known eruption in the Sierra Nevada (Yuba River drainage) occurred 38 million years ago. Eruptions were few and far between, and they had all but ceased by 4 million years ago, which was about the time that the trailing south end of the Juan de Fuca plate finally passed north beyond our area. Here I should note that the Farallon plate once again split apart, this time about 27 million years ago. The northern section—the Juan de Fuca plate—migrated north as the San Andreas fault system lengthened and separated it from the southern section. Today the Juan de Fuca plate dives beneath the Pacific Northwest's coast and is generating volcanism in the Cascade Range. Back in the Sierra Nevada, while eruptions were occurring on the surface, plutons were forming several miles beneath them, but a few million years may pass before erosion uncovers any of these.

The frequency of eruptions was probably no greater than that of today's Cascade Range, and it might have been less. The eruptions can be grouped into five periods, defined mostly by the general type of volcanic rock produced. The first period lasted from about 38 to 16 million years ago, and eruptions produced an extensive cover of rhyolite tuff. Due to the viscous nature of rhyolite, it produces very violent eruptions, unlike Hawaii's basalt, at the other end of the volcanic spectrum, which produces slow rivers of lava. Rhyolite explodes across the landscape, destroying life for miles around in a matter of minutes, as the airborne, pasty material finally settles and congeals to form tuff. The very destructive 1980 Mt. St. Helens eruption, of less viscous dacite lava, pales in comparison. Though eruptions were widely spaced in time and the Sierran land was generally clothed in forest green, they were still extensive enough to bury the granitic land near Sonora Pass under 1200 feet of rhyolite tuff. In the Sierra foothills, which were far from the near-crest sources, the tuff mantle was only a few hundred feet thick. Today, one sees just a few exposures of this rhyolite tuff in Carson-Iceberg Wilderness, for most of it has been eroded away. One easily reached remnant is found along the County Line Trail to Sword Lake (Chapter 14's Route TD-3).

Because eruptions were few and far between, streams and rivers were able to cut considerable canyons in the landscape. As much as 1500 feet of relief was carved into the Sierran land before the start of the second period. This period actually overlapped the first, beginning about 20 million years ago and continuing until about perhaps 10 million years ago. Eruptions were mainly of andesite lava, and the lava often mixed with water—perhaps from summit snowfields or from lava-dammed lakes—to produce *lahars,* or volcanic mudflows. This type of eruption is quite common in today's Cascade Range. Major eruptions occurred around Sonora Pass and lands a few miles to the southwest and to the southeast, and in this vicinity the series of lava flows accumulated to a thickness of as much as 3000 feet. In Carson-Iceberg Wilderness, much of the lower slopes of volcanic peaks and ridges are composed of rocks from this period.

The third period was short-lived, producing three major flows somewhere between 9½ and 9 million years ago. Again, large canyons had been cut in the land before this period com-

The Dardanelles and Dardanelles Butte are remnants of flows that coursed down the ancient Stanislaus River canyon

menced, the relief being as much as 2000 feet. Our area's most notable feature, The Dardanelles, is a part of the flows. This volcanic palisade is seen from viewpoints along both Highways 4 and 108 as well as from many vantage points along trails. Today, the steep-sided walls of The Dardanelles stand about 3000 feet above the Clark Fork Stanislaus River. One must realize that the flows comprising The Dardanelles coursed down a canyon whose walls have been eroded away. Once lying on a canyon floor, The Dardanelles today form a high ridge, a classic case of *inverted topography*. Perhaps as much as a mile of granitic rock has been eroded since the flows coursed down the ancient Stanislaus River canyon. This amounts to about one foot of downcutting every 2000 years.

The fourth major period came quickly on the heels of the previous period and lasted at least until perhaps 5 million years ago. It produced mostly andesitic mudflows and andesitic autobrecciated flows. The latter type of flow is a slowly moving one that fractures as it solidifies, producing a very broken appearance, which is best expressed in the Raymond-Reynolds peaks area just northwest of Ebbetts Pass. In Carson-Iceberg Wilderness these rocks make up virtually all of Disaster Peak, Arnot Peak and the ridge between them.

The rocks of the final period are mostly dacite and rhyolite, and these sticky lavas were extruded about 6 million years ago in the Highland Lakes area, about 5 million years ago in Noble Canyon, and about 4 million years ago along the Highland Peak-Silver Peak ridge.

As you can see, the volcanic history of Carson-Iceberg Wilderness is very complex. After the Juan de Fuca plate left our area about 3½ million years ago, volcanism still continued, the most recent eruption being the Columns of the Giants basalt flow (Chapter 16's Route EV-1), which I believe occurred

about 120,000 years ago. It certainly will not be the last flow, since magma can take up to 25 million years to cool to form a solid pluton.

The Sierra Nevada Rises and Its Crest Forms

Since the Nevadan orogeny the Sierra Nevada seems to have been rising continually, although for tens of millions of years erosion outpaced uplift so that the net effect was a decline in the elevation of the surface. With the inception of volcanism some 35-40 million years ago, this trend was reversed and uplift began to outpace erosion. The net uplift at first was very slow, the altitude of the land being increased more through the accumulation of volcanic deposits.

The rate of uplift increased over time, and by 7 million years ago our area was of sufficiently high elevation to allow giant sequoias, migrating from western Nevada, to reach as far southwest as the Lake Alpine vicinity. Back then, neither the lake nor its granitic basin existed, the area instead being buried under about 1000+ feet of volcanic deposits. I estimate the elevation of this volcanic landscape to have been over 6000 feet at this locale and 7000–9000 feet along the zone that later would become the Sierran crest. Today, giant sequoias exist along both sides of the North Fork Stanislaus River in Calaveras Big Trees State Park, and they grow best at about 4500–5000 feet elevation. However, 7 million years ago the local climate was about 10–15° warmer, and so sequoias thrived only at the higher elevations, which were cooler. Not until between 5 and 6 million years ago, late in our area's volcanic history, did uplift begin in earnest, which led to continued migration of the sequoias.

While the sequoias had been migrating southwest from high lands into the Sierra Nevada, Nevada lands were extending westward. As I mentioned above, a wave of volcanism swept across the Great Basin (essentially Nevada) and with it came extensional faulting—the upper crust was stretched, broken and thinned. In this process, the former, relatively high landscape was transformed into one of tilted fault-blocks that through time led to today's "Basin and Range" landscape. By about 10 million years ago, the western Nevada part of the Sierra Nevada was being slivered away through faulting. The range was being chipped away as faulted blocks of crust tilted and/or sunk. Between 3 and 4 million years ago, the wave of faulting had reached the lands in the eastern Carson-Iceberg Wilderness, and they began to sink. The modern Sierra Nevada crest came into existence. However, it is not a permanent feature. The prediction is that the range will continue to rise and that faulting will continue to chip away at its east flank.

Glaciation

Throughout most of the Sierra Nevada's history, the climate has been too warm to spawn glaciers. Then, about 5 million years ago, the earth chilled briefly. If during this spell there was a "Mt. Shasta" in or around the Carson-Iceberg area, it could have harbored some small glaciers high on its flanks. The earth then warmed again, and stayed that way until about 2½ million years ago, and from then on the climate has been quite cold most of the time. Fortunately for mankind, we're in a warm, though short, interglacial period.

About 2½ million years ago, there were probably some Carson-Iceberg peaks that exceeded 8000 feet in elevation, and their north or northeast slopes likely had minor glaciers. Though these were probably well under a mile long, they were probably strong enough to slightly scallop the peaks' slopes, and over time these slopes would develop into deep glacial basins, or *cirques*.

It appears that by 2 million years ago glaciers became extensive in the High Sierra, that is, from about Yosemite National Park south through Sequoia National Park. In our area they may also have been quite extensive, despite its lower crest. The largest glaciers in the Sierra Nevada formed during the Sherwin glaciation, which occurred about 800,000–900,000 years ago. At this time crest elevations were within about 500 feet of their present altitudes, and because the Coast

Ranges were considerably lower than they are today, more precipitation—mostly in the form of snow—reached the Sierra Nevada. Glaciers developed in cirques at the crest and grew outward and downward, joining other glaciers and burying most of the landscape. In the North Fork Stanislaus River drainage, most of the ice came from the Mokelumne River ice field, north of our area, and the combined ice flow swept as far southwest as Calaveras Big Trees State Park, stopping at what is about 3500 feet elevation today. On this book's map, this spot would be about 13 inches (13 miles) beyond the left edge of the map. In the Middle Fork Stanislaus River drainage, the glacial system was perhaps even more dramatic, for it advanced about 9 miles down-canyon below the Beardsley Reservoir's dam, stopping at what is about 2000 feet elevation today. On this book's map, this spot would be about 18 inches (18 miles) beyond the bottom edge of the map. One must bear in mind that in the ensuing 800,000 years since the Sherwin glaciation there have been over a half dozen additional glaciations. Those more recent glacial systems, together with rivers during interglacial times, likely have appreciably downcut both the North Fork and Middle Fork canyons by hundreds of feet. Therefore, a more conservative estimate of the lowest elevations reached by the Sherwin glaciers would be about 4000 feet for the North Fork and 2500 feet for the Middle Fork.

One can say a lot more about the last glacial period, the Tioga, since its evidence has not been swept away. East of the crest, the evidence has not been studied in detail. West of the crest—in the Stanislaus River drainage—I spent 90 days in the field during the summers of 1990 and '91 gathering evidence to reconstruct the basin's glacial history. Glaciers originated about 26,000 years ago, reached their maximum about 20,000 years ago, and began to retreat before 15,000 years ago. Most of today's lake basins became ice-free and filled with water between that time and 13,000 years ago, by when glaciers had entirely melted away.

A small ice cap formed in the Highland Lakes area, and it grew sufficiently thick to almost bury Hiram and Folger peaks. Various glaciers grew from this developing ice cap. One flowed east across the low Sierra divide into the Wolf Creek canyon, advancing about 10 miles to the East Carson River. Two others flowed south into Disaster Creek and Arnot Creek canyons to join the Clark Fork

Stanislaus River glacier. Another flowed southwest down the Highland Creek canyon, and also one northwest down the North Fork Mokelumne River canyon.

The North Fork Mokelumne River glacier deserves special attention. Near its start by Highland Lakes, it was about 1300 feet thick—great enough to spill north into Noble Canyon. Just northwest, it spilled north across the Sierra divide in a 3-mile-wide swath that was about 500 feet thick in the Ebbetts Peak Area. This glacier was augmented by a small ice cap in the Milk Ranch Meadow area, and a glacier advanced about 9 miles down Noble Canyon. The North Fork Mokelumne River glacier nearly inundated both Peep Sight and Lookout peaks. And on the gentle highlands north of Highway 4, a large ice cap developed, sending glaciers south to join the North Fork Mokelumne River glacier. This system then swept southwest across Pacific Grade Summit into the headwaters of the North Fork Stanislaus River drainage, burying the Mosquito Lakes vicinity under some 1300 feet of ice. This system was so thick that it overrode most of the ridge above Highway 4 between these lakes and Lake Alpine. The 8600-foot crest north of Lake Alpine was completely buried, indicating a minimum depth at the lake of 1300 feet. Westward, by the Big Meadow Campground, the glacier was about 700 feet thick. At the map's west edge is the CalTrans Cabbage Patch Highway 4 station, and just off the map the glacier spilled north through a low divide. At Lake Moran, also near the map's west edge, the top of the glacier was at about the 6900-foot elevation. Down-canyon, the glacier narrowed and then ended about where Little Rattlesnake Creek joins the North Fork, about 6 miles southwest of the map's west border.

The Highland Creek glacier, originating from the Highland Lakes and Milk Ranch Meadow ice caps, joined the North Fork Stanislaus River glacier, although part of it spilled south between The Dardanelles and Whittakers Dardanelles as a 3½-mile wide, 1000-feet-deep lobe that joined the Middle Fork Stanislaus River glacier. West of here there were two smaller spillovers that did not reach the Middle Fork glacier.

This Middle Fork glacier had its origins in the Sonora Pass area as well as around Granite Dome, a prominent mountain that is about 6½ miles south of Kennedy Meadows Resort. The two source glaciers met by this resort, and the ice here was about 1500 feet

thick. About 8½ miles down-canyon, where the Clark Fork glacier joined the Middle Fork, the thickness was about 1400 feet. If you visit the Donnell Vista Point, on Highway 108 about 3 miles west of the Clark Fork Road junction, the ice would have been about 250 feet thick at the vista point's railing. The glacier continued several miles below Donnell Reservoir, ending before Beardsley Lake.

Just as the Highland Creek glacier spilled over into the Middle Fork, so too the East Carson River glacier, originating on the flanks of Sonora Peak, spilled into the Clark Fork. This occurred between the lower south slopes of Boulder Peak and a point (about 9,760 feet) on the Sierra crest some 2½ miles to the south.

The East Fork Carson River canyon is the longest Sierran canyon east of the crest. During a time of maximum glaciation, it had an 18-mile-long glacier flowing through it all the way to Silver King Valley. The Silver King canyon, lying just east of this canyon, fared rather poorly; it only had an 8-mile-long glacier. This is because ridgecrests west of it intercepted a lot of precipitation, hence not much was left to build a glacier in the Silver King canyon. Eastward, the Corral Valley drainage failed to produce any sizable glaciers, though small ones, up to a mile long, grew on the northwest slopes of Antelope Peak.

Glaciers deepened and widened our area's river canyons, and generally made the canyon wall's steeper and more dramatic. Glaciers also excavated depressions in granitic bedrock, and when they retreated, the resulting bowls became lakes. One wishes there were more lakes, but the jointing planes, which largely dictate how a granitic landscape will evolve, are not, like in the adjacent Emigrant Wilderness landscape, very conducive to lake formation. Glaciers did one more thing: they bulldozed away most of the pre-existing soils, leaving most of the landscape barren when they retreated. This desolation is particularly true in the lower, western part of the wilderness, where there are a lot of barren, granitic outcrops, these bounded by linear jointing planes. Weathering and erosion have been effective along the "joints," and glaciers had deposited sediments along them as they retreated headward. Today, these joints support linear stands of trees, but the barren outcrops between them have changed very little—in both erosion and lack of vegetation—since the last glaciers left this area about 13,000–14,000 years ago.

Chapter 4 Plants and Animals

Introduction

To adequately cover Carson-Iceberg Wilderness' plants and animals, their interrelationships and their influences on the environment in only a few pages is an impossible task. Stephen Whitney's *A Sierra Club Naturalist's Guide to the Sierra Nevada,* at over 500 pages, is the most comprehensive natural-history guide applicable to our area, yet even it is too superficial for serious use in the field. If you're really interested in natural history, you'll need a book or two on each major kind of Sierra life form and its natural history: on wildflowers, on shrubs, on trees, on birds, on mammals, and so on. The "Biology" section of "Recommended Reading and Source Materials," at the end of the book, gives you quite a selection.

If you're a plant lover interested in saving weight and space, you should get four small guides published by Nature Study Guild: *Pacific Coast Fern Finder, Sierra Flower Finder, Pacific Coast Berry Finder* and *Pacific Coast Tree Finder.* Altogether they weigh about 9 ounces and they can fit in two shirt pockets. If you can't get copies of them locally, you can order them through Wilderness Press, which distributes the books nationally. If you're a *serious* plant lover, you can get a very complete coverage of Sierra Nevada vascular plants in one compact book, 12 ounces light, Norman Weeden's *A Sierra Nevada Flora.* For serious botanizing, this is the book I depend on most. A professional flora to Carson-Iceberg Wilderness and adjacent lands isn't available, but if it was, it would be quite similar to Gladys Smith's *A Flora of the Tahoe Basin and Neighboring Areas.* I also recommend Niehaus and Horn's wildflower guides. The first has excellent line drawings, and is useful from Baja California to British Columbia. The second has good-to-excellent photographs of Sierra Nevada flowers, and it is probably the easiest wildflower guide to use.

In a given locale, you're likely to see the same plants year after year, though in some years certain species—annuals in particular—may be very prominent, while in others they may be very sparse. Nevertheless, plants are usually reliable enough that I often mention characteristic species in Chapters 7–12's route descriptions.

Plants stay in place while you're trying to identify them; animals often don't. Consequently, I have minimized the mention of animals in this book. Certainly, there's no guarantee of seeing most animal species in the same spots year after year. Fortunately most mammals, reptiles and amphibians are fairly easy to identify, at least to the Genus level, since there aren't that many species to choose from. You can certainly recognize a bat or chipmunk when you see one, but unless you're well versed in the subject, you can have difficulty determining the *species*.

Birds are the animal group that most makes its presence known. However, you're often likely to hear but not see the birds, since they often frequent treetops or dense brush. If birds interest you, I recommend you carry National Geographic Society's *Birds of North America.* And Gaines' *Birds of the Yosemite Sierra* has very useful information for Carson-Iceberg species. Many "birders" still swear by an old standard, Peterson's *Field Guide to Western*

Birds, which is still an excellent reference but was published long before the American Ornithologist's Union (A.O.U.) 1983 Check-list. This is now *the* standard for bird classification, and it differs substantially from previous check-lists in emphasizing genetic characteristics rather than outward appearances. For example, under this new classification, finches and sparrows are put into *separate* families, the sparrow family now including some finchlike birds—towhees, grosbeaks, buntings and juncos—plus warblers, blackbirds, orioles, tanagers and a number of other kinds of birds.

Plant Communities and Their Animal Associations

When you hike in the mountains—or anywhere, for that matter—you expect to see certain plants and animals in a given habitat. You quickly learn, for example, that junipers, firs and all pines except lodgepoles don't grow in wet meadows, but willows, alders and corn lilies do. The meadow plants, in turn, don't grow on dry slopes. Likewise, in summer you would expect to find belted kingfishers and American dippers along swift streams, but not up in subalpine forests, where Clark's nutcrackers and dark-eyed juncos reside. Hence you can put plants and animals sharing a common environment into a group. Such a grouping is usually named after the dominant plant species in an environment, simply because these are the most readily observed life forms. A collection of life forms in an environment is called a *plant community,* even though animals are included.

Because animals move, they can be a problem to classify. Birds in particular typically have a wide, usually seasonal range, and one species may be found in many plant communities. In the following list of communities, a species is mentioned in the one in which you, the summer visitor, are most likely to see it. In addition, only the most prominent and/or diagnostic species are mentioned. The following plant communities are listed in the approximate order of ascending elevation and decreasing temperature, which is what you'd experience if you drove east up either Highway 4 or 108 to the Sierra crest. Along this ascent, annual precipitation generally increases. Along the fairly steep eastern descent from the crest, temperature rapidly increases while precipitation rapidly decreases.

1. White-Fir Forest White firs are fairly common on our area's lower lands and even on some moderately high eastern lands. However, as a plant community, the white-fir forest lies mostly west of Carson-Iceberg Wilderness. It is well expressed along only two routes: the Wheats Meadow Trail, with its side trip to Burgson Lake (Chapter 14's Route TD-1), and the lower part of the Seven Pines Trail (Chapter 16's Route EV-2). White fir is the dominant conifer, but other conifers usually present include sugar pine, incense-cedar and Douglas-fir. Below our area, ponderosa pine is locally very common, while in the lower part of our area, this tree is replaced by Jeffrey pine, an adaptable species that occurs in several plant communities. Also, to be in a *bona fide* white-fir forest, I think you've got to see one particular broad-leaved tree, the black oak. To stroll through this plant community where it's best expressed, visit Highway 4's Calaveras Big Trees State Park, which includes another very notable conifer, variously known as the giant sequoia, big tree and Sierra redwood.

Of all this book's habitats, this is the one most likely to erupt into a mammoth forest fire. *Natural* fires are definitely associated with it. These fires, if left unchecked, burn stands of mixed conifers about once every 10 years. Between fires, brush and litter do not accumulate enough to result in a damaging forest fire; only the ground cover is burned, while the trees remain generally intact. Thus, through small burns, the forest is protected from going up in smoke. Some plants are adapted to fire, and rapidly invade in the aftermath. A patch of white-fir snags is likely to be quickly overgrown with tobacco brush, green-leaf manzanita and, briefly, fireweed.

Many plants and animals found in the white-fir forest are also found in the red-fir forest. Bird watchers, however, might note a few species that definitely prefer the white-fir forest. On its conifers, white-headed woodpeckers punch through the bark to reach wood-boring insects with their long tongues. White-breasted nuthatches descend the trunks head-first, looking for insects in bark crevices, while brown creepers spiral upward looking for them. Hermit warblers prefer to stay in the tree foliage, hunting insects among the branches and needles. High up in the trees, western tanagers, like Hammond's flycatchers, dart out from the foliage to capture flying insects, though at berry time they're more likely to forage in nearby shrubs. Competing for the berries are band-tailed pigeons and gray foxes. Pigeons, acorn woodpeckers and western gray squirrels all eat black-oak acorns.

2. Jeffrey-Pine/Huckleberry-Oak Woodland

In areas of deep, moist soils, white-fir forest grades upward into red-fir forest. Jeffrey pine, a constituent of both, comes into its own where soils become thin, dry or actually bedrock. You may see a healthy specimen seemingly growing right out of a rock slab and, if the day is warm and a gentle breeze blows your way, you may detect the faint butterscotch odor coming from the furrows of its rusty bark. In spots, shaggy-barked western junipers share the dry, bedrock environment, exuding their own subtle odor.

Both conifers exist on both sides of the range, though their associated plants differ widely. In general, there's a sequence, starting with huckleberry oaks in the west, followed by mule ears, western mugwort, sagebrush and bitterbrush (antelope bush). Mule ears, aromatic in its own right, also exist on both sides of the range, and it reaches its apex in volcanic soil.

But far and away the most common shrub associate *west* of the Sierra crest is huckle-

Western mugwort, an aromatic sunflower

berry oak (east of the crest, it's sagebrush). Usually about waist-high, this drab, dusty, evergreen oak can form dense, almost impenetrable thickets with occasional Jeffrey pines breaking the monotony. Such thickets are most likely to form on dry, granitic slabs and benches. They rarely grow on volcanic soils. Lost and Sword lakes, both occupying shallow depressions on a dry, corrugated, granitic bench, offer prime examples of this plant community. As soils deepen and become able to retain more water, other shrubs appear: greenleaf manzanita, tobacco brush and bitter cherry. If the soil deepens but remains very dry because it is so gravelly or so sunny, then snow bush, with its spiny-tipped branches, joins the huckleberry oaks and Jeffrey pines. All these plants occur together on the sunny, south-facing slopes of the Clark Fork and Middle Fork Stanislaus River canyons. The brush is so dense below The Iceberg, in the Clark Fork canyon, that this granitic monolith has rarely, if ever, been climbed. Once I tried a climbing approach through this brush. It was so thick that at times I had to "swim" from bush to bush, for the shrubs were too dense for me to touch ground. One does not intentionally do cross-country routes through this plant community.

On granitic slabs, the brush is less dense, and wildflowers seasonally add specks of color. Perhaps the most diagnostic one of this community is mountain pride (Newberry's penstemon). Few wildflowers care to share its habit, but four that do are mountain jewel flower, spreading phlox, woolly sunflower and Sierra stonecrop. This dry, rocky environment is ideally suited for western fence lizards, who do push ups to "scare" you away, should you get within their territory. The western rattlesnake is another resident, but chances of seeing one are very slim. In this community the golden-mantled ground squirrel is its main prey.

The sagebrush lizard, which is a western fence lizard look-alike, prefers dry, gravelly soils to dry rock slabs. So do a lot of wildflowers. Sunflowers lead the way with asters, daisies, pussytoes (everlastings), yarrow and Anderson's thistle. However, Bridges' penstemon, showy penstemon, Applegate's paintbrush, scarlet gilia, Leichtlin's mariposa lily and western wallflower are also bound to catch your attention in gravelly soils. In very gravelly soils, pussy paws, jewel flower and Brewer's lupine sometimes reign to the exclusion of all others. And although relatively common, nude buckwheat and other eriogonums lack a showy floral display, and hence are often passed by unnoticed. One eriogonum, sulfur flower, does stand out, thanks to its dense clusters of small, lemon-yellow flowers.

A few Sierran birds definitely prefer this dry, often shrubby environment. Fox sparrows and, to a lesser extent, green-tailed towhees flit about the shrubs, while coveys of mountain quail dart about on the ground. On rockier ground, junipers are invaded by Townsend's solitaires when their berries ripen, while Jeffrey pines are occasionally visited by Lewis' woodpeckers.

3. Red-Fir Forest On the broad, gentle-sloped uplands between the Sierra's major western river canyons, the red-fir forest can form large, almost pure stands. This is certainly true of the relatively flat terrain between Highland Creek and Highway 4 (Chapter 7) and the gentle uplands around The Dardanelles and Dardanelles Cone (Chapter 14). Near the Sierra crest, red firs become less dominant, and eastward the plant community

Top left: cones of ponderosa pine (top), Douglas-fir (right) and sugar pine (bottom). Top right: cones of western white pine (left) and red fir (right). Bottom: white-fir branches (left) versus red-fir branches (right).

is increasingly replaced by what I call the eastern white-fir/Jeffrey-pine forest (plant community #9). West of the crest, red firs share the environment with lodgepole pines and, to a lesser extent, western white pines. East of the crest, the two pines seem to dominate.

Most of this book's routes go up canyons which, excluding eastern lands, are largely fir country. You typically start out among white firs and with increasing elevation end up among red firs. These canyons were scoured by glaciers, which then left abundant till (earth) behind when they retreated. On the deep, gentle-sloped soils, red firs do best. On the flat bottom lands, where water content is high, lodgepoles take over, but these mavericks also thrive on steep, gravelly slopes and on rocky outcrops.

Generally, the classic red-fir forest is a shady one, and needles seem to cover the forest floor more so than do bushes or wildflowers. Indeed, in the forest shade, wildflowers are few in both kind and quantity. However, two plant families—the wintergreens and the orchids—thrive in subdued light. Each family has several species that can grow even in the absence of light, for these particular species derive their nourishment from soil fungi of their own or from soil fungi associated with the roots of other plants. Never numerous, the most common saprophytes are pinedrops, snow plant, spotted coralroot and striped coralroot. More exciting, rare finds are sugar stick, fringed pinesap and phantom orchid. As a group, these plants are easily recognized because, lacking chlorophyll, their stems are not green but white, yellow, orange or red. Their green relatives, particularly the prince's pines and wintergreens, are so unobtrusive that people rarely notice them.

Most lowly plants on the dry floor of a red-fir forest seek sunny sites. The most conspicuous wildflower is alternately known as single-stemmed senecio (or groundsel), and tower butterweed. Another common one is Brewer's golden aster, which is not a true aster, and like the senecio has yellow sunflowers. Two shrubs common here are pinemat manzanita—the Sierra's only dwarf manzanita—and bush chinquapin—with spiny seed capsules and evergreen leaves that are gold on their underside. The great majority of shrubs and wildflowers in the red-fir forest seek moist, sunny sites—namely, creeksides. This streamside life is so different from that of the red-fir forest proper that it is described separately under the next category, riparian vegetation.

From a bird's or a mammal's viewpoint, there is little to eat on the relatively sterile floor of the shady red-fir forest. Hence they usually stay high in the firs and pines. Dropping cones left and right, the diminutive Douglas squirrel, or chickaree, busily cuts far more cones than it can possibly process, thus helping to propogate conifer seeds. This squirrel probably evolved in conjunction with montane conifers—specifically, giant sequoias—which owe a great deal of their existence to the squirrel's seed-dispersing habit. Keeping these talkative rodents in check, the marten—a member of the weasel family—runs them down, leaping from tree to tree when it's not playing havoc with nesting birds. Look for its dens in rotted-out trunks and snags. Where the forest is more open, golden-mantled ground squirrels and lodgepole chipmunks comb the ground for various seeds, which they store in their rock or log burrows.

Nesting near them among brush is this forest's only ground-dwelling bird, the blue grouse, which in summer has a highly varied diet but in winter limits its consumption mainly to pine and fir needles. This forest is also woodpecker country, and you can see at least a half-dozen species. You may also see the red-breasted nuthatch, which descends conifer trunks head-first in search of bark insects, then flies to an adjacent trunk to repeat the process.

From the lower foliage in dense stands, the western wood pewee darts out after flying insects, while higher up in the same foliage its close cousin, the olive-sided flycatcher, does the same. Where the forest is more open, the dusky flycatcher fills their role. Gleaning insects off branches, twigs and needles, the tiny golden-crowned kinglet, together with several warblers, peruse the crown. Pruning the tree's seeds and buds are the pine siskin, pine grosbeak, Cassin's finch and red crossbill—all finches.

4. Riparian vegetation The first three plant communities cover large tracts of land. The riparian-vegetation community differs in that it hugs the creeks that flow down mountainsides and canyons, coursing through several plant communities. It is found as high as about 10,000 feet, and it extends well below the bounds of Carson-Iceberg Wilderness. While it can be seen along just about every flowing stream in the wilderness, it stands out best where it contrasts with dry-land vegetation, which generally happens east of the Sierra crest. Snodgrass Creek, one of the eastern-most streams, is a good example (Chapter 13, Route RF-2). A trail descends along the creek's entire length, and you're treated to lush, creekside vegetation on your left, to Jeffrey pines, mountain mahoganies and sagebrush on slopes on your right.

In this community shrubs typically line the creeks. At higher elevations you may see a number of willows: caudate, dusky, Geyer's, Lemmon's, MacKenzie's and Sierra. Mountain alders are almost always present, and other fairly common constituents include American (creek) dogwood, western serviceberry and Sierra currant. Lower down, below the red-fir forest, one can expect western azalea and thimbleberry to join the ranks. Mountain ash, in lesser abundance, makes its presence known in early fall when it produces bright scarlet berries. About this time, aspens, black cottonwoods, dogbanes and bracken ferns—all thriving on seeps as well as creeks—turn a blazing yellow.

In this moist, usually windless environment, a few wildflowers grow to chest height or more: red-orange-blossomed alpine lily, yellow-blossomed arrowhead butterweed, and blue-violet-blossomed monkshood and lark-spur, both in the buttercup family. Notable waist-high buttercups are the red columbine and the distinctly nonmeadow meadow rue, which is *dioecious,* that is, it has male flowers on one plant, female flowers on another. This is a rare trait for Sierra wildflowers. Other wildflowers you are likely to note at stream-sides are Richardson's geranium, great red paintbrush, Lewis' monkey flower and broad-leaf lupine, this lupine occurring in a wide variety of environments having abundant soil moisture.

As a rule, you don't see the community's mammals, which are rodents and insectivores that are mostly small and secretive. Hidden under cover are western jumping mouse, bushytail woodrat, shrew-mole, Trowbridge shrew and northern water shrew. The water shrew is an avid swimmer, and like the American dipper, this mammal will hunt under-water, even in trout-inhabited lakes. The aplodontia, which is misnamed the mountain beaver, also readily swims in creeks, but does not hunt in them. A larger mammal is the porcupine, which browses on willows, alders,

aspens and cottonwoods when it's not girdling nearby firs and lodgepole pines.

One creature you may like to see—the beaver, North America's largest rodent—you rarely do, unless you sit patiently by a lodge. You can find beaver lodges at spots along many east-side streams, including Noble Creek, Wolf Creek, East Fork Carson River, Silver King Creek and Snodgrass Creek. Beavers eat the bark of aspens, cottonwoods, willows and alders, and fell lodgepole pines for dams. All these tree species are plentiful on the east-side streams. Fairly recently, beavers became established at Asa Lake.

Some birds find good foraging in stream-side vegetation. The red-breasted sapsucker lives up to its name as it drills horizontal rows of holes in aspens, alders, black cottonwoods and other trees, such as Scouler's willow. Robins compete with bears for berries while a flurry of feathered friends—house wrens and MacGillivray's and Wilson's warblers—make inroads on insect populations. The bird most adapted to this streamside habitat is the American dipper, which is a drab, chunky bird that actually forages for aquatic insects on the bottom of swift streams, competing with the local trout.

5. Mountain lakes Most wilderness travelers come to our area's relatively few mountain lakes to fish, to swim, or just to admire them. In our area, lakes and ponds are "pocket-size" communities that dot the larger red-fir-forest and subalpine-slopes communities. In the red-fir belt, lakes are usually bordered by lodgepoles and willows; higher up, also by mountain hemlocks, mountain spiraeas and a host of heaths. From the plant family that brings you sun-loving, dry-ground manzanitas, the diverse heath family also brings you the snow- and water-loving huckle-berries. This family's red mountain heather and Labarador tea are common shrubs around many of this area's lakes, the "tea" being easily recognized in any season by the turpentine odor from its crushed leaves. At the highest lakes, white heather, or cassiope, displays its tiny, white, bell-shaped flowers.

Glaciers heavily scoured the local bedrock to carve the basins that filled to become lakes and ponds about 15-13,000 years ago. Within these bodies there are very specialized vascular plants, the most conspicuous one being the yellow pond lily. You'll find this large-leaved water lily mostly in ponds in the western part of the wilderness and in those west of the wilderness. It also occurs in shallow lakes such as Utica Reservoir and Duck Lake. It grows in water that is waist-deep or less, and may be joined by arum-leaved arrowhead and water starwort. Grasses and sedges, able to grow deeper, often line lake bottoms in all but the highest lakes.

Duck Lake, with its abundant shoreline grass, is likely to attract nesting mallards and spotted sandpipers. In late summer, another water bird, the eared grebe, flies in to browse at these lakes. Pursuing aerial insects, several species of flycatchers dart out over a lake's shore, while the violet-green swallow swoops across its waters. As evening approaches, bats—particularly the little brown myotis— take over the insect-harvesting chores, occasionally aided by a leaping trout. And perhaps for most visitors, trout are what lakes are all about. The next chapter is entirely devoted to them—and how to catch them. Where trout are absent, such as in the high-elevation Whitecliff, Wolf Creek, Chango and Hidden lakes, mountain yellow-legged frogs fill their role.

6. Mountain Meadows Often meadows go hand in hand with lakes, though either can exist without the other. There's been a fairly persistent "geologic folk tale" that meadows are just lakes which have been completely filled with sediments. Given enough time, this will surely happen, but our mountain lakes have existed only for about 15-13,000 years, and in that "short" time, most lakes have received only a foot or two of sediment. In all probability, the mountain meadows you see today were never lakes. At best, they were marshes, something like Duck Lake is today. Likewise, given enough time, forests supposedly supplant meadows through a slow process of invasion by water-loving pioneer species, such as the lodgepole pine. But in reality, there is a seesaw battle between forest and meadow, and in times of wetter climate, a meadow will expand at the expense of its encroaching forest. Another glacial period is due relatively soon, and once again most of Carson-Iceberg Wilderness will be scoured clean of all vegetation. Afterward, the lakes, meadows and forests will have to develop once again.

Pristine meadows abound with wildflowers, heavily grazed ones do not. Cattle and sheep in our area date back to mining days, to as

early as the 1850s. By the 1870s extensive damage had been done to High Sierra meadows, particularly by the sheep, which when untended will crop an area until it's barren. Although William Brewer and others collected plant specimens in the 1860s, no one did a detailed collection, so it is hard to determine how many species, if any, have become extinct. The meadows certainly changed their proportional composition in species, perhaps increasing in sagebrush at the expense of grasses, sedges and wildflowers. Most of the major meadows east of the Sierra crest are still grazed today, though now only by cattle. Meadows are much less common west of the Sierra crest, though cattle, in lesser numbers, graze these land too. Along many wilderness trails you're likely to see these animals.

You can avoid the cattle by visiting the wilderness before July, which is the best time for trout fishing. But my God, what mosquitoes! Hordes of them. And their numbers unfortunately tend to peak just when wildflowers are at their best. But while you may curse these needling females (males don't suck blood), you should bear in mind—as you try to identify a meadow's wildflowers or to fish in a nearby lake—that many of the small-flowered species may in part rely on mosquitoes for propagation. Lungworts and rein orchids are known to be mosquito-pollinated.

Thumbnail-sized Pacific tree frogs aid a number of birds in cutting down the mosquito population: white-throated swifts, violet-green swallows and cliff swallows soar and dive overhead while dusky flycatchers and western wood-peewees sally forth from trees and shrubs in and about the meadow. Lincoln's sparrows, dark-eyed juncos and Brewer's blackbirds search wet meadows for seeds as well as insects, joined in drier meadows, such as those east of the Sierra crest, by chipping sparrows. Aiding bees, flies, beetles, butterflies and mosquitoes in pollinating a meadow's flowers are rufous hummingbirds, which sometimes compete with large sphynx moths, particularly for long-tubed flowers such as penstemons, paintbrushes and monkey flowers, all belonging to the figwort, or snapdragon, family. Northern harriers (marsh hawks) and American kestrels (sparrow hawks) prey on numerous meadowland birds and mammals, while their larger relatives, the red-tailed hawks, soar overhead in search of a hapless rodent. At dusk, great horned owls emerge from the forest's edge for the meadowland's "graveyard shift" rodent patrol.

Meadowland is rodent land, and an amazingly large population of white-footed mice, deer mice, meadow mice and voles inhabit and harvest it. In the drier meadows Belding ground squirrels join in the harvest, as do pocket gophers. Both burrow underground, but the gopher creates an extensive tunnel system while it grazes meadow plants from below. In a mountain meadow a gopher population can churn up tons of soil each year. This process has its benefits, for it leads to the development of a richer soil, which in turn can benefit the meadow's flora.

Often, the beauty of wildflowers attracts botanists to mountain meadows. This is generally not true for our area, perhaps because of heavy grazing. If you want to do some fair botanizing, visit the western meadows. I found the extensive meadowland around Duck Lake somewhat interesting, and Paradise Valley, between Arnot and Disaster peaks, even better. Still, they pale when compared to the prime mountain meadows of Desolation Wilderness and Yosemite National Park. In our area, the meadows not invaded by sagebrush are overwhelmingly composed of sedges and grasses, which are not showy. One prominent, very common wildflower, at least in the wet, western meadows, is the corn lily. It's usually seen before it flowers, and can be easily recognized by its cornlike leaves.

7. Subalpine Slopes In many books you'll find this plant community identified as "subalpine forest". Often it's not a forest. Its tree cover can at times be quite discontinuous and, as you approach its upper-elevation limit, the trees are reduced to shrub height—hardly a forest. Most of the high peaks and ridges in the wilderness and along its border fall in the subalpine-slopes category. This includes The Dardanelles, Dardanelles Cone and Bull Run Peak in the western part of the wilderness, Iceberg, Airola, Hiram, Arnot, Disaster, and other peaks in the central part, and virtually all the peaks 10–11,000 feet high east of the Sierra crest. Some of the foregoing peaks may be devoid of any apparent trees, and hence appear alpine in nature, but their collections of shrubs and wildflowers identify them as truly subalpine.

All of this chapter's plant communities can be subdivided into smaller ecological units, and the subalpine-slopes habitat is no exception. The terrain around Wolf Creek Lake, east

below Sonora Peak, offers you an opportunity to view the four major subdivisions: forest, meadow, rock and gravel.

At 10,090 feet, Wolf Creek Lake is the highest lake in the Sierra north of Highway 108. It is also in the most typical part of the subalpine slopes community. On the western slopes above the lake are clusters of snow-loving mountain hemlocks. You may note a few lodgepole pines, but these are mostly below you in lower Wolf Creek canyon. The overwhelmingly dominant trees are whitebark pines, which are the timberline species in our area. If you climb up to the nearby windswept saddle, you discover that the pines are smaller. If you were to continue west up toward the summit of Sonora Peak or east up to the White Mountain ridge, you'd find the trees quickly diminish to dense, knee-high, icy-wind-cropped shrubs. This form of tree is called *krummholz,* meaning crooked wood.

Immediately west of the lake lies a subalpine meadow that is, like others of its elevation, almost always soggy. In such meadows, for starters look for marsh marigold, Eschscholtz' buttercup, alpine shooting star, Newberry's gentian, elephant heads and alpine aster.

The meadow is bordered on both sides by granitic bedrock, the logical environment in the subalpine zone in which to look for high-altitude ferns. Three to look for here and at other sites with damp, dirt-filled cracks among granitic bedrock are alpine lady fern, rockbrake (parsley fern) and brittle fern.

In the preceding paragraph, granitic bedrock has been emphasized because they produce more sterile soil than does the overlying volcanic bedrock of nearby Sonora Peak. The soils derived from volcanic rock are more fertile in part because this rock fractures into smaller pieces than granitic rock, creating a greater water-storage capacity. This benefit is magnified, since the soil contains very fine,

Whitebark pines on Bull Run Peak

clay-rich particles that not only hold a lot of water in their interstitial spaces, but also absorb water into their clay structure. Furthermore, this soil, derived from rocks rich in dark minerals, is more nutrient-rich than granitic soils are. And being darker in color than their granitic counterparts, volcanic-derived soils absorb more heat, which is very important to plants at these high, cool elevations.

In the subalpine-slopes community, wildflowers seem to do best in seeps, which are miniature wet meadows usually watered by snow patches. In some you may see a nearly homogeneous bed of a particular wildflower. For instance, the tall mountain helenium, a sneezeweed, may locally paint an otherwise drab hillside yellow with its multitude of yellow-blossomed plants. On a smaller scale, common monkey flowers and chilly-feeling mountain monkey flowers locally dab the landscape a vibrant yellow. Then too, there's the delicate Drummond's anemone, its stems almost icy from a drippy snow patch. And what amateur botanist wouldn't be thrilled to find—perhaps along with ferns—a band of Sierra primroses or a cluster of rockfringes, both adding pink to an icy, somber environment? This high, cold, wet area is saxifrage country. Up here you're likely to find alumroot, mitrewort, grass-of-parnassus, gooseberry, currant—all in the saxifrage family—plus a number of true saxifrages, particularly the thumb-sized Sierra and bud saxifrages. Consider your botanizing day a success if you come across ankle-high alpine willows.

As gravel gives way to broken rock, leptodactylon may replace spreading phlox, which is more common in gravelly and rocky areas at lower elevations. You may also see sunflowers such as silky raillardella, cut-leaved daisy, Fremont's butterweed and woolly butterweed. Other rock-loving plants include timberline phacelia, mountain sorrel and Davis' knotweed. The last two are in the buckwheat family, which has a number of species that especially love the high, dry, granitic ridges in the eastern part of the wilderness. The more common buckwheats are Lobb's, frosty, marum-leaved and oval-leaved eriogonums. Shrubs up in the dry subalpine areas include bush cinquefoil, ocean spray, timberline sagebrush and several species of rabbitbrush and goldenbush.

The plants growing in gravelly or rocky areas are harvested by alpine chipmunks, pikas, yellow-bellied marmots and golden-mantled ground squirrels. Only the first two

are true high-elevation species, the two others extending their range down to about 6000 feet. Weasels, northern goshawks, sharp-shinned hawks and red-tailed hawks prey in particular on the two smaller rodents, the chipmunk and the pika. The most noticeable subalpine bird, however, is the gray Clark's nutcracker, a large, noisy relative of the Steller's jay, which is found below in open conifer forests. It typically feeds on whitebark- and lodgepole-pine seeds. Other birds commonly seen up in the subalpine environments—as well as in the lower ones—are robins, juncos, mountain chickadees, and chipping and white-crowned sparrows. Cassin's finch eats conifer buds, seeds and berries, as does its red-fir-forest cousin, the pine grosbeak.

In the drier, eastern part of the wilderness, lodgepole and western white pines mingle quite freely with all but the highest stands of whitebark pines. Here the conifers definitely make up a forest canopy. This forest is woodpecker country, and you may see about a half-dozen species. One of note, Williamson's sapsucker, goes after sap rather than wood-boring insects. It especially prefers the sap of lodgepole and western white pines and, where available, mountain hemlocks. The red crossbill, a finch, devotes its energies to eating lodgepole seeds, and its population can drop dramatically if a needle-miner moth outbreak decimates these pines.

8. Alpine Consider yourself in the alpine realm if you see a rosy finch; it seems to prefer only the highest mountaintops. Mountain bluebirds frequently join it, as do horned larks and water pipits, though less frequently. In my opinion, only Sonora Peak, White Mountain and, very marginally, Wells and Lost Cannon peaks, all about 11,000 feet, are in the alpine realm. Stanislaus Peak is above 11,000 feet, but I think its flora is more subalpine than alpine.

On our area's highest summits, look for cushion eriogonum, dwarf cryptantha, Coville's phlox, Davidson's penstemon, cushion stenotus and alpine gold, plus many of the subalpine species mentioned above. And now for a prediction: Over most of the last 2 million years, the climate of the northern hemisphere has been colder that it is now. Another glacier-spawning cold spell is due in the "near" future, and when it comes, the alpine plants in our area will greatly increase their range, dropping to perhaps 8000 feet. Birds will augment the seeding process, while insects will guarantee fertilization. And the more distant future looks even brighter—i.e., colder—for over the next few million years our crest lands should rise another 3000 feet. Carson-Iceberg Wilderness will become a largely subalpine and alpine landscape.

9. Eastern White-Fir/Jeffrey-Pine Forest I believe it's necessary to include this hard-to-define plant community. Here, in the lands between Ebbetts and Sonora passes, generalizations are much harder to make than in the lands to the south. The reason is simple: the topography is more complex. From about Tioga Pass south to Mt. Whitney, the Sierra rises quite evenly as you travel east to the crest, then drops quite steeply and directly to high-desert land. Not so in our area. First of all, the Sierra crest is very low around Wolf Creek Pass, about 8400 feet, and the topography is so gentle that the vegetation on both sides of the pass is essentially identical. The crest fails to make a sharp dividing line.

Second and more important, the lands east of the crest drop to the high desert in a series of ridges and valleys parallel to the crest. The extreme example is seen in an eastward traverse from Boulder Peak, which is a minor high point on an anomalously low part of the Sierra crest in the center of the wilderness. If you were to fly perpendicular from the crest-line east-northeast to Walker, you'd cross five canyons or valleys and five ridges before reaching the town. And the first ridge is between 1–2000 feet higher than the Sierra crest.

The result is that white firs and Jeffrey pines occupy a lot of the eastern landscape below 8000 feet and a few places above it. Your routes up Noble, Wolf Creek, lower Silver King Creek and Snodgrass Creek canyons are overwhelmingly shaded by these two trees, except beside the creeks themselves, where lodgepoles take over. The same is true of the High Trail over to the East Carson River canyon. However, one can't help but notice the difference of the forest floor compared to that of the western Sierra white-fir/Jeffrey

pine forest. Just east of the crest, the under-story is largely sagebrush, but eastward, mountain mahogany, bitterbrush and even pinyon pine appear. Conditions are obviously drier, and the wildflowers are less numerous, less showy, and more adapted to drought.

10. Open Sagebrush The easternmost, driest plant community in Carson-Iceberg Wilderness is dominated by sagebrush, punctuated here and there by specimens of western juniper. Dense groves of aspens may mysteriously appear, but they are tapping volcanic aquifers that produce local "oases." Along the community's eastern perimeter, mountain mahogany and pinyon pine assert themselves. The community is best expressed at Rodriguez Flat and on the broad, gentle ridge west of it. It is also expressed quite well in Corral, Coyote, and Upper and Lower Fish valleys, and even locally in the lower half of the East Carson canyon.

In its "type locality," on the ridge west of Rodriguez Flat, the vegetation appears to be a sea of sagebrush. Actually, the community is quite complex, and you'll find an assortment of shrubs, including rubber rabbitbrush, mountain snowberry and bitterbrush. Mule ears is the most common wildflower, perhaps followed by coyote mint (mountain monardella). One can easily spy at least a dozen other wild-flower species, but most of these have gone to seed by the time summer visitors arrive. These plants can't rely on midsummer snow patches to water their roots; what little snow falls up here is mostly gone by late May.

Like the alpine community, this one is likely to grow larger in the future, first, because the Sierra crest is rising, and second, because lands east of the crest are increasingly sinking. Thus the Carson-Iceberg Wilderness is becoming more extreme in its range of temperature and precipitation. The western lands may become wetter and snowier, the crest lands colder, and the eastern lands drier. This increasing diversification should benefit most plants and animals, since there will be more niches to fill.

Chapter 5   Fish and Fishing

Introduction

At least 80% of the visitors to Carson-Iceberg Wilderness carry some form of fishing gear. But many visitors never uncase their rods because they are doing other things or simply don't get around to it. Many others who would enjoy a battle with a trout and would savor a tasty dinner don't know how to succeed. These half-serious anglers go out at midday and give up early, before the evening feeding. Serious anglers, on the other hand, arise at dawn to tempt the hungry trout, then rest, swim or perhaps even climb rocks during midday, then go fishing again in the magical evening hour near dark. The success rates of serious and half-serious anglers are vastly different.

Methods of catching trout vary somewhat with the species sought. The most popular and abundant trout is the brook trout (technically a char). Found in 11 lakes and reservoirs in and about Carson-Iceberg Wilderness and in nearly all the wilderness' permanent streams, brook trout are arguably the best eating. Rainbow trout are stocked and also occur through natural reproduction in at least eight lakes and nine streams. Rainbow are the most energetic and the most fun to catch. Cutthroat are stocked in three lakes and are self-perpetuating in one lake and six streams. Records suggest that brown trout are found in five or six streams but no lakes. Brown trout probably are more common than people realize because their secretive nature and wariness cause undercounting. In competition with other trout, browns emerge as kings of the hill. Browns are hard to catch and they live long lives. These factors combine to form a population of brownies that is expanding at present in California as a whole and probably in Carson-Iceberg Wilderness in particular.

Fishing Tactics

In general, to have the best chance of success regardless of species, one should present a bait, lure or fly with minimal disturbance. At dawn and at dusk, hungry trout cruise shallows in lakes and frequent the heads of pools in streams. At other times of day, trout generally hug the bottom of both lakes and streams, feeding very little. The offering presented to the fish must be close enough for it to see, because trout are primarily sight feeders. Get your bait down to the fish's level. In the clear waters of Carson-Iceberg Wilderness, use light tackle and great care. This cannot be overemphasized.

In fishing streams, avoid showing yourself. Don't wear white or bright-colored clothing. Neutral shades of beige, brown and green are unobtrusive. Avoid casting a shadow on the water. Sneak up on pools; creep and crawl if necessary to stay out of sight.

The best lake fishing occurs within two weeks after the ice melts, which is usually in June. A period from late September through October is nearly as good, but don't forget that anglers have been depleting the available fish supply since ice-out. Streams also have a "best" time after the high runoff from snowmelt subsides. For both lakes and streams, midsummer, which is when most visitors are in the wilderness, requires special methods. For brooks and cutthroats, one must

This chapter was written by James H. Ryan, Associate Fishery Biologist, California Department of Fish and Game.

Lakes and Reservoirs in and about Carson-Iceberg Wilderness

Lake or Reservoir	Elev. in Feet	Surface Acreage	Depth in Feet	Species of Trout
Alpine, Lake	7,303	180	45	rainbow
Asa Lake	8,550	2	15	brook
Boulder Lake	8,140	2.5	10	brook
Bull Lake	8,635	6	21	cutthroat
Bull Run Lake	8,333	8	30	brook
Elephant Rock Lake	6,922	11	20	rainbow
Heenan Lake	7,084	130	35	cutthroat (catch and release only)
Heiser Lake	8,350	3	15	brook
Highland L., Lower	8,584	32	50	brook
Highland L., Upper	8,613	11	40	brook
Kinney L., Lower	8,499	36	102	cutthroat
Kinney L., Upper	8,670	18	74	cutthroat
Kinney Reservoir	8,353	35	30	rainbow
Lost Lake	6,890	4	20	rainbow
Mosquito L., Lower	8,045	3	15	rainbow
Mosquito L., Upper	8,050	3.5	12	rainbow
Noble Lake	8,870	4	12	brook
Poison Lake	9,180	4.5	60	brook
Rock Lake	7,315	8	15	rainbow
Spicer Meadow R., new	6,614	2000	220	brook and rainbow
Summit Lake	7,068	14	15	brook
Sword Lake	6,859	6.5	30	brook
Union Reservoir	6,850	200	38	rainbow
Utica Reservoir	6,819	(emptied annually, not stocked)		

get the offering into deep water. Rainbow may be nearer both surface and shoreline. For deep-water fishing, an inflatable raft is worth the weight of carrying it. Several manufacturers make lightweight rafts, of 3 to 7 pounds, which are suitable for two persons. Air mattresses have been used for many years; so have log rafts and inner tubes. These improvisations are not as satisfactory as an inflatable raft, and they can be dangerous in a sudden wind.

Trolling from a small inflatable works well for one or two people. Oars are essential. Paddles don't generate enough thrust, and are difficult for trolling in a straight line. The most effective terminal tackle is a large multibladed flasher followed by a single worm on a size 4 hook. The worm should be within 12 to 18 inches of the last flasher blade. Let out enough line to stay just off the bottom. Occasionally touching the bottom indicates your bait is where it should be for success. Go so slowly that the blades just barely revolve. Nearly as effective as blades are the smallest available

gold-colored Flatfish. At times a black woolly worm towed on the surface will take nice rainbows. A gentle breeze creating a riffle seems helpful when one is surface trolling.

Wilderness visitors quickly pass beyond the boundary waters planted with catchable-size (8–10″) rainbows. Among these nonwilderness waters, Lake Alpine, the Mosquito Lakes and Kinney Reservoir are examples. A variety of lures work well, and so do worms and salmon eggs.

Among the most productive brook-trout streams, Highland Creek between Upper Highland Lake and Spicer Meadow Reservoir is among the best. Slinkard Creek, outside the wilderness near Coleville, is probably the best, for fish over 12 inches are fairly common. It has undercut banks and deep holes that are ideal for brooks. Wolf Creek and Noble Creek below Noble Lake are also quite good, but not equal to Highland or Slinkard.

Excellent rainbow streams include Clark Fork Stanislaus River, lower Arnot Creek, North Fork Mokelumne River up and down

Lake Alpine, viewed from Inspiration Point

from Highway 4, and the Mill Creek tributary to the West Walker River, near the town of Walker.

Natural Bait

The best natural bait for stream fishing is commonly called "hellgrammites," a term used generically by anglers referring to aquatic stages of dobsonflies, alderflies, and stoneflies. True hellgrammites are larvae of dobsons, which are scarce and hard to find. Stoneflies are the most abundant and most easily captured.

The larger specimens are ¾ inch long and their color varies from black through brown to beige. Half-inch individuals make good bait, but larger ones are better. As the name implies, the preferred habitat is under stones, and you'll find them in abundance in flowing streams with riffles. When the larvae reach maturity, they crawl out of the water onto rocks and vegetation. They metamorphose into adults by splitting out of their case, which remains behind, and emerging as large flying insects called "salmon flies," "stones" or other terms. As adults fly around, they quickly mate, then lay eggs in the water and die. The adult form may live one or two days but the nymph may live in the water up to two years. During their entire lives, stoneflies are important trout food. The nymphs are a major constituent of the normal downstream drift of all kinds of insects that trout feed upon. When a large hatch of adult stoneflies begins to emerge, trout may go on a feeding frenzy and gorge on both the maturing nymphs and the adult forms.

Methods of capturing nymphs for bait are easy to master. Simply turn over rocks and pick the nymphs from the underside. A quicker method is to hold a 12-inch length of window screen across the current while your partner kicks over rocks just upstream. A piece of fiberglass screen is very light and compact.

In using stonefly nymphs for bait, thread them on a thin wire hook and drift them through the heads of pools and deep areas. I like to cast them on light monofilament with no added weight. This produces no disturbance other than the slight "plop" when the bait hits the water. Try it and get ready for some action. This technique also works well with night crawlers.

Artificial Lures

Among good artificial lures are Mepps spinners in bright nickle finish with or without a bucktail-covered hook. Other good lures are too numerous to mention. I think that most anglers have a few favorites they are familiar with, and they know how to get the most effective action from each. In general, use small sizes for both streams and lakes.

For flies, the method of presenting them to trout seems more important than the pattern. I stick to grays, yellows and a few black patterns in sizes 12 and 14. Dry flies are fine, but wets work very well for me, and I never have to worry about lack of action. I believe stealth is the most important element. I recall once fishing Silver King Creek in Long Valley (Chapter 13, Route RF-4) with a small, gray fly on the end of a six-foot piece of four-pound-test monofilament, which was tied to the end of a willow I had cut at the stream's edge. In an hour I caught and released 18 rainbows ranging from 8 to 12 inches. I had crept up to the stream on my belly, and fish never knew I was there until they were flopping on the bank. These days I keep a coil of mono and a half-dozen flies in my pack. When the flies eventually get too ratty to take fish, I simply scrape the remaining thread and feathers off and use the hooks for stonefly larvae. After 10 to 12 hookups, the artificial flies lose so much body from sharp teeth that they don't resemble their original appearance.

Lake fishing with artificial flies can be done effectively from shore by spin-casting a bubble with the fly on a dropper above the bubble or as a trailer behind it. Don't forget the best results will be obtained at first or last light of day. Again, be unobtrusive and wear neutral-colored clothing.

Trout Natural History

Historically, before the arrival of white men there were only three game fish in Carson-Iceberg country. The Lahontan cutthroat and the Rocky Mountain whitefish inhabited interior streams draining into now dry, former Lake Lahontan. West-slope streams contained rainbows. On both sides of the Sierra crest, most lakes and streams above falls were barren. During the 1870s and on into this century, the California Fish and Game Commission operated a great many trout hatcheries and widely planted fingerling trout by pack train throughout the wilderness. Success was remarkably high, and it thoroughly obscured the original distributions of trout species. Introduction of brook trout began about 1877, imported from New Hampshire and Wisconsin. Brown trout were brought in from Michigan in 1894 and '95. Introductions of west-slope rainbows into east-slope waters had an immense impact on Lahontan cutthroats, driving them to the brink of extinction except in a few, mostly closed waters where cutthroats still cling to a precarious niche.

Paiute cutthroat inhabited about 10 miles of Silver King Creek in the Carson River water-

Fishing at upper Highland Lake

shed. Lahontan cutthroat occupied the entire Truckee and Walker and most of the Carson River watersheds plus possibly others before the turn of the century, inhabiting 334,000 acres of lakes and 3,600 miles of streams. Total numbers then are of course unknown, but probably were in the millions. The source of these fish, based on fossil evidence, is believed to have been the Columbia River basin of interior Washington and Oregon. Their spread southward was facilitated by the Ice Age. In the Great Basin large lakes formed during glacial times, reaching their maximum usually near the end of each glacial cycle as glaciers were rapidly melting away. In such lakes the species evolved along with a rich forage base of native minnows. On these the cutthroats fed, and they grew to large sizes. The record fish was from Pyramid Lake, Nevada. It weighed 41 pounds and is now on display in the Nevada State Museum in Carson City. Weights of 60 pounds have been mentioned by historians, but these may have been exaggerated.

The decline of the cutthroat was in part caused by gradual drying up of the lakes that nurtured it. But the main cause was, as previously mentioned, competition from introduced rainbow, brown and brook trout during the 1890s to 1940s. Pack trains loaded with baby trout ranged widely throughout the Sierra, "seeding" every likely stream and lake with large numbers of fish. This action doomed the noncompetitive cutthroats, and

Fishing at Asa Lake

they rapidly disappeared. In Carson-Iceberg Wilderness, remnant populations of 6–12" fish exist in the East Carson River above Carson Falls, and in the river's tributaries of Murray Canyon, Golden Canyon and Poison Flat. Bull Lake and its outlet have had a reproducing population since 1957, and they provide excellent fishing for one- or two-pounders. Anglers who catch these rare fish are urged to release them for others to enjoy. Please read regulations carefully before fishing for cutthroat.

In 1992, Poison Flat creek, Poison Lake, Bull Lake and its outlet Bull Creek, and Tamarack Lake were open to fishing for all species of trout. Fish now present in Tamarack Lake include both Lahontan and Paiute cutthroat. The Lahontans originated from a plant of fingerlings horse-packed to the lake in 1988. The fish came from genetically pure brood stock in Heenan Lake that originally lived in Sierra County's Independence Lake. Paiute cutthroat in Tamarack Lake and in Poison Lake were planted in 1991 as part of the Recovery Plan for Paiute cutthroat described on page 136. Poison Lake receives aerial fish plants annually, alternating between brook and Lahontan cutthroat. Bull Lake has not been planted since 1957. See page 111 for details.

If you would like a flashback to the cutthroat fishing of old, try Heenan Lake, north of Carson-Iceberg Wilderness. From a junction of Highways 89 and 4 about 5 miles southeast of Markleeville, drive east on 89 about 4 miles toward Monitor Pass. Watch carefully for a Heenan Lake Wildlife Area sign on the south side of the road. There is an access road blocked by a locked gate that is

open during the months of September and October for the "catch and release fishery." Open fishing days are Friday, Saturday and Sunday of each week. A modest access fee is charged to defray the cost of an attendant who supervises the fishing program. In the early 1990s the attendant was a retired California Department of Fish and Game fishery biologist who worked for many years in the Carson-Iceberg Wilderness on research and management of Paiute and Lahontan cutthroat. He welcomes questions and draws on a wealth of personal knowledge. Non-anglers who visit the lake year-round for hunting, nature study and sight seeing can slip through the gate and freely enjoy the wildlife area.

From a lake-view parking area, walk a few minutes southeast down to Heenan Lake. This 130-acre lake's dam was built in 1929 in order to store water to irrigate lands of the Dangberg Land and Cattle Company. Since 1940 the California Department of Fish and Game has operated the lake as a brood-stock lake for Lahontan cutthroat eggs. Around two million eggs are taken each spring from adult fish and used to produce fingerlings for stocking other lakes. At Heenan Lake, only artificial lures with barbless hooks may be used (artificial flies are defined as lures). The fish average 2½ pounds, and are easy to catch from shore or from nonpowered boats.

The ancestral trout of the west slope of Carson-Iceberg Wilderness was the rainbow, a beautiful and spectacular fighter much sought by anglers. Rainbows apparently evolved from a primitive cutthroat-like trout in the last two million years. During this time, when most of the Sierra Nevada was rapidly rising, its river gradients steepening, and cascades and falls developing, the rainbow changed from being a sea-going migratory form (an anadromous fish) to a resident form.

Sexual maturity in fish is a function of age rather than size. A three-year-old brook trout under conditions of extreme stunting may be capable of spawning, even if only 6 inches long. However, its production of eggs may be fewer than 100. Normal egg production would be 200 at 8 inches, 400 at 10 inches, and 800 at 12 inches. This holds true in general for all species in Carson-Iceberg Wilderness; larger fish produce more eggs.

Cutthroat, rainbow and brown trout are obligatory stream spawners. In the wilderness, spawning of cutthroat and rainbow takes place in May and June. In streams where both species occur, there may be subtle differences in areas chosen, maintaining reproductive isolation. In some streams both species spawn in the same areas at the same time, and cross breeding may then occur. The resulting hybrids are fertile and make fine sport fish, but eventually such fish populations tend to become more and more rainbow-like as the cutthroat influence gradually disappears. Brown trout spawn in the months of October and November. Brooks do too, but they can spawn successfully in lakes. In fact, this adaptation often allows brookies to persist successfully in lakes many years after stocking has ended. There is no evidence that brown trout and brook trout ever cross in the wild, and they must be considered reproductively isolated. Brook trout are chars, a group that includes Mackinaw trout, Dolly Varden, Arctic char and bull trout. None of these occur in our area, although Mackinaw trout is found just north of it, in Lake Tahoe, where this species constitutes 50% of the catch. All chars are very important sport and commercial species in other parts of the United States.

All trout are opportunists where food habits are concerned. All feed on insects and other invertebrates plus other fish, including their own species. Growth is dependent on the amount of food available, so growth rates are highly variable.

In summer months, many shallow lakes contain fish with a muddy taste. This taste is due to a material called geosmin, which is derived from blue-green algae in the water and bacteria in the sediment. It permeates the entire fish musculature and cannot be removed by skinning or by soaking in salt water, wine or other preparations. Smoking tends to obscure the taste but does not eliminate it. In the autumn and during the cold months, geosmin is not present, and affected fish rapidly lose the bad taste. If you catch muddy-tasting trout, either stop fishing at the lake or release your catch. Releasing live fish will let them become good eating later on.

Looking Ahead

Long-term human usage of Carson-Iceberg Wilderness will undoubtedly rise, including use by anglers. Hence every angler should keep only as many trout as he can use immediately. The bag limit for trout in Carson-Iceberg Wilderness is five per day regardless of species or size. Added to this is a bonus limit of ten brook trout eight inches long or less. Anglers should obtain a copy of the angling regulations from the Department of Fish and Game or from sporting-goods stores and carefully read provisions on gear and possession limits.

When you catch a fish, try to handle it gently and carefully if you plan to release it unharmed. Using artificial lures and flies rather than worms and salmon eggs will help ensure lower mortality from hooks. More than three fourths of all fish caught on salmon eggs are hooked too deep to survive if released. Fish caught on artificials, even those with treble hooks, are generally hooked only superficially, and more than 90% survive. Think about it, and make allowance for others in the immediate and the long-term future.

Chapter 6   History

The First Inhabitants

Before the arrival of European man, the Washoe Indians were the primary visitors to the eastern part of this High Sierra region. Although the focus of their world was Lake Tahoe, with its excellent fishing, they also ranged south up the Carson River and even crossed the Sierra crest to descend to the headwaters of the Stanislaus River. They were a small group, perhaps 3000 individuals at most, who moved with the seasons. Leaving the Carson Valley, a family or a group of families would slowly work its way up canyons in late spring as snow retreated and certain food became abundant. In early June these foods included trout and large suckers, both of which spawned in East Fork Carson River. Later, as fish-spawning in the river declined, the Indians ascended mountain canyons in search of game on the slopes, vegetable food in the meadows, and trout in the high streams and lakes. On these excursions they were likely to have unfriendly encounters with west-slope Miwok Indians, who had been progressing east toward the crest, following retreating west-slope snowfields.

With the approach of autumn, the Washoe returned to the Carson Valley and other eastside valleys. This season was a time of plenty, thanks to a harvest of berries, seeds and pinyon nuts, followed by hunts of rabbits, deer and antelopes. Doves, quail, sage grouse and rodents were also hunted. Their bountiful harvest had to last until spring, when they could gather wild lettuce, wild spinach and wild potatoes. The Washoe understood their environment and lived totally within its structures, not seeing any need for change.

The Miwok were more diverse than the Washoe geographically, culturally and linguistically. They ranged from Marin County east across the Central Valley and seasonally up to the Sierra Crest. The particular Miwok subgroup that claimed the lands drained by the Mokelumne, Stanislaus, Tuolumne and Merced rivers, like the Washoe migrated up to and then down from the crest lands.

Washoe Indians probably visited the East Carson canyon every summer

The First Crossing of the Sierra Nevada

Though a few Spanish and Mexican parties forayed into the lower Sierra Nevada, there is no evidence that any approached or crossed the Sierra crest. In 1806 Gabriel Moraga, a Spanish Army lieutenant, traveled along the lowest elevations of the Sierra foothills and came to a river with many Indian skulls along its banks. He named the river for the skulls, or *calaveras,* and later Calaveras County would be named for the river. A few years later, and a full 275 years after Juan Rodriguez Cabrillo had sailed along and superficially explored the entire California coast, no European yet knew whether the white cap of the High Sierra was composed of snow, white rock, or both.

The first documented case of a Sierran crossing is that of Jedediah Smith. In November 1826 Smith and his trapper party, in search of beavers, arrived in southern California. They found respite from the winter weather at San Gabriel Mission, but in January 1827 were ordered out of the Mexican-ruled land by Governor Echeandia. Rather than backtrack, as he was told to do, Smith took his company north into the Central Valley, doing some trapping and encountering "a great many Indians," which fortunately for him were friendly. The party attempted to cross the unknown Sierra Nevada, probably via the Kings River drainage, but deep snow forced them back down to the valley floor. They worked and trapped northward, and made a second trans-Sierra attempt, this time up the American River drainage, but were defeated once again. Then they backtracked a bit, and on May 20, Jedediah Smith, Silas Gobel and Robert Evans left most of the party behind on the lower Stanislaus River while

they made a third attempt. This one, mostly up the Stanislaus River drainage, was successful, crossing the Sierra crest somewhere around Ebbetts Pass after about a week of riding. Exactly where the Smith and companions crossed the Sierra crest is not known; however, they probably descended to East Fork Carson River, which they then followed a ways down-river before striking east toward Utah.

Forging through the Carson-Iceberg Country

Another early known crossing in our area was by a mining party led by Major John Ebbetts, who in April 1850 crossed the pass that now bears his name. An approximation of his route would later become Highway 4. Then in October 1853 Ebbetts crossed the Sierra for another reason: to scout a railroad route from San Francisco to Las Vegas. His party took a route up to Pinecrest that is similar to the one Highway 108 follows now. From there Ebbetts turned east and ascended to Relief Valley and Emigrant Meadow before descending north to Leavitt Meadow and up Lost Cannon Creek. In that vicinity (Chapter 18's Route PM-3), which is the eastern edge of today's Carson-Iceberg Wilderness, he recognized the terrain and realized that he had been there in 1850. Although the trip east into Nevada was a failure, he holds the distinction of being the first known individual to scout the lands bordering the wilderness.

Meanwhile, toll roads were under construction, aiming for the Sierra crest and beyond. By 1856 a pre-Highway 4 road was completed east from Calaveras Big Trees up to Hermit Valley, from where it continued northward via Faith and Charity valleys to Hope Valley. There it joined the Carson Pass road,

Lower Highland Lake, Highland Peak and Wolf Creek Pass, from Hiram Peak. Jedediah Smith may have passed through this area in 1827.

which descended northeast to Genoa and other Mormon settlements in the southern Carson Valley.

The Mining Era

More than anything else, the history of our area is one about the rise and fall of its mining industry. On January 24, 1848, James Marshall discovered gold at Coloma, a Sierra foothill settlement outside our area, and immediately hordes of men, usually in small groups, began to scour the Sierra's western slopes. By spring 1848 men were flocking to the foothills to pan Sierra streams. Among them were George Angel and John Murphy, who discovered gold along the Stanislaus River, and their camps quickly grew into the booming mining towns of Angels Camp and Murphys.

In the area covered by this guidebook, gold and silver were discovered in limited amounts east of the Sierra crest in the late '50s, and soon the towns of Markleeville, Monitor, Mogul and Konigsberg sprung up. Jacob Marklee founded Markleeville in 1861 and until his murder in '64 operated a toll bridge he had built across Markleeville Creek. By that year, the town had a population of over 2600 individuals. Monitor and Mogul, both just north of the junction of today's Highways 4 and 89 in the East Fork Carson River canyon, were much smaller. Konigsberg, founded by Scandinavian miners in 1862, grew to almost 3000 by late in the following year; its name was changed to Silver Mountain City and it became the county seat when Alpine County was created in 1864.

In summer 1863, miners were rushing east along the road from Calaveras Big Trees, continuing through Hermit Valley and over Ebbetts Pass, then down to Silver Mountain City, which lay at the base of its namesake. A stage-coach line ran east only as far as Silver Valley—today's Lake Alpine. From it, saddle trains continued eastward. Not everyone taking the route was a miner. William H. Brewer, a botanist working for the Whitney Survey, was also taking the route. In mid-July Brewer's party left the raucous mining town of Aurora, headed west on a pack trail, completed the previous year, up to and over Sonora and Saint Marys passes. Then the men followed it down the Clark Fork Stanislaus River and over to the Pinecrest area, from where the party took the main road down to Sonora. As the party was taking this route, a wagon road was being built from Pinecrest to Sonora Pass. The route, completed in '65, was essentially the same one taken by Highway 108 travelers today. Brewer arrived in Silver Mountain City in early August, and in the following passage he gives us an insightful view of what the town was like.

Silver Mountain (town) is a good illustration of a *new* mining town. We arrive by trail, for the wagon road is left many miles back. As we descend the canyon from the summit, suddenly a bright new town bursts into view. There are perhaps forty houses, all new (but a few weeks old) and as bright as new, fresh lumber, which but a month or two ago was in the trees, can make them. This log shanty has a sign up, "Variety Store"; the next, a board shanty the size of a hogpen, is "Wholesale & Retail Grocery"; that shanty without a window, with a canvas door, has a large sign of "Law Office"; and so on to the end. The best hotel has not yet got up its sign, and the "Restaurant and Lodgings" are without a roof as yet, but shingles are fast being made.

On the south of the town rises the bold, rugged Silver Mountain, over eleven thousand feet altitude [actually lower—see Chapter 11's Route NC-3]; on the north a rugged mountain over ten thousand feet. Over three hundred claims are being "prospected." "Tunnels" and "drifts" are being run, shafts being sunk, and every few minutes the booming sound of a blast comes on the ear like a distant leisurely bombardment.

Perhaps half a dozen women and children complete that article of population, but there are hundreds of men, all active, busy, scampering like a nest of disturbed ants, as if they must get rich today for tomorrow they might die. One hears nothing but "feet," "lode," "indications," "rich rock," and similar mining terms. Nearly everyone is, in his belief, in the incipient stages of immense wealth. One excited man says to me, "If we strike it as in Washoe, what a town you soon will see here!" "Yes—*if*," I reply. He looks at me in disgust. "Don't you think it will be?" he asks, as if it were already a sure thing. He is already the proprietor of many "town lots," now

Miners in search of gold and silver combed the slopes of Noble Canyon during the 1860s

worth nothing except to speculate on, but when the town shall rival San Francisco or Virginia City, will *then* be unusually valuable. There are town lots and streets, although as yet no wagons. I may say here that it is probably all a "bubble"—but little silver ore has been found at all—in nine-tenths of the "mines" not a particle has been seen— people are digging, *hoping* to "strike it." One or two mines *may* pay, the remaining three hundred will only *lose.*

Brewer's words about the "city's" fate were prophetic, for perhaps only about $200,000 in gold and silver were recovered here. Silver King (Chapter 13's Route RF-2), a small town near Rodriguez Flat, probably fared even worse. Monitor and Mogul had better luck, the two yielding several million dollars in gold and silver. Still, this is not a large sum when compared to many Sierra foothill towns. Angels Camp, Jamestown, Sonora and Soulsbyville all produced on the order of $30,000,000 each, while Columbia produced about $100,000,000. And Grass Valley, north of today's Interstate 80, produced over $300,000,000 in gold, making it the richest gold-mining district in California.

After the Mining Bust

By the mid-60s it had become apparent that very little precious metal was going to be found at Silver Mountain City. By 1868 the town's population was down to 200, then in 1872 down to 30. The demonetization of silver in 1873 further depressed a nearly dead economy, and the county seat, along with a few buildings, was moved to Markleeville in 1875. By 1886 Silver Mountain City ceased to exist. Silver King suffered a similar, though quicker fate, the town being abandoned in 1874. Likewise, the population of Alpine County dwindled almost to nothing. From a high of more than 11,600 in 1864, it dropped to about 1,200 in 1875, and for the first half of the 1900s was generally below 300. Monitor and Mogul, producing gold, silver and copper, fared better, operating through the '80s and then on a lesser scale through much of the first half of the 20th century. Actually, the most productive mine in the area produced a product most miners shunned as worthless—sulfur. Located about 2½ miles north of Monitor Pass, the Leviathan Mine produced over a half million tons of sulfur before the mine was closed in 1962.

Despite the wane of mining in Alpine County, silver mining at Virginia City was still quite lucrative, and the county supplied that city with both scrap wood for steam-driven machinery and heating and lumber for buildings and mine timbers. During times of high water, timber was floated down East Fork Carson River to Empire, Nevada, from where it was transported to the city.

The lumber industry fared even better on the western slopes of the Sierra Nevada, for mines were generally active through the 1930s. The baby-boom years after World War II created a demand for housing, which is still growing, and so lumbering is an important activity in much of the western Sierra Nevada today. Fortunately for outdoor enthusiasts the western half of what is now Carson-Iceberg Wilderness was spared the ax, at first because of its remoteness from any market, then later because of the poorer quality of its forest. Glaciers had removed much of the area's soil, so the trees were too thinly spread to be logged profitably.

Since mining times, and still today, the grazing of livestock has been important at almost all elevations in the part of the Sierra Nevada between Highways 4 and 108. Today, cattle are grazed, though in the second half of the 19th century sheep were very numerous. Cattle owners despised the sheepherders because sheep would utterly denude a mountain meadow if not regulated—and they were not. One ethnic group, the Basques, became particularly identified with sheep in the region of the Carson and Walker rivers. At the beginning of the gold rush they began to specialize in the open-range sheep industry, and by the 1880s they had become known as the finest sheepmen in the American West. Basques were still herding sheep in the 1970s, though on my field work in the area in 1986, I saw not a trace of shepherd or sheep. In the 1970s they worked in the United States on three-year contracts. They didn't come to the United States with a sound background in sheepherding; rather, they came with a strong determination to earn money so that they could return to northern Spain with a good economic future. In the eastern part of Carson-Iceberg Wilderness, you may see old tree carvings and stone monuments created by the lonely, isolated shepherds while they were "doing their time."

The Recreation Era

The United States was still recovering from the Great Depression at the outbreak of World War II, and California offered many folks defense-related jobs. After the war, these people stayed on and more came, basking in the State's amenable climate. From about 1940 to 1970, the State's population tripled, to about 20 million. Our local Mother Lode towns increasingly became tourist attractions and the Carson-Iceberg country increasingly became an outdoorsmen's haven.

With the backpacker "revolution" of the '60s came a cry for more open space. About a generation later, in 1984, it was finally answered, as far as our area is concerned, with the creation of Carson-Iceberg Wilderness, which preserves the finest mountain scenery between Highways 4 and 108. This 160,871-acre wilderness also serves as a sanctuary for mid- and high-elevation plants and animals. For some animals, such as the California grizzly, the wolverine and the wolf, preservation came much too late. The same holds true for an undetermined number of meadowland plant species that were grazed to oblivion by sheep before any 19th century botanist could catalog them.

An arri mutillak, or stone boy, built by one or more lonely Basque sheepherders. This one is near the start of the Driveway Trail (Chapter 13, Route RF-1).

The original Spicer Meadow Reservoir

Carson-Iceberg Wilderness is mostly devoid of lakes, and the few present are quite small, so most of the open-water use has been outside the wilderness at P.G.&E. reservoirs: Spicer Meadow, Utica, Union and Alpine. A major reservoir, opened to the public in 1991, certainly dwarfs all the other reservoirs: the new Spicer Meadow Reservoir. This project is the brainchild of the Calaveras County Water District, which saw a major hydroelectric project as a means of generating money and jobs for the county. P.G.&E. and Friends of the (Stanislaus) River fought the project, which had its conception in the mid-'60s, until a final court decision in March 1984. Construction began in 1985, and after the 6½-mile-long lake was completed, it had about 50 times the volume (189,000 acre-feet) of its predecessor. While this project was a loss for environmentalists, it is definitely a tremendous gain for fishermen. The lake has the potential to support more trout than all the area's other lakes and reservoirs combined.

The 1970s and '80s have seen, in addition to increased recreation and tourism, an increased year-round population. In general, the lower Sierra Nevada towns, particularly those along the Mother Lode, have attracted quite a number of retirees, and with them, businesses to cater to them. As these towns overflowed, eastern, higher-elevation settlements grew. This is particularly true along Highway 4. Calaveras Big Trees State Park is now flanked by the montane settlements of Arnold and Dorrington, which have cooler summers than the lower Mother Lode towns of Angels Camp and Murphys. Along Highway 108, Sonora has expanded east to what is called East Sonora, and from it you pass one community after another until you're past Long Barn, as exasperated weekend travelers can attest.

Another change, which may have gone unnoticed to most wilderness visitors, was the acquisition of all the private inholdings in the eastern part of Carson-Iceberg Wilderness. Much of the land from Carson Falls north along the East Carson River canyon to the wilderness border was in private ownership, as were some lands between Poison Flat and Tamarack Creek. Purchases in 1990 and '91 transferred the former lands to the Forest Service and the latter to the California Department of Fish and Game.

The future will undoubtedly bring more urbanization to this part of the Sierra Nevada. Outside road-free Carson-Iceberg Wilderness, more roads will be built for logging and for settlements. Much of the low- and mid-elevation native plants will suffer serious depredations as they are replaced by garden and landscape plants. And the highways will probably receive additional straightening and widening, so they can carry even greater numbers of people to Carson-Iceberg Wilderness and adjoining recreation lands. For many of these people, Carson-Iceberg will become increasingly precious as a place of refuge—if for only a fleeting moment—where they can experience a simpler way of life.

Part Two
Route Chapters

An old, stunted Jeffrey pine growing on glacier-polished, granitic bedrock above Slick Rock Road

Chapter 7   Spicer Meadow

SM-1   Union Reservoir Shoreline

Distance
1.3 miles to end of Road 7N01 above
  adjacent Elephant Rock Lake

Trailhead Start east on Spicer Meadow
Road 7N01, which leaves Highway 4 just 0.2
mile northeast of Hells Kitchen Vista Point
and 3.5 miles southwest of Bear Valley. In 3.0
miles you reach Stanislaus River Campground, along the river's north bank, then in
4.9 miles reach a junction with Road 7N75,
climbing left. Take it 1.8 miles to road's
end.
    Note that along this road you first meet,
after 0.7 mile, Road 7N17, which through
1986 was an ORV route to Utica Reservoir
that continued beyond, ending at Highway 4
near the west shore of Lake Alpine. The first
part of this road has been upgraded and paved
so that now all vehicles can drive to Utica
Reservoir. Beyond, the route will still be
somewhat primitive, and will definitely be
ORV-only north of the Stanislaus River, which
is the end point of Route LA-2. Also note that
0.3 mile farther along Road 7N75, as you start
a descent toward Union Reservoir, you'll meet
a rough road, on your left, which parallels
yours as it descends a gully to a primitive
campground along the south tip of the
reservoir. A similar primitive campground,
with a boat ramp, lies just below Road 7N75
near its end.
    If you want to follow Route SM-1 in the
reverse direction, start from the Elephant
Rock Lake trailhead—Route SM-2.

Introduction Although this is an official
Forest Service Bike Route, most of the use
appears to be by those on foot. If you're
camping along Union Reservoir and want to
visit other lakes on foot, this trail gives you a
way to Elephant Rock, Summit and Rock
lakes. You can also use this trail as part of a
mostly cross-country loop around Union
Reservoir. From the primitive campground at
the reservoir's south end, walk over to the
nearby dam, which prevents the reservoir from
spilling over to adjacent Utica Reservoir. You
can then explore the northern reaches of Utica
Reservoir or the west shore of Union
Reservoir. The latter's north shore is generally
unattractive, and you may want to head back
the way you came. Both of these shallow
reservoirs have numerous rock-slab islands
worth swimming or rafting to. Be aware that
both reservoirs suffer a drastic reduction in
size in late September, and then are quite
unattractive.
    Fishing in Union Reservoir is poor to fair in
early season, just after the ice melts, for 10–
12″ rainbow. The lake is planted annually with
7000 catchable (8–10″) trout during midsummer. It was planted with fingerlings starting in
the mid '50s and lasting until '77. In '78,
fingerlings were abandoned in favor of the current program. Although most are caught immediately, a few winter over and are caught the
following year. Some bullhead catfish planted
many years ago by stock herders persist as
stunted 6–9″ competitors for the scanty food
supply. Bullheads provide tasty meals for
those willing to clean and prepare them.

Description From the end of Road 7N75
you follow a narrow old road ⅓ mile northeast, to where it is replaced by trail tread.
From this spot you can descend to an adjacent
point that juts out into Union Reservoir. This
idyllic site, with spacious camping, has for
decades been used as a summer camp by Boy

You can swim to one or more of Union Reservoir's many islands

Scouts. From this site a shoreline trail heads southwest back to a primitive campground just below your trailhead.

Leaving the unofficial BSA camp and its nearby islands, we first dip into a gully, then climb a short distance up to a shallow gap with a low granitic knoll on the left. Just beyond the knob we arrive at an open bench, from which most of the reservoir's many islands are visible. The trail then stays fairly high above the reservoir for ¼ mile before reaching a major gap with a more prominent knoll on the left. If you want to explore the reservoir, leave the trail here, head west across the knoll and down to the shoreline. If you continue north to the reservoir's inlet, you'll find it shallow and uninviting, though you can continue on without much difficulty to bays, points and islets along the west shore.

Along the trail, Jeffrey pines—so common on these slopes—diminish in numbers as we

pass through an old logging area and then descend into an almost flat-floored forest. Now only ¼ mile from our destination, we hike northeast until **Elephant Rock Lake** appears. From a roadend very near the lake, you can drop to its southeast shore. Given its proximity to the popular roadend, the lake may have more fishermen than trout. The lake at first appears too shallow for swimming, but you'll see it is not if you walk around to its west shore. From the southwest tip you have another opportunity to head over to the inlet of Union Reservoir: head cross-country more or less due west.

To visit Summit Lake, go 0.8 mile up Road 7N01 to a 170-yard-long trail that leads west to the lake. This spot along the road is also the trailhead for Route SM-4, which can get you to Rock Lake. A shorter way to Rock Lake is to continue east from Elephant Rock Lake, following Route SM-3.

SM-2 Elephant Rock Lake to North Fork Stanislaus River

Distance
1.3 miles to North Fork Stanislaus River

Trailhead Start east on Spicer Meadow Road 7N01, which leaves Highway 4 just 0.2

mile northeast of Hells Kitchen Vista Point and 3.5 miles southwest of Bear Valley. In 3.0 miles you reach Stanislaus River Campground, along the river's north bank, then in

4.9 miles reach a junction with Road 7N75, climbing left. You continue straight ahead and in 0.1 mile leave the Spicer Meadow Road, which veers right, and wind southeast over to Spicer Meadow Reservoir. Onward, you reach the Summit Lake trailhead for Route SM-4 in 3.2 miles, then in 0.8 mile more reach road's end just above Elephant Rock Lake.

Introduction This trail offers the shortest way in to secluded camping along the North Fork Stanislaus River, a creek that provides good fishing for both rainbow and brook trout. Because the trail is unmaintained, only experienced pathfinders should attempt it. (Finding the river really isn't much of a problem, even if you can't follow the trail; the problem is finding your trailhead once you're ready to leave the river!) The stretch of trail north of the river is easier to follow, partly because the terrain is different and partly because it receives more use. Route LA-7 describes this longer, more popular way, which begins by Lake Alpine.

Description Your route-finding problems begin almost immediately, for there are a number of use trails just north and east of Elephant Rock Lake. From the roadend, take an obvious trail northeast, which quickly arrives at the lake's eastern arm. Here you can take a trail, which for the first few paces can be downright wet in early season, and follow it northwest along the shore to the lake's outlet. Alternatively, you can continue northeast to a nearby trail junction and work west toward the

lake's outlet creek. Look for the trail on the creek's opposite bank about 60 yards below the lake. If you have lots of trouble finding the trail, turn back—the route's worse ahead.

You now arc briefly northwest, paralleling the outlet creek and entering Carson-Iceberg Wilderness just before you recross the creek. Downstream, you'd reach the inlet of Union Reservoir in 0.5 mile. Northwest, you can reach a seldom visited stretch of North Fork Stanislaus River in 0.3 mile by crossing a low ridge. The trail, however, turns northeast, upstream, heading up the gully at first, then leaving it for a fairly short, ducked climb up partly barren slopes to a stagnant pond atop an open ridge. Along this ascent you can look southeast and see why Elephant Rock is so named.

Your descent continues briefly northeast, jogs momentarily west, then descends briefly north to a lodgepole-pine flat. Here a low, granitic ridge deflects our course momentarily east before we can turn northeast through a gap to a boulderhop or logcross of **North Fork Stanislaus River.** Once on the opposite bank, you'll find a campsite just on the downstream side of the trail. More can be found both up- and downstream, and the farther you get from the ford, the more likely you'll have the place to yourself. The North Fork provides good fishing, and on hot summer afternoons it offers a number of pools for brisk bathing. The ducked, open route ahead gradually veers away from the North Fork, and it is described in the opposite direction in Route LA-7.

SM-3   Elephant Rock Lake to Rock Lake

Distances
0.9 mile (approx.) to Elephant Rock
1.9 miles to Rock Lake
2.1 miles to Highland Creek Trail

Trailhead Same as the Route SM-2 trailhead

Introduction Located a leisurely hour's hike from the trailhead, Rock Lake is the most accessible lake in Carson-Iceberg Wilderness. Despite being quite shallow overall and backdropped with trees rather than cliffs or mountains, it nevertheless attracts a good crowd of fishermen and bathers. Elephant

Rock, whose base is skirted early on the hike, is also a worthy goal, though only for climbers. The summit provides an excellent panorama of the adjacent countryside and also offers interesting glacial evidence. You'll certainly want a rope, preferably 50 meters long, if you intend to climb to and then rappel from the summit.

Description From road's end, start north-northeast on a trail, which quickly takes you to the shallow south arm of Elephant Rock Lake. You rapidly cross the lake's seasonal inlet creek, and then in a few paces meet a trail on the right, which dead-ends, and one on the left,

Elephant Rock and Elephant Rock Lake

which goes over to the lake's outlet creek. Ahead we go briefly north, then turn east and skirt below the imposing south face of Elephant Rock. About 250 yards past it, after you come alongside the inlet creek, you'll note a conspicuous gully. Here, 0.6 mile from the trailhead, is the spot where climbers leave the trail.

Elephant Rock

To climb to the summit of this monolithic mass of olivine basalt, first you have to reach its east face. While this can be done by a variety of routes, I prefer climbing directly up granitic slabs to a narrow crest, then walking along it to the nearby face. Watch your step along this easy scramble for, although it's unlikely, you could meet a rattlesnake. You'll note a loose, exposed route, about Class 4 in difficulty, going up a short crack system. This

is your best bet, though you can also head 70 yards left across talus and start up a longer, poorly protected route toward some junipers. This route is your rappel route.

Once on top of **Elephant Rock,** note the other volcanic ridges and blocks to the northwest and southeast which, like Elephant Rock, were part of volcanic flows and/or volcanic sediments that buried the granitic landscape mostly during a period lasting from about 10 to 5 million years ago. If you descend from the summit to the brink of the south face, you'll come to a small field of granitic boulders. These are erratics; they were carried by a glacier that left the scene roughly 14,000 years ago. How thick was the glacier that dropped these summit erratics? You can calculate the answer knowing that the surface of the glacier was about 8500–8600 feet in elevation.

From the brink you have a fine panorama of lakes to the south and west, whose basins were sculpted by glaciers emanating from the Bull Run Peak environs, 5 miles to the northeast. Elephant Rock Lake appears to be just a stone's throw away, though if you hit the lake with a stone, you'd make the *Guinness Book of World Records.* Behind this lake lies Union Reservoir, which in turn lies in front and left of Utica Reservoir. From about 1990 on, peak baggers were also presented with a view of the new Spicer Meadow Reservoir, beyond and left of Union Reservoir. Summit Lake, considerably closer, also lies to the left of this reservoir.

Few will take the above diversion, but rather will continue traversing east along the

Glacier-transported granitic boulders (erratics) atop Elephant Rock

Rock Lake, viewed from southwest end

trail. About ⅓ mile east of Elephant Rock we cross Elephant Rock Lake's miniscule inlet creek, and then our trail starts to climb. Soon it turns northeast to ascend a gully, and not far up it we recross the often dry creek and enter Carson-Iceberg Wilderness. After a ¼-mile moderate ascent, with views back the way we came, we cross the creek for a final time and soon have an almost level traverse through a pine forest. We keep just south of a low divide and in a few minutes arrive at the southeast shore of **Rock Lake.** This popular lake attracts too many campers, who formerly camped along the shore. Due to overuse, the shore is now off limits and one must camp at less desirable sites. Hence, it is better to day hike to the lake rather than to backpack to it.

Due to its popularity and small size, the fishing pressure on the lake's trout is quite great, so don't count on a meal. This 8-acre lake is annually planted by air with 1000 rainbow fingerlings. From time to time it has been planted with brooks, and in '85 mistakenly with goldens. Primarily, fishing is for rainbow with flies.

The lake, however, does offer some fine swimming once you wade out a bit. From about mid-July through mid-August it warms in midafternoon to the high 60s, sometimes the low 70s. If you continue along Rock Lake's southeast shore, you'll quickly arrive at the **Highland Creek Trail,** the junction lying immediately south of the lake's outlet creek. This Trail 20E04 is described in Route LA-6, which starts near Lake Alpine and arcs 4.5 miles southeast to this junction—certainly a longer way in, but still within reach of a day hike.

SM-4   Summit Lake to Highland Creek Trail

Distances
1.3 miles to Highland Creek Trail 20E04
2.5 miles to Rock Lake
4.5 miles to upper Spicer Meadow Reservoir

Trailhead   See the Route SM-2 trailhead

Introduction   Formerly signed the Sand Flat Trail, this trail (signed 18E16 at its start but 18E05 at its east end), doesn't really visit any sandy flat. What it does is provide the shortest access to the upper part of Spicer Meadow Reservoir. This is a worthwhile goal through July, but after that the reservoir can turn into

an ugly, muddy bowl. Also, the trail offers an alternate, slightly longer route to Rock Lake with more shade and a bit less climbing than the previous route. You can put the two routes together for a loop trip—say, starting at Elephant Rock Lake, climbing to Rock Lake, descending to Road 7N01 near Summit Lake, and then taking the road 0.8 mile down to its end—a total distance of 5.4 miles.

Description   From parking space opposite a short trail west to lodgepole-fringed Summit Lake, your eastbound Trail 18E05 first passes a seasonal swamp and soon is joined at a jog

south by a mountain-bike route. Almost immediately your trail jogs east, leaving the bike
route, and you start a climb east-northeast
along the southern base of hill 7502. You top
out at a minor saddle, dip and climb to another
one, and then wind down in a few minutes to a
junction with **Highland Creek Trail 20E04.**

This trail is described in Route LA-6, so
consult that route if you are heading 3.2 miles
over to the **upper part of Spicer Meadow
Reservoir.** If you are going in the opposite
direction, left, then you could use a brief
description. Trail 20E04 climbs north, paralleling Wilderness Creek at a distance and soon
skirting across an open, gravelly slope that
hosts a carpet of mat lupines. This open slope
may be the Sand Flat after which our Trail
18E05 was originally named. The route ahead
has only a little climbing, and in under a mile,
after crossing two seasonal creeklets, you
arrive at a trail junction immediately before
the seasonal outlet creek of Rock Lake.
Expect good swimming, fair fishing and, above
the lake, adequate camping. See the previous
route for a description to the lake from the
Elephant Rock Lake trailhead.

SM-5   Spicer Meadow Reservoir to Twin Meadows Lake and Wheats Meadow

Distances
3.3 miles to junction with Twin Meadows
  Trail
4.3 miles to Wheats Meadow
4.6 miles to Twin Meadows Lake
(Note: The above mileages are estimates only,
based from the northwest corner of the new
Spicer Meadow Reservoir's dam.)

Trailhead   Start east on Spicer Meadow
Road 7N01, which leaves Highway 4 just 0.2
mile northeast of Hells Kitchen Vista Point
and 3.5 miles southwest of Bear Valley. In 3.0
miles you reach Stanislaus River Campground, along the river's north bank, then in
4.9 miles reach a junction with Road 7N75,
climbing left. In 0.1 mile the Spicer Meadow
Road veers right. You take this 0.9 mile to a
fork right, the route ahead going to nearby
Spicer Meadow Reservoir Campground, on
the left, and just beyond it to the boat-ramp
parking loop. On the right-forking road you
drive past a group camp in 0.3 mile and pass a
parking area just before reaching the reservoir's dam in another 0.6 mile. Now you drop
0.7 mile to a junction with a gated road across
Highland Creek, just down-canyon from a
large building.

Introduction   The new Spicer Meadow
Reservoir, opened to the public in 1991, is
almost 50 times the volume of its predecessor.
When the lake level is high (not too likely in
drought years or in late season), the lake is a
magnet for fishermen, who ply it in myriad
watercraft. Hikers are few and far between.
The only trail in the area worth hiking is this
Route SM-5 to Twin Meadows Lake—but it
isn't for everybody. The trail goes only as far
as Twin Meadows, and from there you're
basically on your own, since the route you
take will largely be governed by how swampy
the meadows are. In late spring you'll have to
take a lot of evasive action around the
meadows; in late summer you'll have a fairly
straightforward course through them. Be fore-
warned that before August you may be
pestered by hordes of mosquitoes, so bring a
tent for refuge if you plan to camp then.

However, this route may be eclipsed by a
shorter route for those with boats. About 2
miles northeast from the dam, just before the
reservoir narrows at the mouth of Highland
Creek canyon, you'll find the reservoir's only
large south-shore bay. This extends 0.4 mile
south, and from its end, one will be able to
climb 150 feet up to a broad, flat bench and
follow it ⅓ mile southeast to Twin Meadows
Lake. This lake, ideal for swimming and sunbathing, has never been pristine, at least not in
the last 20 years, and with probably increased
use, it could become even cloudier. Therefore, I strongly recommend daytime use
only—no camping. In like manner, Lost and
Sword lakes will be easily reached from a bay
about one mile northeast past the mouth of
Highland Creek canyon, and these lakes
should also be visited only on a daytime
basis.

In the past the old Spicer Meadow Reservoir had been planted annually by air with 5000 fingerling brook trout. Fingerlings planted in July grow to 8-10 inches by the following year. Bullheads are also present in fair numbers, and are often caught on worms by trout hopefuls. The stretch of Highland Creek above the reservoir contains a self-sustaining brook-trout population in good numbers. Some of these trout move into the lake and enter the catch. Planting in the new Spicer Meadow Reservoir is based on 200 fingerling trout per acre. Since the reservoir is about 2000 acres, the planting amounts to about 400,000 fingerlings, of which half are rainbow and half brook. Management of both species provides a surface fishery in summer for rainbow and a deep fishery for bottom-loving brooks. Because of extreme drawdown each fall, the number of trout surviving to the next year can be low. In Highland Creek just below the dam, brook trout fare better than rainbow, due to low temperatures and high flows.

Description　　You can cut about ½ mile off your hike if you walk across the dam. This assumes that the spillway is dry, which it usually is. From the far southeast end of the dam, make a short scramble up some blasted bedrock and then from a nearby gully, diagonal east about 250 yards up slopes. Ideally, you should climb only about 80 feet above the dam before topping out. Ahead you have, hopefully, only a brief descent to the trail. Your goal is to reach it where, after making a moderate descent northeast, it abruptly turns southeast. If you go high on your cross-country route, you'll end up walking down a stretch of trail. This however, is better than going too low and missing the trail entirely. The bend in the trail is near a gully and is about 400 feet from the reservoir's high-water line.

If you take the trail, first bridge Highland Creek just below the dam and then take a road south. This quickly ends at the spillway's broad channel. From its far side you continue on a gravel bed/poor road which curves west and quickly ends. Next you take a creekside trail 120 yards to where the stream bends from west to northwest. Here you might see the old route across the broad stream, which used to cross at this point. Now you first climb southwest on Trail 18E04 in a forest of lodgepole pines and white firs. After about 300 yards up alongside a snowmelt creeklet, you angle east

and climb in steps, reaching in ⅔ mile a flat divide with a seasonal pond. A brief walk to the north to glaciated granitic bedrock presents you with a view of Spicer Meadow Reservoir, which can be rather unsightly when the water level is way down.

Ahead you descend rather steeply north-east ¼ mile to the abrupt turn mentioned in the first paragraph. You immediately cross a tributary just above where it joins a seasonal creek, and this you now follow. The trail climbs 400 feet in elevation up through a red-fir forest, and after 1.0 mile it tops out at a saddle below the north end of Whittakers Dardanelles. This unseen volcanic ridge contains the same sequence of lava flows, volcanic mudflows and stream sediments as do the more famous Dardanelles, 3 miles to the east-northeast. Some 20,000 years ago an arm of the Highland Creek glacier completely filled this space as it flowed down to the Middle Fork Stanislaus River glacier. Also worth noting is that both Dardanelles are sections of volcanic deposits that filled an ancestral Stanislaus River canyon over 9 million years ago, causing a major change in drainage that led to today's river system.

From the saddle we start down a minor gully, then leave it and pass a nearby spring that arises at the contact between the over-lying volcanic sediments and the underlying granitic bedrock. After a few more minutes of slight descent we cross a spring-fed creeklet that waters a garden of aspens, alders, corn lilies and wildflowers. Just beyond it we pass a seasonal pond, on our left, which signals our impending entry into Carson-Iceberg Wilderness. Then, after winding southward ¼ mile, we touch the north end of a typical wet meadow, which supports the standard meadow vegetation of corn lilies and arrow-leaved senecios, plus many lupines.

Immediately east of it we vault a low ridge and make a short drop to an obvious junction with the **Twin Meadows Trail.** Ahead, the main trail follows Wheats Meadow Creek 1.1 miles southeast at a generally leisurely pace down to Wheats Cow Camp. Since few folks will be descending this stretch, it won't be described in detail. If you do take it, be aware that when you reach the first long, often wet meadow, the trail diagonals across it, then climbs south over a low, adjacent ridge, only to drop into nearby Clover Meadow. Here you could lose the trail again, but head south through the meadow to where an east-flowing

Author at Twin Meadows Lake

tributary joins Wheats Meadow Creek. Cross in this vicinity and follow the trail ⅓ mile southeast over to an often obscure junction in **Wheats Meadow** immediately before a ford of the creek. Wheats Cow Camp lies just south of this crossing; the Wheats Meadow trailhead lies 3.2 miles east.

Twin Meadows Lake

Most people will skip Wheats Meadow for Twin Meadows Lake. Heading north on Twin Meadows Trail 18E06, you immediately climb past a 5-foot-deep lakelet and soon crest a minor saddle. After a short descent, your 0.4-mile-long trail ends at the south edge of Twin Meadows. Ahead, the most direct route to Twin Meadows Lake is about 0.9 mile long. Expect a longer distance. I have visited the lake on several occasions, and each cross-country route has turned out different from the previous one. Perhaps the route that assures you the best chance of finding the lake is to start north-northwest along the meadow's edge, reach a low, forested divide, and follow it north to the next meadow. From there

onward, try to stay on the northwest edge of the meadows you pass as you head northeast ½ mile to granite-slab-and-lodgepole-rimmed **Twin Meadows Lake.** The lake, plus your route to it, bears the dubious honor of being one of the most mosquito-ridden places in Carson-Iceberg Wilderness. However, the mosquitoes largely disappear by late July, and from then through mid-August you can expect the 3-acre lake to warm in midafternoon to as high as the low 70s. But the lake is warm enough even in early July, and if you can protect yourself from the hordes of mosquitoes, you'll avoid the horde of hikers who come later. Because glaciers scoured the area, the granitic bedrock surrounding the lake is quite smooth, making some nearly level slabs ideal for sunbathing. And, from several spots by the slabs you can dive directly into the lake, which in my opinion is the best way to enter any lake. Leave your fishing rod behind, for Twin Meadows Lake and its outlet, Wheats Meadow Creek, are barren of trout. Bullheads may be present in the lake, but if so, their number is too low to support a fishery.

Chapter 8   Lake Alpine

LA-1   Osborne Point Scenic Trail

Distances
0.8 mile to Osborne Point
1.5 miles to junction with Emigrant Trail

Trailhead   Along Highway 4 about ¼ mile east of Silvertip Campground and ⅓ mile west of Road 7N17, which leads to Lake Alpine Campground and Marmot Picnic Ground. Parking for three vehicles. An alternate trailhead lies at the upper (south) part of Silvertip Campground. No trailhead parking.

Introduction   In a half hour or less you can make an easy climb to Osborne Point for good views of the Bear Valley-Lake Alpine environs. You can get better views from atop Inspiration Point (Route LA-4), but the elevation gain on that route is twice as much, and the last part of the route is a bit too exposed for many people.

Description   The trail heads west across relatively flat ground which, due to a high water table, supports lodgepole pines and meadow wildflowers. After about ¼ mile, we come to a fork, from which a de facto trail heading northwest quickly dies out in a small meadow by Silvertip Campground. Red firs are also known as silvertip firs, whence the campground's name. In 100 yards we come to a second fork, this one with a trail that dies out after only a few yards northeast. We now climb at an increasing grade, and in a few minutes reach a volcanic crest, just under ½ mile from our trailhead, where we join a trail from the campground. This trail begins between campsites 6 and 7, climbs south about 160 yards to the campground's conspicuous water tank, and then continues about 130 yards farther to our junction.

Southbound, we climb briefly but moderately above a cliff, which is composed of layers of volcanic sandstone and conglomerate. Millions of years ago these sediments were deposited here by ancient streams that were eroding volcanic formations to the east. The vegetation is now quite different from that seen lower on the trail, being composed of aromatic species such as coyote mint and mule ears, which like drier conditions.

The trail momentarily levels off, then makes a brief, moderate climb to **Osborne Point** (called Osborn Hill on the USGS 7.5′ topo map). Up here you'll note some pale gray boulders—granitic in nature—which like others you may have seen along the trail were transported here by a former glacier. Since Osborne Point stands at least 500 feet above the Lake Alpine environs, the glacier must have been at least that thick to leave the boulders stranded up here. However, this summit just gives a minimum thickness for the glacier. If you were to climb to the 8605-foot summit you see 1¾ miles to the northnortheast, you would find several granitic erratics up there. Some higher summits lack erratics, so the top of the glacier was, in the Lake Alpine area, about 8600–8700 feet.

In contrast to the granitic boulders is the dark volcanic soil, which is rich in nutrients and supports a diverse assemblage of drought-resistant wildflowers (at their best in June). However, most people hike to Osborne Point not to botanize, but to take in the views. Since you've climbed only about 300 feet above your trailhead (about 200 feet, if you've started from Silvertip Campground), your views aren't all that spectacular. Nevertheless, you do have a 360° panorama. The most eye-catching features lie on the southeast skyline: The Dardanelles, blocky Peak 9070, seen through a gap in The Dardanelles, and pyramidal Dardanelles Cone, above the east end of The Dardanelles. One giant lava flow, which originated east of the present Sierra crest about 9¼ million years ago, makes up the bulk of these features. The view east, somewhat blocked by conifers, is of Lake Alpine, which is a Pacific Gas and Electric reservoir that floods former Silver Valley. To the north and northwest is a paved road, California Route 207, climbing up to the Mt. Reba Ski Area, which lies hidden in a large glaciated bowl on the back side of the prominent ridge 2 miles away. The settlement of Bear Valley, off to the west, lies at the base of this ridge.

Most folks won't travel farther than the viewpoint, but the trail does continue onward, descending ½ mile along the crest and offering additional perspectives and plant species before turning east from atop a cliff. The trail descends moderately for ¼ mile, becoming vague as it approaches a meadowy saddle. Here you'll meet the **Emigrant Road**, Route LA-3, which received heavy use in the mid 1860s but is seldom trod today.

LA-2   Slick Rock Road

Distances
0.8 mile to junction with Emigrant Trail
0.9 mile to junction with Lakeshore Trail
2.0 miles to lowest Silver Creek campsite
3.1 miles to Slick Rock
3.4 miles to Silver Creek crossing
3.7 miles to bridge over North Fork Stanislaus River

Trailhead   Along Highway 4's junction with Road 7N17 south to nearby Lake Alpine Campground. This junction is about 0.3 mile west of Lake Alpine Lodge.

Introduction   For hikers this route has a minimal appeal, since it is an official ORV route. However, from late April through early June there is enough snow along this jeep road to stop ORVs, yet not enough to stop hikers. During this period, campsites 1¾–2 miles from Highway 4 are particularly appealing, though you should adequately prepare yourself for an onslaught of mosquitoes (bring repellent and carry a tent). If you don't mind an occasional ORV, then the route is adequate for a summer hike.

Description   By late June you can easily drive 0.6 mile to the last summer home along the Lake Alpine shoreline, then can usually drive an additional ¼ mile southwest to a small flat containing the start of the **Emigrant Trail** (next route). However, before this time, particularly in April and May, your Road 7N17 can be mostly snowbound. From the flat the road's condition quickly deteriorates as it drops 230 yards to the southwest end of the **Lakeshore Trail** (Route LA-4). Ahead, Road 7N17 parallels Silver Creek, usually at a distance, descending at a gentle-to-moderate grade. After about 1.6 miles from the highway you emerge from the shady forest and, in late springtime, leave most of the snow behind. Here the true 4WD route begins. Over the next 0.4 mile, the road is close to the creek, and you'll spot several appealing campsites. From the **lowest Silver Creek campsite** the road abruptly bends southwest.

Ahead, the granitic terrain has been considerably fractured, the major fractures being along a southwest-northeast orientation. Past glaciers have quarried along these fractures, leaving a series of linear gullies, down which your route proceeds. Besides quarrying the gullies, glaciers have removed former soils, so plants must eke out a living on the barren bedrock or on nutrient-poor glacial deposits.

About 0.6 mile beyond the lowest Silver Creek campsite Road 7N17 bends south-southeast to cross a boggy flat. After about a 100-yard slog across the flat the road resumes its southwest course and after a couple of hundred yards leaves lodgepoles and muck behind. Shortly, our route bends east, then begins a steep, brief descent across appropriately named, glacier-polished **Slick Rock**. The views from this vicinity give you an appreciation of just how thoroughly the latest glaciers scoured the land, for around you lie large tracts of barren granitic bedrock.

From Slick Rock we descend moderately for several minutes, then soon angle east to nearby **Silver Creek**. In the past you could find a fallen tree to cross it. However, trees come and go, so you may have to wade. Also in the past you could head about 0.2 mile downstream to easily the best campsite along this route—a spacious spot at the confluence of Silver and Duck creeks. Other campsites are in between these two creeks. In 1986 work was begun on the North Fork Diversion Dam and Diversion Tunnel. The 35-foot-high dam, now completed, can create a small reservoir that may lap against the prime campsite. However, water is diverted only while there is a high flow. After that, the North Fork Reservoir, which is not stocked with trout, is drained and the stream continues down its natural channel. The diversion tunnel, 2.2 miles long, connects this reservoir to the new Spicer Meadow Reservoir.

The North Fork Stanislaus River Hydroelectric Development Project was opened to the public in 1991, and now the North Fork takes a mighty unnatural course. First, it exits the wilderness to Union Reservoir, which overflows into Utica Reservoir, which spills into a short stretch of a natural stream bed. The North Fork then *during snowmelt runoff* goes through the diversion tunnel *under* Utica Reservoir, is joined by Hobart Creek (from Summit Lake), and then flows down a straightened channel to Highland Creek's mammoth new Spicer Meadow Reservoir. Leaving the reservoir via hydroelectric turbines, the North Fork flows down Highland Creek, which after a few miles joins the North Fork's natural, though greatly diminished, course. But another major diversion awaits downstream.

From the Silver Creek crossing your jeep road winds eastward, passing some ORV campsites just before meeting a **bridge over North Fork Stanislaus River.** Beyond the misnamed Duck Creek Bridge across this stream you climb briefly up granitic slabs to meet a road that heads down to the dam. In the opposite direction, graded Road 7N17 first climbs about 230 yards to a junction, from which a secondary road climbs northeast to Utica Reservoir's nearby dam. Primitive camping is allowed in this area. Onward, Road 7N17 heads 1.2 miles over to just above the reservoir's south end, where a spur road north gives access to more camping. After 0.9 mile Road 7N17 ends at Road 7N75, the road to Union Reservoir.

LA-3   Emigrant Trail

Distances
0.4 mile to junction with Osborne Point
   Scenic Trail
1.4 miles to Highway 4 by Bloods Creek

Trailheads   Start south on Slick Rock Road 7N17, which leaves Highway 4 about 0.6 mile east of Silvertip Campground and 0.3 mile west of Lake Alpine Lodge. By late June you can easily drive 0.6 mile to the last summer home along the Lake Alpine shoreline, then can usually drive an additional ¼ mile southwest to a small flat—the trailhead. An alternate, western trailhead is where Highway 4 crosses over Bloods Creek, which is 0.9 mile northeast of the Bear Valley Road junction and 0.5 mile southwest of the Alpine Ranger Station. Minimal parking at each trailhead.

Introduction   You can relive a bit of history by taking this short stretch of former road. In early summer 1863, miners were rushing east along it, continuing through Hermit Valley and over Ebbetts Pass, then down to Silver Mountain City, which lay at the base of its namesake. A stagecoach line ran east only as far as Silver Valley—today's Lake Alpine. From it, saddle trains continued eastward.

Description   From a small flat, which may be boggy in early season, the Emigrant Trail makes a brief, moderate climb southwest away from Road 7N17. It quickly curves northwest, and soon reaches a nearby meadow on a minor saddle. The westward climbing **Osborne Point Scenic Trail** begins just within the forest along the north edge of the meadow, though the trail's start, due to lack of use, is usually obscure.

From the obscure junction the trail heads 230 yards southwest to a spring that is seasonally cloaked in a yellow garland of monkey flowers, then it momentarily begins to curve west for a descent past the base of a volcanic cliff—the south end of Osborne Point. Beyond the cliff our viewless trail winds westward at a moderate grade, first through a red-fir forest, then past a meadow being invaded by lodgepole pines. The trail then curves northwest for a short spell, only to curve southwest and immediately come to a gate just 40 yards

from **Highway 4** and just north of Bloods Creek. The creek, like the broad, flat meadow of Bear Valley, is named for Harvey S. Blood. In 1864, at the youthful age of 24, he took over responsibility for the completion of the Big Trees-Carson Valley Turnpike (the Emigrant Trail). In Bloods Meadow he set up a toll station, where he collected tolls until about 1889, by which time the mining activity in nearby eastern lands had all but ceased.

LA-4   Lakeshore Trail

Distances
0.4 mile to Inspiration Point Trail
1.2 miles to Lake Alpine's dam
1.7 miles to Slick Rock Road 7N17

Trailhead   Take Lake Alpine's east-shore road, which leaves Highway 4 immediately east of Chickaree Picnic Ground. That picnic ground is just above the lake's east tip. On the 0.4-mile-long east-shore road you quickly pass the Backpackers Campground, on your left near Silver Creek, which is a convenient place to camp at if you're doing long-distance backpacking along the Tahoe-Yosemite Trail (see Route LA-6). Just past the creek is a short spur road right, which goes 110 yards to the Pine Marten Campground entrance, then deadends 110 yards past it. For Routes LA-4 and LA-5, park here, by the road's end. For Routes LA-6 and LA-7, continue briefly ahead on the east-shore road and park immediately before a sharp bend to the right. The Highland Creek Trail begins at the bend, and the Silver Valley Campground lies just beyond the bend.

Introduction   Next to the Emigrant Trail the Lakeshore Trail is probably the least scenic one in this chapter. However, it is probably the most popular, for it provides ready access to Lake Alpine for the throngs of fishermen who flock to the campgrounds of Lake Alpine Recreation Area. (The lake is planted annually with 25,000 catchable-size rainbow. Fingerling plants were abandoned several years ago because of intense competition from abundant golden shiner minnows and bullheads. The shiners were illegally released into the lake, presumably by anglers using them for bait.) The trail also provides access to the start of the Inspiration Point Trail (next route).

Description   The Lakeshore Trail begins from the right (northwest) side of the spur road, winds southwest almost to a small bay, and then heads south for almost 200 yards to a shoreline junction with a use trail. Now we head about 230 yards south-southwest along the shoreline to a junction with the **Inspiration Point Trail,** which is described in the next route.

From here we have a 0.6-mile traverse just above the lake's southeast shore. One could also start a swim from various points along this shore, though swimming is far better from the opposite (northwest) shore, since that shore is blessed with granitic slabs suitable for sunbathing after a swim.

Our shoreline traverse ends as we make a brief ascent southwest up a shallow, bedrock gully. This we quickly top, then begin a descent southwest down another gully. If you want to visit **Lake Alpine's dam,** head a few paces northwest and you'll see the east end of the dam, less than a stone's throw away.

You will probably stop here unless you want to circle the lake for the exercise, or continue over to the Slick Rock and Emigrant trails (Routes LA-2 and LA-3). The Lakeshore Trail switchbacks north out of the gully near its lower end, quickly regains its southwest tack, and in a moment or two reaches Silver Creek, which drains Lake Alpine. We boulderhop the creek, then skirt along a bench past brushy slopes and granitic outcrops. After this short traverse we cross a seasonal tributary of Silver Creek and in a few yards reach **Slick Rock Road 7N17.** For a pleasant day hike with rewarding views, follow this road 2.1 miles to Slick Rock. Alternately, you could head about 200 yards up the road to a small flat containing the start of the Emigrant Trail.

To complete a circle of Lake Alpine, follow Road 7N17 up to the Marmot Picnic Ground entrance and from the east (far) side of the parking loop, take a trail southeast down to the shoreline. A walk northeast along the lake's bay-blessed northeast shoreline is preferred to a walk along Highway 4. Perhaps you'll want to stop at Lake Alpine Lodge, just above the highway, for a drink or a snack before you return to the trailhead or to your campsite.

LA-5   Inspiration Point Trail

Distance
0.7 mile to Inspiration Point

Trailhead   See the Route LA-4 trailhead

Introduction   Situated about 620 feet above Lake Alpine, largely barren Inspiration Point lives up to its name by providing a 360° panorama of the countryside. However, the last part of the trail could turn back some people, for it is a potentially dangerous, intimidating uphill traverse across steep, exposed, rubbly slopes. If you're unsure about hiking across such terrain, then take Route LA-1, the Osborne Point Scenic Trail, which offers similar, though definitely inferior views.

Description   First, see the first paragraph of the previous route's description for the 0.4-mile stroll to the start of the Inspiration Point Trail. The stroll ends there, as you start a steep climb south through forest toward a saddle west of Inspiration Point. Two thirds of the way up to the saddle, you reach an opening and can stop for a view of the lake and a chance to catch your breath. You then re-enter forest only briefly, ending your climb to the saddle up a steep, rubbly slope of a volcanic mudflow.

Similar though steeper slopes lie ahead, and if they prove to be too intimidating, you can still get some rewarding views by climbing easily to the top of the ridge immediately west of the saddle. If you successfully negotiate the footpath to **Inspiration Point,** you can share William H. Brewer's sentiments, when his party probably topped this point back on July 31, 1863. He noted that the point "had a fine view, commanding a wide extent of country— the snowy Sierra lying along east of us, a wild, rocky, and desolate landscape."

When Brewer viewed the landscape, it was a bit more wild than it is today. It didn't have Highway 4 climbing to a low point on the northeast horizon, but rather had a newly constructed, rather inconspicuous wagon road. And the only easily discernible lakes to be seen were marshy Duck Lake, in the meadow by the east base of our point, and Union Lake, to the south. The latter was a slightly smaller version of today's Union Reservoir. Just right of it was a small precursor of today's Utica Reservoir. Elephant Rock Lake and Summit Lake were both visible, then as now, by those with sharp eyes who scanned the lowlands to the south-southeast (both lakes lying just left of today's Union Reservoir). But Lake Alpine, by the west base of our point, was in Brewer's time only "a pretty, grassy, mountain valley." Utica and Union reservoirs, which we see to the south, had yet to be built. Hikers can also see part of the area's largest body of water, the new Spicer Meadow Reservoir, which lies beyond Union Lake.

Union (left) and Utica (right) reservoirs, from Inspiration Point

But most features appear unchanged, and thanks to 1984 Federal legislation, most of the Sierra crest lands will stay that way. Our area's most prominent geographical feature, The Dardanelles, still stands unblemished 6½ miles to the southeast, as does smaller Elephant Rock, below it and a third the distance away. Both were remnants of giant lava flows, which were first studied in some detail back in the summers of 1895 and '96 by Leslie Ransome of the U.S. Geological Survey. You'll also see a prominent summit, Reynolds Peak, 11 miles to the northeast, just left of rather indistinguished Pacific Grade Summit. This peak was formally named in 1929 for G. Elmer Reynolds, who had long been an advocate of forest conservation.

Boulders dropped by the last glacier are strewn along your point's south ridge. Some 20,000 years ago the top of that glacier lay about 700 feet above Inspiration Point, and it covered all but the highest ridges that you see.

If you are adept at rock scrambling, you need not return the way you came. Instead, you can head briefly northeast along your ridge, to where it drops off in all directions, then find a suitable chute to the left (north) to downclimb about 20 feet to gentler terrain. Then, the walk along the crest to a saddle to meet the Highland Creek Trail (next route) is a snap.

LA-6   Highland Creek Trail to Bull Run Creek Trail

Distances
1.1 miles to Duck Lake, north shore
2.0 miles to junction with Duck Lake access trail
3.0 miles to North Fork Stanislaus River
4.5 miles to Rock Lake
5.7 miles to junction with trail west to Summit Lake trailhead
8.9 miles to upper Spicer Meadow Reservoir
10.2 miles to junction with Bull Run Creek Trail
10.6 miles to junction with Dardanelles Creek Trail

Trailhead   See the Route LA-4 trailhead

Introduction   In the past this section of Highland Creek Trail 20E04 was used mostly by folks with one of two goals in mind: following all or part of the long-distance Tahoe-Yosemite Trail, or heading over to campsites at Gabbott Meadow. The latter, a prime attraction, now lies under as much as 60 feet of water, the depth depending on the water level of the new Spicer Meadow Reservoir, which can drop dramatically by hunting season, and then the meadow may be "resurrected" as an unsightly mud flat. However, before August, the lake's level is quite high, and the Gabbott Meadow part of the reservoir may be best reached by non-motorized watercraft (motorized watercraft are prohibited in the lengthy, mostly narrow, upper part of the reservoir).

Description   From the bend in the road immediately before the Silver Valley Campground entrance, we start southeast up a broad, gentle trail through a wildflower-floored lodgepole-pine forest. After about 270 yards we pass a stretch of the Emigrant Trail on our right which winds westward ½ mile down toward Lake Alpine, ending on a spur road. In another 100 yards we pass its continuation on our left. This stretch climbs 5.3 miles to the western, upper Mosquito Lake. Since this mostly viewless stretch of trail parallels Highway 4, it is not described as a separate route, although it and its laterals are shown on the book's topographic map. The Emigrant Trail provides a way to reach other trails—including two into Mokelumne Wilderness. However, since one could start from Highway 4 trailheads, the hiking merits of this historic trail are in doubt. It nevertheless will be briefly described.

Emigrant Trail

The Emigrant Trail climbs about 0.8 mile to a junction with a lateral trail that goes 0.6 mile over to the Woodchuck Basin trailhead parking area. Onward, the Emigrant Trail climbs about 0.7 mile farther to a second junction, this one with a lateral trail that climbs 0.1 mile to Highway 4's Cape Horn viewpoint. Then 1.9 miles farther it crosses a spur road that leads to the start of Route PG-1. About

0.8 mile past the spur road and just past the upper end of Stanislaus Meadow, the Emigrant Trail gives rise to a lateral trail climbing 0.5 mile north-northeast to a corral that is about 50 yards east of Highway 4's Sandy Meadow trailhead. Both the Woodchuck Basin and Sandy Meadow trails provide access to Mokelumne Wilderness' Wheeler Lake.

Just beyond the Emigrant Trail junction Highland Creek Trail 20E04 climbs to a crest saddle, which marks our entrance into Carson-Iceberg Wilderness. We briefly walk along its crest and soon start a descent to a nearby switchback. Here we leave the main tread, which has widened to a road as our Trail 20E04 (part of the Tahoe-Yosemite Trail) descends eastward through a white-fir forest to a notch in a low granitic ridge. From it we head south-southwest a bit before veering east through a lodgepole-pine forest, missing the north shore of swampy **Duck Lake** by 100 yards. For almost a mile we now meander eastward across flat, mosquito-ridden lands, the trail staying close to the base of glacier-smoothed outcrops on our left. Nearing the end of this stretch we parallel a seasonal creek and then cross it to meet a south-bank junction with the **Duck Lake access trail.**

Duck Lake access trail

This unmaintained though relatively easily followed trail heads west across flat land that is largely boggy and mosquito-ridden before late July. Initially this 1.1-mile-long trail starts west along the creeklet you just crossed, but then quickly enters the creeklet, veering away from it after about 300 yards. After 0.3 mile it crosses meadow-lined Duck Creek—a boggy area in early season but like the creek dry later on—and then the trail skirts a seasonal pond, on your right. Just past it, and just before a gap in a low granitic ridge, you can leave the trail, head north over the ridge, and arrive at the south shore of Duck Lake. This mucky bottomed lake, with a rich crop of pondweed, is mostly less than waist-deep, and probably has few admirers other than serious naturalists. From the gap, the trail heads 0.3 mile west to a junction, just south of a cluster of tall aspens, with an old trail to Elephant Rock Lake.

Staying on Highland Creek Trail 20E04, we continue to follow the seasonal creek

upstream, crossing it after a minute, passing its seasonal pond, and then recrossing it thrice in rapid succession near its headwaters. Now the trail veers southeast for a short, winding ascent to a small snowmelt pond and an open-lodgepole saddle. Ahead we face a moderate, south-curving descent almost ½ mile down to a small campsite on the bank of **North Fork Stanislaus River.** A midsize campsite lies on sloping ground on the opposite bank. For some of the most secluded, yet easily reached, camping in Carson-Iceberg Wilderness, either head southwest, downstream, reaching the vague, old Elephant Rock trail in about 1¾ miles, or head north, upstream, reaching well-defined Trail 19E02, bound for **Bull Run Lake**, in about 2½ miles. If you choose the latter, then save time and effort by leaving the Highland Creek Trail just after you start your descent toward the North Fork.

Keeping to the trail, you face the only "major" ascent along your fairly level route. You climb south about 400 feet in two stages: first a short, fairly steep ascent to a minor indent in granitic bedrock, then from a nearby seasonal stream a doubly long ascent up a slackening grade to a scallop in a broad, amorphous minor ridge. Maintaining a south tack, you make a mildly rolling traverse for 0.6 mile then, from a minor ridge clothed in huckleberry oak, you jog momentarily east to a usually dry creeklet—the main "stream" feeding Rock Lake. Sustained almost wholly from melting snow on local slopes, Rock Lake typically loses its influx of fresh water by mid-July, and by late summer can be fairly low and a bit cloudy. In a few minutes we arrive at the shallow, grassy east end of **Rock Lake** and cross the seasonal outlet creek. Just a few yards from it is a junction with a 2.1-mile trail southwest down to Elephant Rock Lake (Route SM-3). By starting along this trail you'll encounter several small campsites on sloping ground just above the lake's edge. A better camp lies near the lake's west end, though due to the use this lake receives, I strongly urge people to day hike to this lake or, if you backpack to it, try to find a find a site well away from the shoreline. The lake, like others in this lake-deficient wilderness, is over-fished, so don't expect a trout dinner. The lake does offer you pleasant swimming, particularly in midafternoon, and the best place to enter the lake is from a peninsula (an early-season island) along its south shore.

The Dardanelles

For most folks, Rock Lake may be as far as they'll want to travel. Your route to it certainly makes a nice day hike. However, some nice country, inspiring views and fine campsites lie ahead, so continue southward on your Trail 20E04. You make a brief climb to a minor gap, cross a nearby seasonal creeklet, and wind for 0.6 mile to a similar creeklet. Then from it you parallel Wilderness Creek downstream, usually at a distance. You quickly enter a sandy flat, which yields to a sandy slope, this vicinity teeming with ground-hugging mat lupines. These seemingly dainty wildflowers are sturdier than one might guess; they are hardy perennials with extensive root systems.

Just after we re-enter forest, our trail swings southwest over to a nearby junction with a westbound, 1.3-mile **trail to a Summit Lake trailhead** (Route SM-4). This trail offers the shortest way in to the upper part of Spicer Meadow Reservoir.

Onward, we wind 0.3 mile southeast down to a crossing of Wilderness Creek, which can be a wet ford in late spring and early summer. Maintaining a southeast orientation, our trail initially climbs past a minor outcrop, soon passes a larger, brushy one, and then crosses a couple of Wilderness Creek tributaries before making a short, winding climb to a saddle. This is a fine lunch spot, if you've brought along liquid refreshment, for the hill to the

Left to right: Hiram, Airola and Iceberg peaks and Peak 9366

northeast is composed of an eye-pleasing array of glacier-smoothed hummocky slabs. From the saddle you descend fairly steeply over 0.4 mile, losing about 300 feet in elevation by the time you reach a trail junction. The descending trail used to drop to Gabbott Meadow, but now it drops about ¼ mile to the shoreline of **upper Spicer Meadow Reservoir.** The shoreline fluctuates seasonally as well as from year to year. The best time for swimmers to visit this vicinity is in late July, after the lake has had some time to warm up, but before its level has dropped significantly. Anglers may want to visit it earlier, although it is unlikely that this upper part of the reservoir will be heavily fished.

If you opt to continue on Trail 20E04, you start a traverse on which, after a spring-fed creeklet that is just before a prominent gully, you soon have views across Highland Creek canyon. The most eye-catching feature is The Dardanelles, which is a massive remnant of volcanic flows that stands high above your granitic canyon. These flows originated near the Highways 120/395 junction east of Sonora Pass, and they streamed down an ancient river canyon about 9–9½ million years ago. Most of the canyon has since been eroded away, though its bottom still survives, lying hidden and inaccessible at the base of the lowest flow. This base is about 1000 feet higher than the bottom of the Highland Creek canyon. The base of the Whittakers Dardanelles, whose end you see about 5 miles southwest down-canyon, is about 2500 feet higher than the bottom of the unseen Middle Fork Stanislaus

River canyon. Such figures give you an idea of how much erosion has occurred since the flows were deposited. Keep in mind that streams first had to remove the original river-canyon's walls and adjacent uplands before they could cut down to form today's drainages.

Our views continue for almost ½ mile of hiking, then we enter a white-fir forest. In ½ mile we first pass several springs and creeklets that may be reliable through most of the summer, and then encounter a gently sloping area just below and right of us, which is suitable for camping. About 200 yards beyond this area we cross the first of two usually brisk branches of Bull Run Creek. The trail then weaves in and out of two dry gullies before quickly reaching a junction with the **Bull Run Creek Trail.** To hike up it and then down to Pacific Valley, consult Route PG-3, which describes the trail in the reverse direction. Before the new Spicer Meadow Reservoir, this trail used to continue down to Gabbott Meadow. Today you may be able to follow it steeply down to the north tip of the reservoir, which from August onward is likely to be a dry.

Onward, the Highland Creek Trail in 0.4 mile first descends eastward to a seasonal stream, then south to a junction with the **Dardanelles Creek Trail.** This junction is situated close to Highland Creek, and you can find a good campsite or two in this vicinity. To continue on either the Highland Creek Trail or the Dardanelles Creek Trail, consult respectively either Route HL-3 or Route TD-5. Both trails are described in the reverse direction.

LA-7   Lake Alpine to North Fork Stanislaus River via old Elephant Rock Trail

Distances
1.1 miles to junction with Duck Lake access trail
1.5 miles to Duck Creek
3.1 miles to North Fork Stanislaus River

Trailhead   Same as the Route LA-6 trailhead

Introduction   This trail is the answer for those who seek mountain solitude, yet don't want to spend more than a couple of hours reaching it. Because the terrain along this

route is quite subdued, lacking both majestic peaks and pristine lakes, the trail receives very little use. Hence, leaving the trail at any point virtually guarantees you'll see nary a soul. But a word of caution is necessary: because the terrain is quite subdued, prominent landmarks are absent, so you had better be expert with map and compass if you don't want to get lost.

Description   As in the preceding route, you climb east to a nearby glaciated, forested ridge, which is part of the northwest boundary of Carson-Iceberg Wilderness. Your route,

Derelict cabin in meadow west of Duck Lake as it appeared in 1985

which had quickly widened to an old road, now briefly traverses the ridge, passing through a gate and quickly descending to a switchback. From it the Highland Creek Trail continues east while you follow the narrow road as it arcs southward down to the west edge of a large meadow. Here you'll find three cabins, only the northern one in respectable condition. You also see Duck Lake, about 300 yards to the east, whose maximum depth is about 4 feet. In dry years this oversized duck pond can all but disappear in late summer, when the southward-migrating ducks arrive. You leave the meadow by a cluster of tall aspens and in a minute arrive at a junction with the **Duck Lake access trail.**

Duck Lake access trail

This easily missed, eastbound, 1.1-mile-long trail quickly crosses a southern, sometimes wet stringer of the Duck Lake meadow then soon passes through a gap in a low granitic ridge. Between this gap and an upcoming, seasonal pond, one can leave the unmaintained trail and cross the ridge to the south shore of Duck Lake. Eastward, one quickly reaches a seasonally boggy crossing of Duck Creek, enters a lodgepole-pine flat, then for about 300 yards walks essentially along (not beside) a snowmelt creek, leaving it just before a junction with Highland Creek Trail 20E04 (previous route). As veteran hikers reading the foregoing description will rightly conclude, this trail goes through prime mosquito land. Be prepared for hordes, at least until late July.

Spurning the Duck Lake access trail, we start a south-southeast traverse through a prime red-fir forest, then soon leave it for a short descent in the same direction down open, ducked granitic slabs. Our descent ends at seasonal **Duck Creek,** which is one's first opportunity to escape to solitude. You could go down the creek for 3 miles, not seeing a sign of civilization until you reach Slick Rock Road 7N17 (Route LA-2). Be aware that the creek can dry up before late July and that mosquitoes can be fierce before then—a "Catch-22" situation. The creek initially heads down a minor, southwest-oriented canyon, then breaches its south wall to find a course down an adjacent canyon. As you can see from this book's map (or from an airplane), the gently corrugated landscape lying between Highway 4 and The Dardanelles has a series of more or less parallel, southwest-draining creeks.

From Duck Creek our trail climbs steeply but briefly southeast up to a narrow ridge clad in huckleberry oak. We next dip a bit before breaching a second, broader, adjacent ridge, then wind down a fairly gentle grade to the headwaters of a Duck Creek tributary. Here is your second opportunity for escape to solitude: follow the tributary just over a mile to its union with Duck Creek.

Just past the tributary, the trail briefly heads southwest, reaching a stagnant, seasonal pond, then turns east to the edge of a nearby lakelet, which, like its eastern twin, is shallow and grassy. From the lakelet we make a moderate descent southeast down a gully as we enter the shallow North Fork Stanislaus River canyon. Our gradient abates as we reach open, granitic slabs, on which our trail completely disappears. Follow a ducked route, which arcs southwest almost to the stream bank, then parallels it about 300 yards downstream to a log or boulder crossing of **North Fork Stanislaus River.** You'll find a campsite along the northwest bank just west of the crossing, but others can be found by heading either upstream or downstream. Enjoy the solitude!

Chapter 9   Pacific Grade

PG-1   Trail 19E02 to Bull Run Lake

Distances
2.3 miles to junction with Trail 19E94
3.6 miles to Heiser Lake and to Bull Run
Lake

Trailhead   From Lake Alpine's east-shore access road, drive 3.9 miles east up Highway 4 to a curve with a spur road branching southeast across an adjacent, level area. From Pacific Grade Summit this spur-road junction is 2.2 miles west down Highway 4. In early season you may have to park near the start of the spur road rather than near a gate; if so, your hike to each of the above destinations will be 0.5 mile longer. The last 125 yards of road are badly rutted, and only those in high-clearance vehicles will want to drive all the way to the trailhead—a gate across the road.

Introduction   Trout-stocked Bull Run Lake is only a two-hour hike for the average backpacker, which gives it the potential for overuse, particularly on summer weekends. To reduce impact on the lake and its adjoining terrain, day hike to it, if possible. The trail starts out very user-friendly—first level, then downhill—which gives you an opportunity to warm up your calf and thigh muscles. These will be challenged by a substantial three-stage climb, but you can cool off with a refreshing swim to the lake's bedrock island.

Description   From a gate at the border of Sections 31 and 36 we start along a route that parallels the west edge of fenced-in Stanislaus Meadow. After ½ mile we leave the meadow and its seasonal herd of cows, and from a brink can look east to a band of cliffs, ¼ mile away, which would please any technical-rock climber. We now make a moderate descent ½ mile south down a wide path, entering Carson-Iceberg Wilderness and generally staying within earshot of the seasonal headwaters of North Fork Stanislaus River. At the base of the slope we encounter two bouldery snowmelt washes, which we cross, and then the route turns east and in rapid succession crosses several more. Through early July these washes may tax your ability to keep your boots dry.

Next, we parallel the Bull Run/Heiser lakes creek lazily upstream for over ⅓ mile before crossing it. This can be another wet early-season crossing. Once across, we make a short traverse up-canyon across a shaded flat. Where we begin to toil up a steep, rocky tread, plentiful conifers yield to scrubby huckleberry oaks and a largely shadeless woodland of junipers and pines. After we perspire up 200 feet of elevation gain, the trail's gradient slackens and forest shade soon returns where we approach a junction with **Trail 19E94.** Up it you could continue 1⅓ miles to **Heiser Lake,** but this would surely be the long way to it; the following route is considerably easier. If after your short but strenuous climb you need a refreshing body of water to cool off in, then go but 300 yards northeast up Trail 19E94, leave it, and head cross-country 100 yards southeast to a hidden lakelet. Its water may be slightly cloudy, and it certainly abounds in aquatic insects, but it is, nevertheless, a refreshing swimming hole.

Starting east-southeast from the aforementioned junction, our Trail 19E02 fords, in 45 yards, Heiser Lake's outlet creek, which in June is a small torrent of white water that you must boulderhop. Continuing in the same direction, we can relax as we stroll across an almost level granitic bench that is laced with a number of snowmelt creeklets. About ⅓ mile beyond Heiser Lake's outlet creek, we angle south, cross several more creeklets, and then face the second of three strenuous climbs. Our usually steep trail proceeds from slab to granitic slab as it climbs and gyrates up alongside a creek. After ⅓ mile of climbing that produces a 350-foot gain, we turn south and amble past a quickly reached snowmelt pond. Before August, its resident swarm of mosquitoes will spur you onward.

Just beyond the pond we commence our final climb, which is convoluted like the preceding one, but is only moderately steep. After ⅓ mile of progress we crest a granitic slab and almost fall into **Bull Run Lake.** After a hot, perspiring climb, that isn't a bad idea. Though swimming tends to be brisk—in the low-to-mid 60s at best, you may find the lake's rock-slab island a tempting goal for a bit of sunbathing. Lying only 40–50 yards from the shore and separated from it by shallow water, this island can almost be reached by wading.

While some visitors come to swim, others come to fish, for with a relatively high elevation and a good depth—30 feet—the lake is an excellent habitat for brook trout. Since 1950, Bull Run Lake, like nearby Heiser Lake, has

been annually stocked with 1000 of these trout. However, angling pressure is quite heavy.

If you've backpacked to the lake, you'll find camping accommodations for about two dozen people. For backpackers the lake provides a base camp for further exploration of the area. From a large, grassy meadow bordering the lake's southeast shore, one can climb ½ mile south up granitic slopes to a saddle and then angle east up a gully to another saddle, this one separating Peak 9352, to the south, from Peak 9413. The latter offers better views and offers a way to slightly higher, dark, volcanic Bull Run Peak, which is almost due east of it. A fairly obvious scramble up its west side leads to the summit. Summit views are given in Route PG-3. Summit views from Peak 9413 are quite similar, and both summits barely protruded during the last glaciation. "Bull Run" names were probably given in Civil War days by local miners who were sympathetic to the Confederate cause, and were commemorating two Confederate victories at Bull Run, Virginia.)

An easily reached rock-slab in Bull Run Lake

PG-2 Trail 19E94 to Heiser Lake

Distances

1.6 miles to a junction with westbound Trail 19E94

2.1 miles to Heiser Lake

2.5 miles to Bull Run Lake Trail 19E02

3.8 miles to Bull Run Lake

Trailhead From Lake Alpine's east-shore access road, drive 5.8 miles east up Highway 4 to a small parking area for a picnic ground that lies just west of Mosquito Lake. This parking area is about 70 yards west of Mosquito Lakes Campground, whose entrance in turn is ¼ mile west of Pacific Grade Summit. This summit, in turn, is 7.8 miles west of Ebbetts Pass. (Note the discrepancy between Mosquito Lake and Mosquito Lakes. Usually, there is one lake, but by late summer the water line drops enough to form two separate lakes.)

Introduction Heiser Lake is second only to Rock Lake as the wilderness' most accessible lake. And because Heiser Lake Trail 19E94 starts from Highway 4 near a popular camp-ground and a roadside lake, rather than from some place miles along a graded road, it receives heavy use. It is a small-scale version of Rock Lake, being mostly shallow and being rimmed by trees rather than having a moun-tain backdrop, as is fairly close-by Bull Run Lake. Despite its small size, Heiser Lake has a relatively large amount of camping space. Those in search of special views have a treat from a viewpoint only a few minutes off the main trail: a view of the elusive Peep Sight of Peep Sight Peak. And climbers who want to hone their skills can do so on outcrops just above the lake.

Description At the picnic ground the start of the trail is not always obvious, especially before late July, when snow patches still lie shaded beneath the clustered mountain hem-locks. Look for old blazes on the trees, which indicate a moderately climbing southeastward route. In about 30 yards or so, the trail should become obvious, and up it we hike on a steepening grade across granitic bedrock that has a veneer of volcanic rocks.

After our first climb we cross a small, broad flat and then make a minor descent south through a typical subalpine forest of red fir, mountain hemlock, western white pine and lodgepole pine. From just west of a grassy pond we start to climb again, though not as steeply or for as long as before. Quickly we reach a windswept, relatively barren, granitic crest, which marks the northern boundary of Carson-Iceberg Wilderness. By walking just 40 yards west to a minor high point, you get fair views of lands to the north and south. Better views are obtained from the broad summit ¼ mile to the west.

From the crest we descend south, generally at a moderate-to-steep gradient, losing about 200 feet in elevation before our hemlock-lined trail reaches a snowmelt creeklet and makes a moderately steep ascent southeast up to a nearby junction. From here **Trail 19E94 goes west** (as well as east), which is not the route you'll want unless you're bound for Bull Run Lake. This 0.9-mile trail segment starts almost level, curves south, and then plunges steeply down slopes, gradually easing to a gentle descent after about 300 feet of elevation loss. You then have an easy, creekside stroll to a junction with **Bull Run Lake Trail 19E02**, from which you follow Route PG-1 1.3 miles up to Bull Run Lake.

But most folks will go to Heiser Lake, so at the first trail junction you turn left, on the east branch of Trail 19E94, and walk about 350 yards up a gentle grade to a junction. The main trail climbs south, but for a view of the Peep Sight, continue east on a use trail, which quickly dies out. This doesn't matter, since the nearby crest is clearly visible. Rather than head to its lowest point, veer left up granitic bedrock to a fine vantage point. From here you see glacier-scoured-and-smoothed Pacific Creek canyon, which contains Pacific Valley near its lower end. Lookout Peak, with a ridge descending toward us, stands in the east-northeast, while right of it stands spreading Peep Sight Peak. You'll see the Peep Sight—a natural bridge about 25 feet high and 40 feet wide— ⅔ of the way down its southern flank. It is quite easily reached, and the route to it is described in Route PG-5. Continuing your scan to the right, you'll note Henry Peak, which is merely a smooth ridgecrest with a steep north-facing escarpment.

Bound for nearby Heiser Lake, one leaves the previously mentioned junction for a short climb, first southwest and then southeast, to a gap in a minor ridgecrest. Here, climbers will be enticed by a 35-foot-high cliff with Class 5 routes ranging from easy to moderately diffi-

Heiser Lake

cult. All others will be enticed by the thought of reaching the nearby lake. The trail heads southwest down slopes, dying out just above several spacious campsites perched above the north shore of trout-stocked **Heiser Lake.** Once known as Lost Lake, this 3-acre lake is quite shallow at both ends, though its center is about 15 feet deep. If you want trout, you had

better come early in the season, for from late July through August, when the lake is warmest, the brook trout congregate at the hard-to-reach bottom in the center of the lake. During this period, when the lake warms to the mid 60s by afternoon, you can console yourself for bad fishing luck with a refreshing swim.

PG-3   Bull Run Creek Trail to Bull Run Peak, Henry Peak and Highland Creek Trail

Distances
3.2 miles to saddle between Bull Run and
    Henry peaks
3.6 miles (approx.) to Bull Run Peak
3.9 miles (approx.) to Henry Peak
7.2 miles to junction with Highland Creek
    Trail
7.6 miles to junction with Dardanelles Creek
    Trail
8.7 miles to junction with Jenkins Canyon
    Trail
17.8 miles for Bull Run/Highland/Weiser
    semiloop

Trailhead   From Lake Alpine's east-shore access road, drive 6.1 miles east up Highway 4 to Pacific Grade Summit, then wind 1.0 mile down it to the Pacific Valley road. This junction is 6.8 miles west of Ebbetts Pass. Head south on this road, passing through stretched out Pacific Valley Campground, which has

tables and outhouses dispersed along the way. If you stay at the primitive campground, you'll have to carry out your own trash and get your water from adjacent Pacific Creek, which can dry up in August. About 0.7 mile from Highway 4 your road reaches a turnaround, and you should park in this vicinity. Just beyond the turnaround is where Pacific Valley Trail 19E43 actually begins.

Introduction   There are at least seven trail routes to the northeast part of the new Spicer Meadow Reservoir. One of the commonest is the Highland Creek Trail, which heads southeast to it from the Lake Alpine environs (Route LA-6). Perhaps the least used is the Bull Run Creek Trail, even though it is about the same length as the Highland Creek Trail, and it has only a bit more total elevation gain. The trouble with the Bull Run Creek Trail is that it makes most of its gain in one rather strenuous, intimidating 1.5-mile climb to Bull Run saddle. From there on, it goes mostly downhill to Highland Creek. Should you take this route in, don't take it out. It is too steep and it can be waterless, and on a hot summer afternoon you could face a real threat of heat stroke. Instead, head 2.6 miles east up the Highland Creek Trail, then climb north up the moderately graded, streamside Weiser Trail.

Some folks may want to climb only to Bull Run saddle and then "bag" Bull Run Peak. This ascent, though very steep, is quite safe, and the views are outstanding. Henry Peak is a much easier ascent, but being flanked by higher peaks—Peep Sight, Lookout, Bull Run and its northwest ridge—its summit views are quite restricted, though still pleasing.

Description The route begins as Pacific Valley Trail 19E43, which is an easy ORV road by 4WD standards. Pickup trucks with high clearance can make the first ½ mile without trouble, passing a creekside campsite or two. But then, immediately beyond a dry wash, the route is briefly steep and bouldery. Just after this short climb we reach a meadow that has been enlarged by logging, and now has a herd of cows. We parallel this fenced-in meadow for ⅔ mile, then soon arrive at a turnaround by a fence. If you've driven all the way to here, you've saved yourself 1½ miles of nearly level hiking, each way. Immediately beyond the fence Milk Ranch Trail 20E01 branches left, climbing 2 miles to Weiser Trail 19E41, both described in the next route. If you plan to make a semiloop trip, you'll return along this route.

Straight ahead the Bull Run Creek Trail (which like the Pacific Valley Trail is also numbered 19E43) climbs gently southeast before the gradient becomes moderate-to-steep and quite shady. Off to your right you'll see where a late '80s rock avalanche broke loose and eradicated some vegetation. About 0.7 mile from the fence we reach the bank of Pacific Creek and parallel it south a couple of minutes before crossing it at the north edge of a spacious meadow. In late summer the creek may be your last source of water until you reach the Highland Creek vicinity, about 5½ miles farther. Straight ahead is volcanic Bull Run Peak, rising a full ¼ mile above you.

Leaving the meadow and its creek, we start a second forested, moderate-to-steep climb, and in ⅓ mile touch the creek bank and enter a meadow of willows and corn lilies. Over the next ⅓ mile the ascent is merely moderate, and we can enjoy the multitude of wildflowers. One species that is extremely common between here and the upcoming saddle is western mugwort, an aromatic herb that is a close cousin to sagebrush. This is a hard species to key out, because even at full bloom, its tiny, greenish sunflowers go unnoticed by the casual observer. Though quite common in many places in Carson-Iceberg Wilderness, it is generally uncommon in the rest of the Sierra Nevada.

Just past several springs, which last through much of the summer, the trail becomes very steep. Surveying the lands below and Bull Run Peak above, you may note a path or two up the peak's scree slope, which is one of two routes to the peak's summit. Soon your ascent moderates and you quickly arrive at a granitic **saddle between Bull Run and Henry peaks.** The Carson-Iceberg Wilderness boundary runs along this crestline.

Bull Run Peak

The broad summit of volcanic Bull Run Peak is a strenuous ½ mile (½ hour) away. To reach it, don't tackle a granitic headwall head-on, but rather head a few yards south down the trail, then start a scramble up the jumble of bedrock and boulders. After several minutes you'll reach a spot where the granitic crest yields to a rubbly volcanic ridge. Proceed up this rubble, then cross a wooded flat and stand face-to-face with Bull Run Peak proper.

You have two choices to the summit: left of the ridge up a rather stable talus slope, or right, around the ridge, to the scree slope you saw back on the trail. The safest way is to go right, though you'll slip and slide as you struggle up the loose scree to the obvious top

Summit view down Pacific Valley

of **Bull Run Peak.** Along this strenuous ascent, you'll want to pause often, and can admire two species of subalpine wildflowers— Sierra primrose and alpine sorrel. Since neither is common, take great care to avoid uprooting these plants. Near the top of the scree slope, the left route traverses over from a shelf between two lava flows to join our route. This alternate route, which began on rather stable talus blocks, involves a scramble up the lower flow to reach the shelf. While easy, this scramble is potentially dangerous, since there are some loose blocks of lava.

Standing atop Bull Run Peak, with a 360° panorama, you may feel you're on top of the world. How different the feeling would have been about 9¼ million years ago, when your summit was only a tiny part of an 80-mile-long flow of latite lava, which had just buried a similar, recently deposited flow in an ancestral Stanislaus River canyon. Just some 20,000 years ago, Bull Run and higher peaks to the north and east stood out as islands above a sea of ice.

Other summit sights include glaciated Pacific Valley, 3 miles to the north, and Lookout Peak, high above the valley's granitic eastern wall. Round Top, the highest peak in Mokelumne Wilderness, is 14 miles away. You also see all the major peaks in the Highland Lakes area plus Highland and Silver peaks, just north of the area. In the south stands a dark, volcanic ridge, which includes pointed Dardanelles Cone and The Dardanelles proper. From about 1990 onward the most eye-catching feature may be an artificial one—the new Spicer Meadows Reservoir, which will flood about a 6-mile stretch of the Highland Creek canyon. Two other reservoirs to the right of it—Union and Utica—will pale in comparison.

Henry Peak

If you want summit views with a minimum of effort, then Henry Peak is for you. Leaving the trail at the saddle, you climb up a broad volcanic ridge that becomes increasingly gentle and forested with elevation, until just before the summit of **Henry Peak,** where you have a 360° panorama. Looking north-north-west down Pacific Creek canyon, you see Round Top—the dark jewel of Mokelumne Wilderness—dominating the skyline. Looking clockwise, you see Lookout Peak, which lies west of a broad, granitic saddle, Willow Flat. Silver and Highland peaks stand behind the western flank of Peep Sight Peak, which in turn is flanked to the east by Folger Peak. East to south the views are quite similar to those obtained from Bull Run Peak—which, however, blocks views to the southwest. See the next route's "Henry Peak" side trip if you want to continue northeast.

If you keep to the trail, you'll quickly start a moderate-to-steep descent southeast, passing two fairly lasting springs along the way. These are your most reliable sources of water between here and Highland Creek. The gradient next slackens briefly for a pleasant stroll through a lodgepole-and-wildflower woodland, then descends fairly steeply to a meadowy crossing of Bull Run Creek. The creek can dry up in mid- or late summer, at least in its upper reaches. A spur trail starts downstream along the creek's northwest bank, ending in ¼ mile at a cow camp, which gives you a hint about the creek's purity.

Our trail continues southeast, climbing to and then traversing the slopes of a volcanic mudflow just before crossing a narrow, granitic ridge. Onward, we descend, sometimes steeply, in a south-southeast direction, getting pleasant views of eastern peaks and canyons. The trail turns south immediately before the east end of a minor ridge, which is worth visiting, for it too has rewarding views. More sometimes-steep descent ensues, this time across slopes with one unreliable spring and an abundant crop of snow bush, which has needle-tipped branches (hikers in shorts—take note). The trail then heads southeast down a usually dry gulch, crosses a low, forested ridge, and quickly comes to a lodgepole-fringed pool that is largely overgrown with sedges. Note that just east of the pool, from where your trail starts to curve southwest, there is a minor, forested gap. From that gap you can make an easy cross-country descent northeast, reaching the Weiser Trail and nearby Weiser Creek in just under ½ mile.

Southwest, we start down a damp, meadowy draw, then have a fairly steep drop into the upper part of a minor side canyon, where we soon cross its seasonal creek. From one mile before the Highland Creek Trail, we make a short stream-bank traverse before veering west to, and descending along, a minor gully. This debouches onto a sandy flat, treed with some mature Jeffrey pines, and you could camp here, getting water by heading east over the adjacent ridge to the creek we just left—if it indeed has water in it! From the flat we go west for a minute or two, then face a 400-foot elevation loss along a generally steep trail. Fortunately it is shaded. Still, by the time you reach the **Highland Creek Trail,** you'll be convinced you won't want to hike back up it. An old stretch of your trail continues about ¼ mile down to the northeast end of the new Spicer Meadow Reservoir, which from August onward—if not earlier—is likely to be water-less.

Chapter 8's Route LA-6 describes Highland Creek Trail 20E04 from Lake Alpine southeast to our junction. Likely you will want to continue east on this trail rather than head out to Lake Alpine. Therefore, start south-east, descending briefly to a gully that contains the seasonal creek you crossed above, then descend ¼ mile southwest to a junction with the **Dardanelles Creek Trail.** This Route TD-5 (Chapter 14) begins by quickly crossing Highland Creek, and in the general vicinity near the creek's north bank you should find a good campsite or two.

To return to Pacific Valley, head southeast up the Highland Creek Trail. This climbs about ½ mile up to a gap in a very low ridge, beyond which you are quite close to a part of Highland Creek that has a deep pool fed by an 8-foot-high cascade. This vicinity is a fine place to camp. The creek contains brook trout from natural reproduction throughout its length.

From here we head east, staying just above the creek and its alluring pools. Junipers, Jeffrey pines, manzanitas and huckleberry oaks quickly give way to cottonwoods, lodgepoles and firs as we reach the west end of an alluvial flat. Two nice camps lie here, and you'll find another one near the flat's east end, where you reach a junction with the **Jenkins Canyon Trail.** The Tahoe-Yosemite Trail route has been on the Highland Creek Trail to this point, but now this lengthy route turns onto the Jenkins Canyon Trail, which momentarily crosses Highland Creek. A boulderhop by late summer, this creek can be quite a challenging ford before mid-July. To continue up the Jenkins Canyon Trail, see Chapter 15's Route CF-1, which describes the trail in the opposite direction. To continue up the next part of the Highland Creek Trail, follow the last part of the next route in the opposite direction.

PG-4   Milk Ranch and Weiser Trails to Henry Peak and to Highland Creek Trail

Distances
3.3 miles to saddle above Marshall Canyon
3.5 miles to junction with Weiser Trail
4.3 miles (approx.) to Henry Peak
7.6 miles to junction with Highland Creek
    Trail
8.0 miles to Hiram Meadow Cabin
9.1 miles to junction with Jenkins Canyon
    Trail

Trailhead   Same as the Route PG-3 trail-head

Introduction   The first two miles of the Milk Ranch Trail take you to a junction with the Weiser Trail, which offers the wilderness traveler a very pleasant, easy, creekside descent through a shallow, forested canyon. The trail's several creekside campsites are enough justification for some to take this route, though most people will want to take the trail to its end, then go briefly west along the Highland Creek Trail to campsites located near Hiram Meadow. What the route lacks is views,

though by making a relatively easy cross-country side trip up to the top of Henry Peak, you'll obtain a 360° panorama of the land-scape, including some views of distant peaks.

Description   As in the previous route, walk, ride or drive (if you can) 1.5 miles south along a nearly level, though primitive road—Pacific Valley Trail 19E43—to a gate at the second fence. About ¼ mile before this fence you'll have a fine view of Henry Peak, to the south-east, which stands above your route up Marshall Canyon. If you drive all the way to the fence, you can subtract 1.5 miles from all the distances mentioned above. Immediately past the gate, which prevents further motor-vehicle travel, Bull Run Creek Trail 19E43 continues south, while your road veers left, northeast, to an immediate crossing of Pacific Creek. This could be a wet ford in early season. Just 85 yards past the creek the road bends southeast, and here you can leave it for a start on rather obscure Milk Ranch Trail

Peep Sight Peak dominates the view northeast

20E01, which begins northeast. It too curves
quickly southeast and becomes very apparent.
Both road and trail bend east and climb
moderately, the two crossing about midway
before trail's end, about ⅔ mile after the start.
Now the old road becomes the only Milk
Ranch Trail, and in 100 yards it passes
through a barbed-wire gate. The gradient
eases, and you momentarily parallel Marshall
Canyon creek just before entering a small
meadow. Not far beyond, you cross Marshall
Canyon's creek, and from this spot one can
climb north for the shortest ascent to the top of
Lookout Peak. However, such a route is
heavily forested and bouldery at first, and it
lacks views. A much more enjoyable, imaginative cross-country route is presented in the
next hike.

The road turns southeast, crosses a nearby,
seasonal tributary, and then climbs southeast
before heading east and dying out. Onward,
you follow a trail south, which climbs quite
steeply through a shady fir-and-hemlock forest
before reaching, without too much effort, a
saddle above Marshall Canyon. You've now
reached the north boundary of Carson-Iceberg
Wilderness, and you can make a mile-long
side trip along that boundary, a ridgecrest,
southwest up to Henry Peak.

Henry Peak

From a small, linear meadow at the saddle,
you immediately enter forest cover as you

start southwest up the broad, poorly defined
ridgecrest. Farther up, the ridgecrest becomes
better defined, and granitic bedrock begins to
crop up. Higher, the forest thins, and one can
gaze east to the Peep Sight, a natural bridge on
the southern slope of Peep Sight Peak. Should
you wish to hike to either the bridge or the
peak, consult the next route.

Higher still, the ridgecrest becomes almost
exclusively granitic bedrock, and the red firs,
mountain hemlocks and western white pines
become sparse. When you encounter your first
volcanic "bedrock"—mudflows and stream
sediments—you know you're getting close to a

Lakelet at the base of Henry Peak

lakelet at the base of Henry Peak. You spy the lakelet just after you cross a small, forested volcanic knoll. From a saddle immediately southwest of the knoll and west of the lakelet, you face a curving band of cliffs that make up the north face of Henry Peak. Unless you've brought along climbing gear and a lot of courage, you'll not continue straight ahead. The cliffs, though impressive, are short enough that climbers with a 50-meter rope should be able to climb virtually any route in just one pitch. However, I believe you should use a top rope to climb the latite-lava cliffs. Lava isn't as solid as granite, and you're quite a distance away from medical help.

One alternate hikers' route is to traverse to the right, across a steep talus slope. This is quite safe except when hard, icy snow is present. From a northwest-descending ridge you then traverse about 50 yards south to an obvious gully, up which you scamper to the top.

The longer, all-season, preferred route is to drop to the lakelet and just east of it start climbing up Henry Peak's northeast-descending ridge. Though fairly steep, it is quite easy and safe, and is not really very exposed. Once on the broad summit of **Henry Peak,** you'll have to do a bit of walking to get in all the views; it is too flat to have one ideal viewpoint. Views are described in the "Henry Peak" side trip of the previous route. If you want even better views, you can walk southwest down Henry Peak's gentle back side to a saddle and then tackle Bull Run Peak (side trip in previous route), or you can return to the Milk Ranch Trail and climb Lookout and/or Peep Sight peaks (side trips in next route).

From the saddle above Marshall Canyon, Milk Ranch Trail 20E01 heads southeast down a small, linear meadow, then through a broader one frequented by range cattle. Immediately beyond it we arrive at a junction with the **Weiser Trail.** If you're bound for Milk Ranch Meadow, Lookout Peak, the Peep Sight or Peep Sight Peak, stay on the Milk Ranch Trail and consult the next route.

Our Route PG-4 branches right onto Weiser Trail 19E41 and in 100 yards crosses the seasonal headwaters of Weiser Creek. After a 0.6-mile creekside descent southeast, the creek is joined by a larger branch, and stream flow from this point downstream is guaranteed. Ahead, we stay either along

Weiser Creek or within earshot of it, and in about a mile we skirt the edge of a 60-foot-deep gorge that the creek churns through. Just below the gorge, near where we enter a grove of mature red firs, the creek is joined by a major, south-flowing tributary.

Immediately beyond the small grove we spy the first Jeffrey pines, junipers, huckleberry oaks, snow bushes and aspens, which certainly represent a change in the vegetation. Only a low ridge separates Weiser Creek from Highland Creek, and if you want to go over to Highland Creek Trail 20E04, you can do so just ahead, where your trail curves from south-southeast to south-southwest. Several large trailside junipers alert you to this stretch of the trail. Going cross-country, you cross adjacent Weiser Creek, then head east over a nearby broad, forested ridge saddle, which stands no more than 80 feet above the creek. Bearing east-southeast, you then drop 280 feet along a ¼-mile descent to the Highland Creek Trail, which in this vicinity runs along the west edge of a broad flat. By heading down the Highland Creek Trail and then back up the Weiser Trail, you add diversity to your trip.

You could also head up-canyon, though following the trail to its end by the Highland Lakes would take you far out of your way. Instead, you can follow the trail up-canyon for just under a mile and then, instead of crossing Highland Creek, keep to its west bank for a leisurely cross-country trek ⅔ mile north to where Highland Creek bends east. Continue north along a creek that flows through a gentle-sloped canyon, and in 1⅓ miles reach the southwest end of Milk Ranch Meadow. Continue following your creek, and soon you should intersect the Milk Ranch Trail, which starts a steep climb just west of the creek. Take the trail 2.8 miles west back to its junction with the Weiser Trail. In several places this lightly used, traversing trail is hard to follow, though the route is a natural one, and you shouldn't lose the tread for long.

Most people will undoubtedly keep to Weiser Trail 19E41, which now descends a minor granitic ridge covered by aromatic-barked Jeffrey pines and drab, scrubby huckleberry oaks. This quite open descent presents us with a view all the way down our canyon to its end at unseen Highland Creek, above which stands the dark, pointed summit of Dardanelles Cone. Just beyond the toe of the minor ridge, we cross a creeklet, and then in 35 yards cross a second one. In a minute we arrive at a spacious lodgepole flat with plenty of camping space; all you have to do is remove its squatters, the cows.

You've dropped about 1000 feet over the last 2.5 miles since we left the Milk Ranch Trail, and you'll drop about 350 feet more over the next 1.6 miles to the Highland Creek Trail. You'll also cross a half-dozen creeklets before you reach a second lodgepole camp, 0.6 mile from the first. You then cross a bouldery wash, immediately beyond which the trail is being eradicated by a westward migrating meander of Weiser Creek. Just beyond this meander is a third camp, from which you make a short climb south while the creek flows through a granitic gorge. Soon we reach the north end of an extensive lodgepole-pine flat. In a few minutes we bend southwest to pass between two small outcrops of slate-like andesite lava. In another minute we reach a junction with the **Highland Creek Trail.** Chapter 10's Route HL-3 describes the 5.2 miles of trail down Highland Creek to this junction.

You'll find a popular campsite just east along this trail, by the west bank of broad Highland Creek. You can try fishing anywhere along the creek, since there is a naturally sustaining brook-trout population along its entire length. On Highland Creek Trail 20E04 we start west, and in a couple of minutes we find another lava outcrop on our right and a creekside campsite on our left. Ahead, we skirt Hiram Meadow as we continue on for a few more minutes and then come to **Hiram Meadow Cabin.** The cabin and its immediate vicinity are for Forest Service personnel and their stock animals, not for campers.

Immediately beyond the cabin you cross a spring-fed creeklet, then your trail bends

Hiram Meadow Cabin

southwest and soon follows a narrow route between Highland Creek and the base of a lava hill. Beyond, our creekside trail first crosses granitic bedrock and then bends south. Here, the creek enters a gorge, which it descends in a series of rapids and small cascades, while we climb briefly to a bench, then make a steep, ⅓-mile-long descent to a junction with the **Jenkins Canyon Trail.** The 7.1 miles of route west to this junction from Clark Fork's Arnot Creek trailhead are described in Chapter 15's Route CF-1. Just east along this trail, by the west bank of Highland Creek, you'll find a well-used camp.

West from the junction, the Highland Creek Trail stays beside or within earshot of its namesake as it heads 1.1 miles down to a junction with the Dardanelles Creek Trail. This stretch is described in the opposite direction in the last two paragraphs of the previous route. What you should know is that about 0.2 mile west along it are two adjacent, creekside campsites, which lie about 200 yards upstream from the start of a string of refreshing pools.

PG-5 Milk Ranch Trail to Lookout Peak, Peep Sight Peak and Milk Ranch Meadow

Distances
3.5 miles to junction with Weiser Trail
4.8 miles (approx.) to the Peep Sight
5.1 miles (approx.) to Peep Sight Peak
6.1 miles (approx.) to Lookout Peak
6.4 miles to southwest edge of Milk Ranch Meadow

Trailhead   Same as the Route PG-3 trailhead

Introduction   The best part about the Milk Ranch Trail is leaving it, for about a mile east of its junction with the Weiser Trail the tread becomes lightly used and can be hard to follow. And if you're trying to reach Milk Ranch Meadow, you're certainly taking the long way in. The meadow is better reached by starting from the Tryon Meadow trailhead (Chapter 10's Route HL-1), or by my preferred route, from the western sites of Highland Lakes Campground (Route HL-2). By leaving the trail not far east of the Weiser Trail junction, you can climb to the Peep Sight, which is one of the largest natural bridges in the Sierra Nevada. I can think of only one that is larger—a feature on the lower southeast flank of Mammoth Mountain, near Devils Postpile National Monument. Additionally, you can climb to the top of Peep Sight Peak, which is not far above the Peep Sight, for some excellent summit views. Or you can climb to the top of Lookout Peak, whose summit views are equally rewarding. No other peak south of Highway 4 offers such a fine overview of Mokelmune Wilderness, which extends north from the highway.

Description   First, follow the previous route 1.5 miles south along the Pacific Valley Trail, then 2.0 miles east along the Milk Ranch Trail to a junction with the **Weiser Trail,** which branches right, downslope. You continue southeast for a traverse past three snowmelt washes and then, ⅓ mile from the junction, bend northeast for a quick traverse over to a nearby, usually reliable stream (get your water here). If you plan to climb only to Lookout Peak, this is the start of your route. If you plan to climb also to the Peep Sight and Peep Sight Peak, you'll want to do those first, then make an easy descent to Willow Flat and climb Lookout Peak.

Lookout Peak

You'll want to start up the west ridge of the gully with the reliable stream, and to do that it's best to backtrack about 50–100 yards to the bend in the trail. This ridge actually separates two gullies, and the one on the left (west) is the one that is more important, routewise. After you climb about ⅓ mile up the ridge, it levels off, and you contour north, intercepting the creek in the west gully where it curves west over to its nearby source, a cattle-frequented, muddy pond. A low ridge lies just west of and above the pond, and you start north on it, then quickly veer left from it as the gradient steepens. You make a relatively easy climbing traverse, then arrive at the headwaters of Marshall Canyon. A gully separates the volcanic rock you've been traversing from granitic rock to the north and west. You head up that gully, staying just east of a low granitic point as you enter a broad,

Summit view toward Henry and Bull Run peaks and The Dardanelles and Dardanelles Cone

The Peep Sight

windswept bench appropriately called Willow Flat. The route ahead is obvious: head west across the narrowing bench and then up granitic, brushy slopes to the block of basaltic lava that makes up the Lookout Peak summit area. The ascent up the lava flow is quite easy, though due to its loose nature you'll want to be especially careful on your descent.

Lookout Peak offers a fairly good view of much of Mokelumne Wilderness. The highest peak in it is 10,381' Round Top, about 12½ miles to the north-northwest, which is the central point on a long volcanic ridge. During glacial times, only the higher volcanic peaks and ridges—and the summit area of granitic 9332' Mokelumne Peak—protruded above a vast sea of ice. We see that peak just north of west, rising above Highway 4's Pacific Grade Summit.

East of Round Top you'll see Elephants Back and also Red Lake and Stevens peaks, both just over 10,000 feet. To the right of them, after a stretch of low crest, stands Freel Peak, 24 miles north of us, which at 10,881 feet is the highest peak along the Tahoe basin rim. Although these northern lands abound in lakes, you see only one, Lower Blue Lake, which lies in a line of sight below Red Lake Peak. The central peak is 9690' Reynolds Peak, which largely obscures 10,014' Raymond Peak, about 1½ miles beyond it.

You can identify dozens of features to the east, south and west by using a compass and this book's map. To the south you see the southernmost peak in Carson-Iceberg Wilderness, Sonora Peak, and even see some high summits in Emigrant Wilderness.

About 20,000 years ago, glaciers inundated most of what you see. The North Fork

Mokelumne River glacier flowed west just below your summit and only about 150 feet below it.

To descend from Lookout Peak you can either backtrack or else head directly down slopes into viewless Marshall Canyon, which is certainly the shorter of the two routes back to your trailhead. While this latter route is not recommended as an ascent route, it is okay as a descent route because you've already gotten fine views and because hiking around large boulders and through a dense forest is a much easier task in the downhill direction.

Continuing east from the gully with a usually reliable stream, Milk Ranch Trail 20E01 traverses briefly across mule-eared slopes, then crosses a creeklet and starts to climb up steepening slopes. The trail becomes vague here, but where the gradient becomes steep, the trail angles southwest and climbs to a switchback that is just below a shallow saddle on a minor, south-heading ridge. If you look north-northeast from the switchback, you'll see a high point that appears to have a large cave. That "cave" is the east side of the Peep Sight. If you plan to visit it, you'll aim for its west side. Continue north up the minor ridge to where the trail bends east to cross a string of seeping springs.

Peep Sight and Peep Sight Peak

You could probably take any of a number of routes up to the Peep Sight, but I prefer a conspicuous chute near the north end of the minor ridge. This chute is quite safe if you're careful—and as long as you don't have a careless hiker above you knocking off loose blocks. The top of the chute takes you directly up to

Pacific Grade

the west side of the **Peep Sight,** which measures about 40 feet across and 25 feet high. This window will probably grow in time until the center of the natural bridge finally breaks away, which is not likely in the near future. This natural bridge stands isolated just a few feet away from the main ridge, and as an isolated summit, it is a strong attraction for any technical climber who might visit it. I saw no sign that it had been climbed, but a really daring person could have climbed its relatively easy, crumbly route and left not a trace.

To reach Peep Sight Peak, continue up along the ridge. Just above the Peep Sight you spy another inviting summit if you're a technical climber: a 30-foot-high pinnacle that is narrower at its waist than at its summit. It looks almost almost as if it would topple over if you tried to climb it.

Not much higher, we reach the top of the ridge, which is separated from a cliff by a shallow notch. The top of this cliff is not the summit, so veer right and traverse along its base, passing below another notch before reaching a third one. The summit is now just a careful climb up a 40-foot-thick piece of latite tuff to the top of **Peep Sight Peak.** Although this short scramble is neither exposed nor difficult, the tuff, like lava which it resembles, can be loose, and this is no place for an injury, even a minor one such as a sprained ankle.

During glacial times, glaciers originated in the area between your peak and Hiram Peak.

The top of this ice cap was about 9600 feet, and only higher features protruded.

Earlier on this route I mentioned that you get a good view of much of Mokelumne Wilderness from Lookout Peak. If you're not satisfied with your view of it from your spot on Peep Sight Peak, then whisk on over there after you've first scanned the terrain to the southwest, south, east and north. As you can see, the route to Lookout Peak is quite easy and very straightforward.

The most notable feature to the southwest is flat-topped Bull Run Peak, which stands above and left of Henry Peak. To the left, in the distance, is the north end of The Dardanelles. A linear ridge, not part of The Dardanelles proper, lies to the left, followed by a true butte, then above it, Dardanelles Cone. Highland Creek canyon spreads below us, and a massif, topped by Airola and Iceberg peaks, more or less makes up its far side, several miles from us. A broad, low gap separates the massif from adjacent Hiram Peak, 3 miles to the east-southeast, and you see through that gap another one, on the distant horizon—Saint Marys Pass. Note on that distant horizon two peaks just left of the pass: Sonora and Stanislaus peaks. Note that Disaster Peak barely pokes above Hiram Peak. Left of both and 5½ miles from us stands spreading Arnot Peak. Next comes Folger Peak, due east of us and only 2 miles away.

Thirty-foot-high pinnacle near the summit of Peep Sight Peak

To the northeast and north the view is very similar to that from Lookout Peak, and includes Highland and Silver peaks, Ebbetts Pass, Ebbetts Peak and more-distant summits. Farther to the left, on the northwest skyline 14 miles away, is Round Top, which is the highest peak in Mokelumne Wilderness. Nearby Lookout Peak, though a little lower than our summit, nevertheless blots out a good chunk of the wilderness, but you still see Mokelumne Peak, over 13 miles away.

With your panorama complete, either descend the way you came or head over to Lookout Peak, then descend directly from it. Although you can descend directly from Peep Sight Peak to the Milk Ranch Trail, I don't recommend it, for the slopes are steep and they have some minor cliffs you must get around. If you descend the way you came, heading toward the minor, south-heading ridge, proceed with caution, for the volcanic-mudflow deposits are quite rubbly.

From the north end of the minor ridge you have a 2.0-mile trek northeast along an open, view-blessed, lightly used stretch of Milk Ranch Trail 20E01. You first traverse past about a half dozen seeping springs, then traverse a granitic bench to two closely spaced snowmelt creeklets. The trail continues across another granitic bench, and then you drop a bit, passing several minor creeklets before starting a brief climb to an adjacent meadow. The trail through it is obscure, but keep on in the same direction, a 50° bearing, and in about 60 yards the tread should reappear. Immediately beyond it you pass through a gate in a fence that runs along your broad, almost flat, volcanic ridge. You then drop almost 200 feet to a seasonal creek, possibly losing the tread along the way, but maintain your bearing as you ascend from it, heading up a northeast-climbing side gully with a prominent granitic outcrop above its southeast side. From the top of the gully climb over to this minor summit for a major view, which includes Folger, Hiram, Airola and Iceberg peaks plus Milk

Ranch Meadow and the Highland Creek canyon.

Now your descent to the meadow begins. The tread is faint in places, and you could lose the trail, though that would not be much of a problem. The trail makes a moderate descent northeast, then steepens and makes a short jog southeast before reorienting and passing beside a very big, very old, thick-branched western white pine. From it the trail jogs briefly southeast again, then heads northeast below a trickling spring and over a minor divide, from which it curves east, then southeast, plummeting very steeply down to an alluvial fan just west of the meadow. From here, you start east, cross a seasonal creek, and then in a couple of minutes reach the **southwest edge of Milk Ranch Meadow.** Here, among lodgepole pines at the meadow's edge, is a suitable camp that is used mostly by cows, which are the meadow's most conspicuous mammal.

To continue onward 2.2 miles to the Tryon Meadow trailhead, consult the first route in the next chapter, which describes this stretch of trail in the opposite direction. Note that you have two other hiking alternatives, both cross-country. First, you can walk south to the meadow's end, then make an ascending traverse southeast to a minor gap in a nearby ridge. From it you then contour around a bowl to the start of a second ridge, and from there make a gradual, easy climb east-southeast to a third ridge. This cross-country route has been done enough times that it has almost become a trail. From the third saddle you can climb directly to the top of Folger Peak, as many people do, or follow a trail east down to the western sites of Highland Lakes Campground (next chapter's Route HL-2 in reverse). The second cross-country route starts at Milk Ranch Meadow's edge and, keeping just west of a creek, follows its relatively gentle gradient all the way down-canyon to Highland Creek, then follows that down to the Highland Creek Trail, which you'll meet at the north end of a large, bouldery floodplain.

Chapter 10   Highland Lakes

HL-1   Tryon Meadow to Milk Ranch Meadow via Milk Ranch Meadow Trail

Distances
0.9 mile to Davis Lake
1.4 miles to northeast end of Milk Ranch Meadow
2.2 miles to southwest end of Milk Ranch Meadow

Trailhead From Pacific Grade Summit follow Highway 4 just 2.3 miles down to a bridge across North Fork Mokelumne River, then 4.2 miles up to a junction with Highland Lakes Road 8N01. If you're coming from the east side of the Sierra crest, you'll reach this junction 1.3 miles west from Ebbetts Pass. Driving west, you could easily miss the junction, so look carefully. Take Road 8N01, which first drops 1.0 mile southeast to Bloomfield Campground, and then continues 2.3 miles to a bridge across North Fork Mokelumne River. Drive 0.8 mile up a steep section of road to the north edge of Tryon Meadow, from where a minor road branches right. This is the recommended "trailhead" for Route HL-1. The real trailhead lies ¼ mile up the steep, poor road, but you won't want to drive to it in an ordinary automobile.

For Routes HL-6 through HL-10, continue 0.9 mile farther, crossing a minor pass before descending to a nearby junction close to lower Highland Lake. Branch east on a short road, which ends in 150 yards at a trailhead parking area by the lake's outlet creek.

For Route HL-2, continue 0.7 mile along the main road to the first of several roads branching right to the western part of Highland Lakes Campground. Drive about 0.1 mile west, to this spur road's end. For Route HL-5,

continue only 0.1 mile farther on the main road to a road branching left, east, just above upper Highland Lake. Follow it to its end in the eastern part of Highland Lakes Campground.

For Routes HL-3 and HL-4, drive to the end of Road 8N01, by the upper lake's outlet, which is 6.0 miles from Highway 4.

Introduction Few hikers take this easy use trail, whose primary users are probably the folks who manage a herd of cattle that graze in Milk Ranch Meadow. Still, the meadow is rather scenic, is within the wilderness, and does have some camping potential.

Description You start north on a narrow road, which quickly turns west and climbs steeply up to a road fork. Keep right and go about 60 yards to a sharp bend in the road. Milk Ranch Meadow Trail 20E01 officially begins here, and if you've driven up to this spot, you'll have saved ¼ mile of walking. With most of your climbing now done, you descend west-northwest past snowmelt creeklets to a creek, then leave a colorful assortment of water-loving wildflowers behind as you climb just ahead to a red-fir/western-white-pine saddle. You then traverse a bowl, crossing four snowmelt creeklets before reaching its far end and laughably signed **Davis Lake**. Willow Spring would be a better name. Still, to the resident frogs it's definitely a lake.

We next traverse over to an adjacent saddle, then make a ¼-mile descent west before angling southwest to a usually flowing creek in the **northeast end of Milk Ranch**

Milk Ranch Meadow

Meadow. If the trail through this part of the meadow is obscure, note that it crosses the creek beside a chest-high granitic outcrop. The route ahead is pleasant, though quite uneventful, as you proceed, mostly along the meadow's edge on a gravelly trail, to the **southwest end of Milk Ranch Meadow.** Here you'll find a cow-visited campsite beneath lodgepoles. Ahead, the trail continues about 200 yards west to where, just past a creeklet, it becomes vague as it makes a very steep climb to slopes below Peep Sight Peak. This climb, plus the rest of the trail and summit views, are described in the last chapter's last route.

HL-2   Highland Lakes Campground to Folger Peak and Milk Ranch Meadow

Distances
1.0 mile (approx.) to Folger Peak
2.0 miles (approx.) Milk Ranch Meadow

Trailhead   See the Route HL-1 trailhead

Introduction   The two Highland Lakes occupy much of a low, broad divide that lies between Folger Peak and Hiram Peak. Though of nearly similar height, Folger is the easier and safer of the two to climb. However, the views from Folger are definitely secondary to those from Hiram. Still, Folger, unlike Hiram, won't scare off acrophobics. And the first part of the route, up to a saddle, is the start of a fairly well-used route over to Milk Ranch Meadow.

Description   From the west end of a road in the western sites of two-part Highland Lakes Campground, a fairly obvious trail makes a ⅓-mile climb west to a shallow saddle. For some, this may be all the climbing they'll want to do, since by walking south from the saddle on a nearly level volcanic ridge, they'll get fine views of the Highland Lakes, Hiram and Airola peaks, and the Highland Creek canyon.

You will note along this ridge, as around the saddle, some large granitic boulders. Although in times past the Highland Lakes area lay under hundreds of feet of ice, the anomalous granitic boulders aren't erratics left by the area's glaciers. Rather, the boulders were carried in fairly fluid flows of andesite lava that originated from a nearby volcano about 7 million years ago. Just above the saddle, on the lower flank of Folger Peak, the boulders die out, which indicates that the granitic terrain eventually was completely buried by these early flows. As you'll note when you climb toward the summit, there were quite a number of these thin, fluid flows.

However, before leaving the saddle, note a use trail starting a westward traverse. Though essentially cross-country, this route provides relatively easy access to the southwest end of **Milk Ranch Meadow.** Perhaps the Forest Service ought to consider building, if it ever gets the funding, a trail to the meadow along this natural, well-graded cross-country route. Then, by revamping the trail segment from the meadow west to a junction with the Weiser

Trail, the Forest Service will give hikers and equestrians alike a fine loop route down to Hiram Meadow and back.

Continuing on your route, leave the saddle for a cross-country jaunt north up the Carson-Iceberg Wilderness boundary. After about the first 300 yards up a generally barren ridge, the gradient increases considerably, and you zigzag up whatever you deem to be the route of least resistance. The ridge then briefly levels before making a minor drop to a saddle, and you confront the final push. This is up a gravelly slope that is sparsely vegetated with lowly subalpine plants such as lupine, phacelia, locoweed and cut-leaved daisy. Try to make a minimal impact on the native flora, particularly higher up, where you encounter some fairly uncommon subalpine wildflowers growing on gentler, gravelly slopes. When you descend these slopes, you'll be very tempted to rush down them, but please don't, for doing so just hastens the soil's erosion and the plants' demise. Bedrock underfooting returns once again as you approach the neat little summit block capping **Folger Peak**. The peak was named for one of two brothers who lived in Markleeville during its early mining days: Robert M. Folger, the town's first newspaper publisher, or Andrew C. Folger, the town's first postmaster.

You'll see the Highland Lakes below you, with Hiram Peak rising above the upper, southwest one and more distant Arnot Peak rising above the lower, northeast one. Between the two, on the distant skyline, stand a pair of pointed peaks: Sonora on the right and Stanislaus on the left. Of all the peaks in the wilderness or along its boundary, they rank number one and three respectively, while the second highest peak—White Mountain—lies to their left, resembling nothing more than a gently convex ridge.

Turning counterclockwise to the east, we actually look down across the Sierra crest, which at 8410′ Wolf Creek Pass is abnormally low. Actually, the location of the Sierra crest shifted back and forth between glacial and interglacial times. During glacial times, the crest was between Highland and Folger peaks, and ice north of this divide flowed east across Wolf Creek Pass, abrading it as the massive glacier continued down Elder Creek, then north down Wolf Creek canyon.

Northeast, we note two high peaks, Highland on the right and Silver on the left.

View southwest down Highland Creek canyon toward The Dardanelles

Scanning left to due north, we spot Ebbetts Pass, which is a minor gap lying in front of the right base of a chaotic jumble of volcanic rocks crowned by Raymond Peak. Behind this jumble stands the highest summit along the Lake Tahoe rim, 25-mile-distant Freel Peak. The Raymond Peak jumble dominates the eastern sector of Mokelumne Wilderness, while to its left, on the northwest skyline, Round Top dominates the central sector. Mokelumne Peak is the highest along the relatively low western sector, and we see this hazy peak just to the right of 2-mile-distant Peep Sight Peak.

Continuing the scan, we view the peaks adjoining Highland Creek canyon. Bull Run Peak is a blocky summit above the canyon's west slopes, while The Dardanelles are the dark ridges above the canyon's end. Dardanelles Cone is the highest point along these ridges, which were originally part of an ancient 100-mile-long lava flow. We conclude our 360° panorama by recognizing the two prominent summits above the canyon's east slopes: Iceberg Peak, with several summits, and higher, closer Airola, with a pyramidal summit.

HL-3 Highland Lakes to Weiser Trail via Highland Creek Trail

Distances

1.4 miles to first Highland Creek crossing
2.2 miles to second Highland Creek crossing
3.0 miles to start of cross-country route to Weiser Creek
3.3 miles to packers' camp
4.0 miles to third Highland Creek crossing
4.5 miles to Champion Canyon creek
5.1 miles to mouth of Hiram Canyon
5.2 miles to fourth Highland Creek crossing and junction with Weiser Trail
5.5 miles to Hiram Meadow Cabin

Trailhead See the Route HL-1 trailhead

Introduction This route covers the eastern part of Highland Creek Trail 20E04. (The trail's western part is covered in Chapter 8's Route LA-6, which begins near the east end of Lake Alpine.) Starting from the Highland Lakes the trail drops too steeply for some folks for the first 1.3 miles, which is something worth considering if you plan to hike back up the trail. However, beyond your first crossing of Highland Creek you have easy, enjoyable hiking all the way to the route's end. You have five cross-country possibilities, four of them leading to isolated camping, though on two of these routes—up Poison and Champion canyons—you'll face strenuous ascents. But then, seclusion in the Sierra Nevada doesn't always come easily.

Description From road's end by the outlet of upper Highland Lake, Highland Creek Trail 20E04 enters Carson-Iceberg Wilderness as it starts a descent southwest through a minor gorge. At first you descend right alongside Highland Creek, for the steep-sided walls preclude any other route. The stretch of creek through this gorge is hard to fish, but can be rewarding because each pool may contain one or more 7–10″ brook trout. Anglers are encouraged to take only enough trout for a meal so that others may be able to do the same. After about ⅓ mile of moderate-to-steep descent past slopes covered with mule ears, sagebrush and coyote mint, the trail curves to the right and gives us the first good views down-canyon. If you plan to take the next route, up Airola and Iceberg peaks, leave the trail here and traverse south to a nearby gully.

The great majority of hikers will keep to the trail, descending westward past more mule ears, which grow well on loose volcanic rubble. Watch your step on this ¼-mile stretch, for it's quite easy to slip here. Next, open volcanic rubble yields to forested granitic bedrock. For about ¾ mile we make a usually moderate descent west, passing several minor gullies before switchbacking down to our first Highland Creek crossing. For campsites off the beaten track, you might continue ¼ mile west to a stream from Milk Ranch Meadow and explore the environs.

Crossing alder-lined Highland Creek usually involves boulderhopping through late July, but after that it is little more than a step across. Bound for the Hiram Meadow environs, we've already lost almost two thirds of our route's elevation loss in just 1.4 miles. On a more forested stretch, we first traverse southwest across a flat, then descend past low granitic outcrops before crossing a broad, usually dry, gravelly wash. Just beyond it we reach a **second Highland Creek crossing**, this one at the upper end of a long, sparsely vegetated floodplain. The wash we just crossed, plus another one down-canyon, together have transported large amounts of loose volcanic rock from the slopes of Airola Peak, creating the floodplain. Among cottonwoods on the east bank of Highland Creek you'll find a small campsite. However, for much of the summer the creek flows through the sediments rather than on top of them, and you might want to walk about 200+ yards upstream in search of campsites and flowing water.

Once across the broad floodplain, we hike southwest along its border, then curve right (west-southwest) and soon make a short, moderate ascent. After a brief traverse, we make an equally short, moderate descent to the first of two snowmelt washes, these about 40 yards apart. These washes alert you to the start of a **cross-country route to Weiser Creek**. Heading northwest, you can climb about 280 feet in ¼ mile to a broad, forested saddle, then drop about 80 feet to nearby Weiser Creek. You'll find the Weiser Trail just above the creek.

We've been out of sight of Highland Creek ever since we left the floodplain, but after the two snowmelt washes our trail turns south and quickly arrives at the creek's bank. You stroll beside the creek for a minute or two, then reach a lodgepole-shaded **packers' camp,** which is about ⅓ mile west of the mouth of Poison Canyon. If you're looking for solitary camping, you're likely to find it in the upper reaches of this canyon.

From the packers' camp the Highland Creek Trail makes a short, gentle ascent south to pass just above a meadow, whose grass grows on water-saturated sediments that have collected behind a granitic outcrop at the meadow's south end. When you reach this nearby outcrop, you'll see something more interesting—a wide swath of trees felled by an avalanche that originated high on the slopes below the end of Iceberg Peak's west ridge. The avalanche didn't stop at Highland Creek, but rather continued west part way up the canyon's slopes.

Willows do very well along the canyon bottom in this avalanche area, probably because when avalanches are most likely to occur, the willows lie dormant and protected under snow. At first our trail skirts above these willows, then it descends to the canyon's flat floor for a 200-yard traverse among them. About a minute or two after you leave this dense growth, you reach a mid-size, lodgepole-shaded, creekside campsite. Then, in a similar time you reach your **third Highland Creek crossing,** at the end of a 50-yard-long meadow. The trail can be vague in this vicinity, but still you shouldn't have trouble finding its continuation above the creek's east bank. Before late July you can expect a wet ford.

From the east bank the trail soon angles south-southeast away from Highland Creek. On this bearing you contour for about ¼ mile,

then head south-southwest for several minutes to **Champion Canyon creek,** which can be a boulderhop before late July. Here's another chance to seek isolated camping. Beyond the creek your trail makes a gentle descent southwest. After about ⅓ mile you skirt the edge of a predominantly sagebrush meadow, which lies about ¼ mile north of the **mouth of Hiram Canyon.** This is your last opportunity for a cross-country hike up into a secluded side canyon.

At the edge of the sagebrush meadow the Highland Creek Trail passes a campsite, and then it briefly descends west along a usually dry wash to your **fourth Highland Creek crossing.** This can be a 40-foot-wide ford through early July but just a mere boulderhop in late summer. As at previous crossings, fish populations tend to be low, due to too many anglers. For better success, try fishing the creek about 200–300 yards up- or downstream. You'll find a popular campsite just above the west bank of broad Highland Creek, and additional camps are found to the west. Only about 110 yards west of the creek you'll meet a junction with the **Weiser Trail.** The 7.6-mile route from Pacific Valley to this junction is described in the previous chapter's Route PG-4.

On Highland Creek Trail 20E04 we first continue west for a couple of minutes, to where the open forest of lodgepoles takes on a grass-and-sagebrush carpet. Ahead, we skirt Hiram Meadow as we continue on for a few more minutes and then come to **Hiram Meadow Cabin.** The cabin and its immediate vicinity are for Forest Service personnel and their stock animals, not for campers, though you shouldn't have too much trouble finding a site or two in the adjacent Hiram Meadow environs. To continue onward, see the last two paragraphs of Route PG-4.

HL-4   Highland Lakes to Airola and Iceberg Peaks

Distances

2.4 miles (approx.) to Airola Peak
3.2 miles (approx.) to Iceberg Peak
4.6 miles (approx.) to Peak 9366

Trailhead   See the Route HL-1 trailhead

Introduction   This route is only for serious peak baggers, since better summit views are

obtained from the more easily reached summit of Hiram Peak—the next route. This doesn't mean that the views from Airola and Iceberg peaks are bad; they're just not fantastic. The route goes all the way along the ridge to Peak 9366, which, due to its considerably lower elevation, doesn't offer prime summit views. However, it does have interesting geology.

Description Consult the first paragraph of the previous route for a ⅓-mile descent through a minor gorge. Where the trail curves a bit to the right, giving you the first good views down-canyon, leave the trail, cross the adjacent creek, and traverse south to a nearby, minor gully. Head up either side of the gully's snowmelt creeklet to an open-wooded saddle. From its environs you see, just to the south, a granitic knoll that has a thick, horizontal dike across its precipitous northeast face. Head toward the knoll, descending first to an adjacent saddle. Rather than climb to the top of the granitic knoll, traverse south across its lower slopes to another granitic saddle. From it you have a choice of two equally long routes.

The more exposed route heads south up an obvious ridge. Near the top, where it becomes intimidating, veer left (southeast) about 20 yards, then climb back up to the ridge to reach its end at an adjacent summit. From there you have a brief descent south to a nearby ridgecrest saddle. Because this Class 3 route is somewhat exposed and therefore potentially dangerous, it is recommended only for experienced mountaineers.

The safer route starts from the granitic saddle by making a descent across gullied slopes until you are just beneath the fairly obvious main gully leading up to the ridgecrest saddle. The gully is easy at first, then it steepens, so you then traverse left into a stand of mountain hemlocks. Above, the slopes are steep but not exposed, and they have a smattering of trees. Above the last trees you traverse back into the gully and ascend it to the nearby saddle.

Leaving the saddle behind, you now make an easy climb south up the ridge to **Airola Peak.** At 9942 feet, it is the highest of this route's three summits, and it offers the best views. To the north-northeast, Highland and Silver peaks stand above "nearby" Hiram Peak, while just west of north, Raymond Peak stands above "close by" Folger Peak. Looking northwest, you'll see Peep Sight Peak topped by 17-mile-distant Round Top, the highest peak in Mokelumne Wilderness. Lookout Peak, which is a little lower than Peep Sight Peak, lies just to the left of these. Continuing a counterclockwise scan, you next see a long ridge with a north-facing cliff. This is Henry Peak. Chunky Bull Run Peak rises to the left of it, and between the two you see gentle-sloped Mokelumne Peak, which dominates the

western part of Mokelumne Wilderness. Next, to the southwest, you see The Dardanelles, which barely break the hazy horizon, then higher, pointed Dardanelles Cone, which rises above your next goal, Iceberg Peak.

Moving on from the southeast to the east, we see Disaster Peak, about 4½ miles away, which appears as a small summit block flanked by two gently sloping ridges. Finally, we conclude our scan by noting bulky Arnot Peak, east-northeast across Arnot Creek canyon. You might study these summits before leaving, and see if you can identify them from the top of Iceberg Peak.

During the last glaciation, an ice cap spread between Peep Sight and Hiram peaks, from which glaciers radiated in all directions. The surface of the ice cap was at about 9600 feet elevation, and west of your summit a glacier's surface was about 9400 feet.

The crest route to Iceberg Peak is quite obvious. From the saddle between Airola and Iceberg, you follow the crest up to a minor summit, and then make a short, relatively easy climb to the 9781-foot summit of **Iceberg Peak.** The origin of its name is a mystery. It is not near Iceberg Meadow or The Iceberg, and the peak certainly doesn't resemble an iceberg. However, during periods of glaciation, the peak, like any other one in the vicinity over 9000 feet in elevation, spawned glaciers. If you look east toward Lightning Mountain, you should be able to delineate a glacier's *trimline,* which stands about 1000 feet above the floor of Arnot Creek canyon and about 900 feet below the summit. Slopes below the trimline are glacier-smoothed, while those above it are rough and unscathed. During its formation, Iceberg Peak was anything but icy. The peak appears to be the eroded remains of a sizable volcano.

After you check out the views, turn around and retrace your steps, unless you're interested in geological pursuits or peak bagging. As you descend southwest from Iceberg Peak, you encounter increasing amounts of vegetation, notably sagebrush and rabbitbrush, but these and other shrubs yield to whitebark pines, western white pines and mountain hemlocks as volcanic soils yield, just before a long saddle, to granitic soils.

From the saddle you first climb southwest to the upper south slopes of a low granitic knob, then make a slightly ascending traverse west to a slightly higher volcanic summit, **Peak 9366.** It appears to be about all that is

On the summit of Airola Peak

left of a minor volcano. The peak's views are not inspiring, but a giant, segmented, volcanic *dike,* which slopes southwest from a point just south of and below the summit, is quite impressive. Like other dikes in this area, this one formed when molten material intruded surrounding bedrock and solidified in place. Dikes tend to be more resistant to weathering, so they typically stand out, as this one certainly does.

The fastest way back to the trailhead is probably via the Highland Creek Trail, rather than a backtrack route along your crest route. Anyway, it visits new scenery. Head northwest down a ridge, then down some short, fairly steep but quite safe slopes. Below them you'll have a rapid descent to Champion Canyon creek, and if you cross to and stay on its north bank you should be able to find a use trail. The trail essentially dies out before reaching the Highland Creek Trail, but that doesn't matter. On that conspicuous trail you hike 4.4 miles up-canyon to your trailhead, gaining about 1300 feet of elevation.

HL-5 Highland Lakes Campground to Hiram Peak

Distances
0.5 mile to ridgecrest
0.8 mile to icy lakelet
1.2 miles to Hiram Peak

Trailhead   See the Route HL-1 trailhead

Introduction   Hiram Peak offers better summit views than any other peak mentioned in this chapter. The views certainly rank with those obtained from the higher, more taxing peaks to the east and the southeast. But there's a caveat: acrophobics will probably balk at a traverse atop a knife-edge ridge or at a short climb up the summit block. However, both are quite safe if you don't spook at the exposure. On my ascent, I met some parents with children and a dog. Maybe they weren't a typical family.

Description   Just beyond the end of the road that climbs past the eastern sites of two-part Highland Lakes Campground, your unofficial trail begins at the base of a fairly steep slope. After an initial, fairly steep climb southeast, your trail curves south and climbs moderately

through a forest of mountain hemlocks, western white pines and red firs. Shortly, it reaches a gully, which more or less separates an open lodgepole-pine forest to the north from a meadowy landscape to the south. You parallel the gully on a moderate-to-steep ascent, though the gradient lessens, and the vegetation becomes more open as you climb to a minor gap in a **ridgecrest.** The route to the summit of Hiram Peak is along the low ridgecrest, which is part of the Carson-Iceberg Wilderness boundary, but the trail continues southeast, straight ahead. Were you to follow it, you'd see, after a couple of minutes, a seasonal, knee-deep pond.

Bound for Hiram Peak, we hike southwest, essentially cross-country, along the low ridgecrest for ¼ mile to the base of a steep talus slope. From this vicinity, one can make a contour along the base over to a milky blue-green, **icy lakelet** and its satellite pond.

Instead, we start up the steep, though safe and unexposed, talus slope, which narrows with elevation, causing several use paths to merge into one. The talus goes almost up to the top of the north end of a lava ridge, where you deserve a well-earned rest. If you look northwest down toward slopes above Highland Creek, you'll see car-size granitic boulders that were swept along in some of this area's numerous volcanic mudflows, which flowed down a now buried canyon some 10–15 million years ago.

Your first stretch along the lava ridge can be a bit scary, for the ridge is only a few feet wide, and it drops off steeply on both sides. If you get past the spot where it is only 2 feet wide, you've got it made. Fortunately, the rock is mostly quite solid, though one should always be wary of an occasional loose rock. As the ridge curves from south to southeast, it widens appreciably, and you skirt past currants, cream bushes and scrubby whitebark pines as well as an assortment of near-alpine wildflowers that include alpine gold, cut-leaved daisy, phlox, phacelia and buckwheat. As you approach Hiram Peak's summit block, it looks increasingly intimidating. However, you needn't tackle it head-on; rather, veer several yards left to a corner, from which you'll see a hidden ramp ascending to the nearby top of **Hiram Peak.**

From many vantage points in the Highland Lakes area, steep-sided Hiram Peak appears to be a volcano. It is—or more correctly, was—and it probably grew at some time during the last 5–10 million years, when eruptions were quite common in this area. The summit of this andesitic volcano may have stood about 1000 feet above its top today, but back when it formed, these crest lands lay, by my estimate, about 3000–4000 feet lower than today's lands.

Virtually all the peaks in Carson-Iceberg Wilderness and along its boundary are merely

high points along a ridgecrest. Hiram Peak stands apart by being a separate mountain. You really feel you are on top of the world. And, given its location, it offers some dramatic views. Looking south and southwest, with one glance you view the deep, glaciated canyons of Highland and Arnot creeks, which are separated by a mighty bulwark, the Airola-Iceberg peaks ridge. Airola Peak, on the left, is the highest, and it almost blots out Iceberg Peak, just to the right. Just right of that peak, standing in the distance, is pointed Dardanelles Cone. Using a compass and this book's map, you can continue your identification of dozens of other features in and about Carson-Iceberg Wilderness.

Outside the wilderness there are other interesting summits worth identifying. Looking south down Arnot Creek canyon, you see a swaybacked summit standing on the distant horizon. This is The Three Chimneys, which lie along the Emigrant Wilderness boundary 15½ miles away. In the southeast at a similar distance away stands 11,569′ Leavitt Peak, the highest peak north of Yosemite National Park (you have to go to northern California's Mt. Shasta to climb a higher peak). In the northwest quadrant you see 9,334′ Mokelumne Peak, the highest summit in western Mokelumne Wilderness, and 10,381′ Round Top, the wilderness' highest peak.

After taking in these views, you may be tempted to make a speedy descent down Hiram Peak's north slopes. Please don't, since doing so can leave unsightly scars on the extensive talus slopes. In early season, when the talus is covered with snow, there isn't this problem, but the snow can be iced over, and you might find yourself making a speedier descent than you had intended.

Airola-Iceberg massif and Arnot Creek canyon

HL-6   Highland Lakes to Upper Gardner Meadow and Arnot Creek Canyon

Distances
1.5 miles to junction with Arnot Creek Trail
at south end of Upper Gardner Meadow
2.8 miles to first crossing of Arnot Creek
4.4 miles to southeast-flowing seasonal creek
5.9 miles to a small campsite on a shady
bench
7.1 miles to junction with Woods Gulch/
Tahoe-Yosemite trail

Trailhead   See the Route HL-1 trailhead

Introduction   This is the first of five routes
from a very popular trailhead. Each of these
routes has one or more close-by goals suited
for day use, and one or more goals that are
suited for overnight stays. For Route HL-6,
the day-use objective is Upper Gardner
Meadow and the overnight-stay objective is
any of several campsites in Arnot Creek
canyon. This route describes the trail south to
a junction with the Tahoe-Yosemite Trail,
along which you can extend your journey by
hiking either west or east and then looping
back to the Highland Lakes area. Both choices
are discussed at the end of the route description. Actually, one need not descend all the
way to make a loop trip. Since the lower part
of Arnot Creek canyon isn't particularly
scenic, I describe, for sturdy hikers, two cross-
country routes northwest out to the Highland
Lakes area.

Description   From a trailhead within sight of
the lower, northern Highland Lake's dam, we
start northeast and in 60 yards reach jump-
across North Fork Mokelumne River. Now our
Disaster Creek Trail climbs east across volcanic slopes, entering an open forest before
making a brief drop into a wildflowered gully.
Our route soon reaches an abandoned jeep
road, and you can take either it or a trail east
up to a nearby granitic gap, where you enter
Carson-Iceberg Wilderness. Just 40 yards
down the jeep road from the gap is a
southeast-descending trail. This is the route to
Upper Gardner Meadow, and both Routes HL-
6 and HL-7 take it. Routes HL-8, HL-9 and
HL-10 keep to the road, which descends about
260 yards to an obscure junction with another
closed jeep road at the north edge of a
meadow. Our Route HL-6 takes the trail down
to the meadow and this jeep road where, if

you're good with a compass, you can easily
reach Half Moon Lake by keeping to a 120°
bearing. This meadow junction is at a point
about 100 yards south of the obscure junction.

Southbound, we follow the road through
the meadow, quickly leave it, skirt a smaller
one on the right, and then arrive at the north
end of expansive Upper Gardner Meadow.
During the summer months this meadow
usually has a sizable cow population, which
certainly detracts from the wilderness feel of
the place. As you progress south along the
meadow's west edge, you have views east of a
bulky mountain, Arnot Peak, whose actual
summit lies out of sight. After a pleasant, level
stroll, you reach the meadow's south end, and
where the jeep road turns east, you should find
a not-always-signed junction, by a low, granitic
outcrop, with the **Arnot Creek Trail**. If you're
bound for Half Moon Lake, Arnot Peak or the
Disaster Creek canyon, stay on the jeep road
and follow the description of the next route. If
you're turning back, you'll appreciate the view
north across Upper Gardner Meadow of the
Tryon Peak ridge.

Those bound for Arnot Creek start south
from the junction and soon make a quick,
steep descent across bedrock. The route ahead
is obvious, though in the opposite direction
one could possibly lose the trail. We continue
south through a linear flat and soon pass just
west of a granitic knoll that has a massive,
pink pegmatite dike cutting across its south
face. Southward, we go along a meadow's
west edge, then veer southeast and cross a
minor gap between two granitic knobs. Again
we turn south, and in a couple of minutes pass
just west of a volcanic hill. For the next 0.4
mile our trail parallels the Disaster Creek
Trail, unseen on slopes just above Arnot
Creek. We keep to slopes just above the west
bank of the creek. Along this stretch we first
traverse through a lodgepole-pine forest, then
from a granitic ridge make a short, fairly steep
descent to a gate by the edge of a small, circu-
lar meadow. This is your last realistic chance
to head east over to the nearby Disaster Creek
Trail.

The Arnot Creek Trail first goes along the
edge of a small gorge, then heads west-
southwest toward towering Airola Peak. A bit
farther, you'll see, off to the right, hulking

Hiram Peak. Your trail then becomes fairly steep as it makes a short drop to your **first crossing of Arnot Creek.** Here, from the creek's north bank, a use trail heads several hundred yards northwest, passing a couple of campsites on a spacious lodgepole-pine flat before dying out at a creek. If you were to follow this creek about 1.3 miles upstream, you'd arrive at its source, the icy lakelet mentioned in the previous route. You could then backtrack along that route for a relatively quick descent to the eastern sites of two-part Highland Lakes Campground.

From the creek crossing the trail winds briefly west almost to the brink of a small though impressive gorge with a waterfall, which lies at the foot of Hiram Peak. You then make a relatively short, fairly steep descent to your second crossing of Arnot Creek, near a large juniper just above a small waterfall—which is a noteworthy hazard for early-season hikers.

The creek here flows southwest, and we stay fairly close to it, passing between it and a willowy spring, on our right, in just under ½ mile. Cottonwoods and white firs now put in an appearance, signaling a warmer climate, and in ⅓ mile from the spring we make our third Arnot Creek crossing. Beyond, the trail goes through a cottonwood grove that is growing on a small floodplain. By mid or late summer, Arnot Creek along here can go dry. We then enter a small meadow and make our last Arnot Creek crossing, about 250 yards downstream from the previous one.

Our trail now hugs the creek, which quickly resumes its surface flow, and in just under ¼ mile we reach a **southeast-flowing seasonal creek,** with two small camps. The seasonal creek offers you a second cross-country route out to the Highland Lakes. Just head upstream, climbing about 1.7 miles up to a saddle that lies just beyond a ragged, granitic cliff, on your left. From here you backtrack along the first 1.2 miles of Route HL-4. You first climb northeast over to a slightly higher, open-wooded saddle that separates a small knoll from the base of Hiram Peak, then descend northwest along a gully, veering north from it when you see a logical route over to the Highland Creek Trail. A short ascent up it gets you to a trailhead, from which you walk 1.1 miles along the Highland Lakes Road, then 150 yards east along a spur road to your original trailhead.

Down-canyon near Arnot Creek, you soon pass some giant junipers, some brush, a grove of white firs, then a lot more brush, which is largely a prickly species with the unlikely name of snow bush. Leaving the brush, you make a fairly steep descent south to a minor ridge just above a bend in the creek, then descend in similar fashion ⅓ mile southwest to a usually flowing creeklet. Here you'll see a **small campsite on a shady bench** just above a pool-blessed stretch of Arnot Creek. The site is large enough for a party of six, and the creek is warm enough, at least in the afternoon, for a brisk romp. The creek is a good stream for rainbow trout. Rainbow are better sport fish than brooks, for rainbow are flashy leapers while brooks are stubbornly bottom-oriented. For a hungry hiker, both are equally acceptable.

For about ¼ mile you stay close to the creek, and then you veer away from it, soon crossing another permanent creeklet. After a short while you pass through a gap shaded by Jeffrey pines, then make a short, fairly steep descent almost to Arnot Creek. You briefly parallel it, then curve over to a meadow to a junction with the **Woods Gulch/Tahoe-Yosemite trail.** Few people would hike all the way down to this junction only to retrace the route back up to the trailhead. However, there are two loop routes that are attractive if you've got two or three days to spare.

The first is to follow the Tahoe-Yosemite Trail 5.5 miles west to a junction with the Highland Creek Trail. This stretch is composed of a climb up the Woods Gulch Trail to a saddle, then a descent from it on the Jenkins Canyon Trail, and it is described in Chapter 15's Route CF-1. You then follow the first 1.5 miles of the Highland Creek Trail up to a junction with the Weiser Trail, this stretch being described in reverse in the last part of Chapter 9's Route PG-4. Finally, you climb 5.0 miles up the Highland Creek Trail to its trailhead at the higher, southern Highland Lake, this stretch being described in reverse in this chapter's Route HL-3. Now you head 1.1 miles along Highland Lakes Road and, at a curve just past the second lake, meet your trailhead spur road and take it to complete a 20.3-mile loop.

The second loop route begins by following the Tahoe-Yosemite Trail southeast for 1.6 miles. This stretch coincides with the lower part of the Arnot Creek Trail and is described in the reverse direction in the first part of Chapter 15's Route CF-1. From that trail's trailhead the Tahoe-Yosemite Trail coincides with Road 7N13, which goes 0.5 mile southwest to a junction with the Clark Fork Road. You could save about 0.6 mile of walking by following Arnot Creek directly south to the nearby Clark Fork Road, but then you'd miss the entrance to Clark Fork Campground, which lies about 230 yards northeast from the junction. However, I prefer linear, roadside Sand Flat Campground, about one mile farther, which has walk-in sites on a bench just

east of the campground proper. Both campgrounds are USFS fee areas. From the Sand Flat Campground you ascend the Clark Fork Road 2.4 miles almost to its end, then take the Disaster Creek Trail back up to a junction at the south end of Upper Gardner Meadow and from there retrace your steps 1.5 miles to your trailhead. The first part of the Disaster Creek Trail is described in Chapter 15's Route CF-2, while the next part is described, in the reverse direction, in the following route. If you don't take any shortcuts along this loop route, you'll cover 20.7 miles.

HL-7   Highland Lakes to Half Moon Lake and Arnot Peak

Distances
2.2 miles to junction with Half Moon Lake trail
2.8 miles to Half Moon Lake
2.9 miles to low gap separating the Arnot Creek and Disaster Creek drainages
4.7 miles (approx.) to Arnot Peak

Trailhead   See the Route HL-1 trailhead

Introduction   Half Moon Lake won't make your heart beat with excitement, and this book describes a route to it simply because a trail to it exists. This small, boggy-shored lake is perhaps best left to diehard botanists and aquatic entomologists. Arnot Peak is another matter. The register at the top indicates it is quite a popular peak. There are at least five safe, relatively easy routes to the summit, and this description mentions two.

Description   See the preceding route's first two paragraphs for the first 1.5 miles to a junction at the south end of Upper Gardner Meadow. Then, leaving that part of the meadow, which is seasonally colored magenta by a field of shooting stars, our jeep road climbs east to a nearby, small gap. It then makes an equally short though steeper descent to the head of a linear gully. As the road heads down this gully, which is separated from Half Moon Lake's outlet creek by only a low ridge, it gradually narrows to a path. After a ¼-walk south, the last part along the edge of a usually soggy meadow, we curve east, then northeast, more or less staying at the meadow's edge. The path is vague here, particularly after you

cross Half Moon Lake's outlet creek—also known as Arnot Creek. From that creek the trail goes about 50 yards northeast and then 45 yards southeast to a very easily missed junction with the **Half Moon Lake trail.** This junction is roughly half way across the meadow.

Arnot Peak alternate route and Half Moon Lake

If you want to visit the lake, but can't find the trail, just head north, staying about 50 yards east of Arnot Creek. The trail should quickly become apparent, particularly once it has entered a nearby lodgepole-pine forest. After about 0.2 mile of forested walking, we curve briefly northeast to cross an often-flowing creeklet, and it offers you the start of an alternate route to the top of Arnot Peak. Just follow it up to steep slopes, above which you'll see a shallow notch in the ridge directly above you. From that notch, start south up the ridge, then soon leave it for gentler, east-facing slopes. This brushy though scenic, ascending traverse gets you to a major saddle at the south end of the ridge, where you join the standard route, described below.

Beyond the creeklet crossing, where we meet a small eastside gully, we're finally forced to cross Arnot Creek to its west bank. A short, moderate climb, almost in the creek itself, gets us to the disappointing outlet of **Half Moon Lake.** The lake lies in a very boggy meadow, which is gradually filling in the lake, so that now most of the lake is little more than a wide creek. Supposedly there are eastern brook trout in this lake, though I didn't see any. Stay along the forest's edge, walk about 0.2 mile northeast to the main part of the lake, and try your luck there. However, my experience was that I sank up to my neck in the bog that lines the lake! If you're just day hiking and would rather not backtrack, then from the shore near mid-lake try to maintain a 300° bearing as you make an easy cross-country jaunt over a low ridge and down to the point where Route HL-6's shortcut trail reaches a jeep road in a meadow.

If you don't want to see Half Moon Lake, stay on your obscure Disaster Creek Trail, which heads south through a fairly large meadow. If you can't follow the tread in the meadow, find it at the meadow's south end, right beside Arnot Creek. Here, a stretch of old road immediately crosses the creek, but it rejoins our trail in about 130 yards. As we continue south in a lodgepole-pine forest, the creek veers away from us, and it is bordered by a wet, linear meadow. If you were to cross the creek in this vicinity, you'd reach, in about 120 yards, the Arnot Creek Trail. About ⅓ mile south of the fairly large meadow we hiked through, we climb over a minor gap, and then descend to a nearby creeklet. Ahead, we go about 200 yards south-southwest before starting a curve south-southeast across a **low gap separating the Arnot Creek and Disaster Creek drainages.** This is your last opportunity to head west over to the Arnot Creek Trail, but more important, it is the start of a cross-country route up to Arnot Peak. This is the route you take even if you've ascended from the Clark Fork Road trailhead (Chapter 15's Route CF-2).

Arnot Peak

To climb cross-country to the summit of Arnot Peak, you climb northeast from the low gap, quickly finding yourself on a low ridge just above the creeklet you recently crossed. Very soon your ridge becomes steep and brushy, and you'll likely make short switchbacks rather than tackle it head on. After about 300 feet of elevation gain, your ridge curves southeast and offers you a comparable ascent up to a brushy flat. On it you can congratulate yourself for being halfway to a saddle, now in view.

Onward toward the saddle, the brush begins to thin, and by the time you reach it, the vegetation has become mostly low, sub-alpine herbs such as ballhead ipomopsis and cut-leaved daisy. Just north of and below the windswept saddle you're likely to find a snowfield, which is a source of fresh water. Folks who took the previously mentioned alternate route or a route off of the Pacific Crest Trail (Route HL-10) join us here.

To the southeast a steep ridge confronts us, so we first climb south along its lower slopes, then east up to a minor saddle with whitebark pines, mule ears and subalpine wildflowers. With the 10,054' summit in sight we now hike the remaining 200 yards up to the top of **Arnot Peak.** Like Disaster Peak 2 miles to the southeast, Arnot Peak is located close to the center of Carson-Iceberg Wilderness. Because of its location, you're very hard pressed to see any sign of man, except for a plaque on the summit, which commemorates Nathaniel D. Arnot, the first superior court judge of Alpine County. You may also find a summit register.

You see, standing in the southeast, conical Stanislaus Peak, which rises directly above Disaster Peak. The former is flanked on the left by gently domed White Mountain and on the right by snowy Leavitt Peak. To the east through northeast we see a line of wilderness-boundary peaks gradually taper in elevation, no major peak riveting our attention. What gets our attention is the straight, deep, glaciated Wolf Creek canyon, which extends 8 miles north-northeast from our summit. A high ridge rises above the canyon's west side, this mass topped by mostly obscured Highland Peak. Summits to the west and southwest are much closer. Right across from us is isolated Hiram Peak, barely breaking the skyline, followed by a ridge topped by Airola and Iceberg peaks. Dardanelles Cone tops off the ridge just south of them.

If you're eager for additional summit views, you can continue east from Arnot Peak along a high ridge that provides continually changing panoramas. After about 3 miles of traversing along the multipeaked ridge, you'll arrive at a saddle above the head of Golden Canyon. Chapter 15's Route CF-3 describes the trail up to this saddle as well as the 0.8-mile climb south to another popular summit, Disaster Peak. You can then return to the saddle and follow the Disaster Creek Trail down to Disaster Creek Canyon and head up it (Chapter 15's Route CF-2), or from the saddle

Left to right: Airola Peak and Hiram Peak, from Arnot Peak's summit

you can descend east to the nearby Pacific Crest Trail and follow it northeast (this chapter's Route HL-10). If snow hasn't been a problem for you so far, then I suggest you take the more scenic latter route.

If you don't want to climb to Arnot Peak but rather want to continue down-canyon, consult the last part of Chapter 15's Route CF-2, which is described in the opposite direction. In brief, the trail continues 2.1 miles southeast to a junction with a trail up to Paradise Valley and over to the Pacific Crest Trail, and then continues 2.9 miles down to the trailhead at Iceberg Meadow.

HL-8 Highland Lakes to Lower Gardner Meadow, Wolf Creek Pass, Asa Lake, Tryon Peak and Noble Lake

Distances
1.4 miles to Lower Gardner Meadow
1.7 miles to Wolf Creek Pass
2.1 miles to Asa Lake
4.0 miles to saddle on the Sierra crest
4.5 miles to junction with Noble Canyon Trail
4.6 miles (approx.) to Tryon Peak
5.0 miles (approx.) to Peak 10,082
5.1 miles to Noble Lake
6.5 miles to Bull Lake

Trailhead See the Route HL-1 trailhead

Introduction As day hikes go, the trip to Asa Lake is one of the easiest and most enjoyable in the Highland Lakes area. Backpackers can continue past the lake to either Noble or Bull Lake. I prefer the latter, from which one can then descend to Wolf Creek and follow the Wolf Creek Trail back up toward your trailhead—a nice semiloop trip. Additionally, you have the opportunity of climbing Tryon Peak, this rewarding goal being a moderately long day hike. Peak 10,082, east of it, is best left to serious peak baggers.

Description Consult the first paragraph of Route HL-6, which guides you east along 0.6 mile of route, first along a trail and then briefly along a closed jeep road to a junction with a southeast-descending trail. Routes HL-8, HL-9 and HL-10 now leave the Disaster Creek Trail as the road winds down to the north edge of a meadow from where an obscure jeep road starts south. Our route is the Wolf Creek Trail, which continues southeast as a jeep road. This route is misnamed, for it descends most of its distance along Elder Creek and ends at a junction just past a ford of Wolf Creek. From that junction, a sign indicates that the trail's name is the Asa Lake Trail, which is also a misnomer, since it totally avoids the lake.

Regardless of what you call it, the road momentarily bends northeast into a lodgepole-pine forest and narrows to a trail just before crossing a quickly reached creek that drains the meadow we just left plus Upper Gardner Meadow. Ahead, we have an easy stroll northeast, mostly downhill, and we cross a verdant swale midway down to **Lower Gardner**

Noble Canyon and Silver Peak, from Tryon Peak's summit

Meadow. Your Wolf Creek Trail heads east through the well-grazed meadow, generally staying close to a seasonal creek. Eastward, the meadow constricts almost to a linear filament, and you hike past a low, blocky lava outcrop, then momentarily spot a small silted-up dam. In a minute or two you reach **Wolf Creek Pass,** which has an intersection with the Pacific Crest Trail. Route HL-9 continues straight ahead on the Wolf Creek Trail, Route HL-10 climbs southeast on the Pacific Crest Trail, and our route climbs north on it.

At first the Wolf Creek Trail stays along the west edge of a meadow, while our Pacific Crest Trail parallels it on slopes just above and west of it. But then that meadow route veers east while we gain a bit of altitude north to a junction. By climbing 0.1 mile north up a steep path, you'll reach the southwest corner of **Asa Lake.** Although the lake appears to be rich in nutrients, and therefore should be able to support a decent trout population, two factors work against your chances of catching a dinner. First, the lake is small—only 2 acres. Second, fishing pressure is great, for it receives a lot of visitors from the Highland Lakes area. The lake is high and cold enough for golden trout, but since it is shallow, only brook trout can survive in a typical winter. For many years it has been annually planted with 500 of these trout.

The lake is also second rate as a swimming hole, for it is fed by a number of icy springs. Anyway, you can expect water temperatures from the low 50s to the low 60s. While such temperatures will deter most folks, they don't deter beavers, who sometimes successfully establish residence in a shallow part of the lake. You can establish temporary residence at one of two spacious campsites beneath red firs.

Most folks probably go no farther than Asa Lake, which is an easy day hike from the Highland Lakes. However, if you want to continue, rather than backtrack to the Pacific Crest Trail, climb directly upslope from the campsites to it. On it you climb briefly west-southwest to a nearby ridge, where we leave Carson-Iceberg Wilderness. Here, at the Sierra crest, you have an excellent view of three peaks. From south-southeast to west-southwest, these are Arnot, Hiram and Folger peaks.

Junipers and sagebrush briefly take over as we start northwest. Then we dip northeast into a glade rich in mountain hemlocks and, through mid-July, snow. Continuing our northward climb, we soon pass just above some easily reached, willow-draped springs, which you may not see but certainly should hear. Beyond them, the gradient slackens and the trail slowly begins to arc northwest across increasingly brushy slopes, offering us unrestricted views of features we've already seen. Finally we reach a **saddle on the Sierra crest.** From here, you have four choices. Continue onward to Noble or Bull Lake; backtrack to your trailhead; climb Tryon Peak; or climb unnamed Peak 10,082, which stands about a mile to the east.

Peak 10,082 and Tryon Peak

Peak 10,082 can be climbed at least two ways: hiking northeast up the aforementioned glade to a level area and then north up steep slopes, or else starting from the Sierra crest saddle and hiking east up along the ridge. Both are quite safe. The only problem is the 20-foot-high summit block of **Peak 10,082.** Getting up the volcanic block is definitely Class 5. Several routes are possible; none were protected in 1990. Views are inspiring even if you don't climb the block.

Tryon Peak is another matter. Though only 112 feet lower, it is an easily attained summit. Simply climb west up the crest, which at first is a fairly steep ascent. After about 400 feet of elevation gain, your route becomes gentle and you speed along to the base of the summit block. Then scramble up talus to the top of **Tryon Peak,** which itself appears to be mostly talus and is mostly devoid of plant life.

Tryon Peak, like the small meadow at the foot of Folger Peak to the southwest, is named for Charles Tryon, who ran stock in the area. Scanning counterclockwise from that peak, you see the blocky Dardanelles just right of pointed Dardanelles Cone, both on the distant horizon above the unseen south Highland Lake. Hiram Peak stands above the north lake, followed by Upper Gardner Meadow, to the left, which lies in front of lowly Lightning Mountain, both to the south. Next comes the prominent mass of Arnot Peak, followed by Peak 10,082, with its summit pinnacle, to the east-southeast. To the northeast you see the nearby area's highest summit, pointed 10,935'

Highland Peak. This is immediately left of what appears to be a more massive mountain, Peak 10,824, which stands high above Noble Lake. Left of these is Silver Peak, and all three make up the east flank of Noble Creek canyon.

From the aforementioned saddle on the Sierra crest we pass through a gate to start a northeast descent through a forest of whitebark pines and mountain hemlocks. After ½ mile of descent we arrive at a junction with the **Noble Canyon Trail.** This name is inappropriate, for although the trail starts in upper Noble Canyon, most of its length is in Bull Canyon. See the last part of the next chapter's Route NC-1 for a description of this trail east to Bull Canyon and **Bull Lake.** You could then continue east down the canyon, then up along Wolf Creek and Elder Creek back to Wolf Creek Pass, making a 13.3-mile semiloop trip—see the next route.

From the junction the Pacific Crest Trail continues on past Noble Lake and upper Noble Canyon to Ebbetts Pass. To reach that lake you're better off starting from the pass or starting from Highway 4 and hiking south up the Noble Canyon Trail (next chapter's Routes NC-1 and NC-2). Still, if you're making an overnight trip to Asa, Noble and Bull lakes, you'll want to know how to reach Noble Lake. The Pacific Crest Trail is misleading in only

Bull Lake and Peak 10,824

one spot, about half way to the lake. The trail, which has been descending north, reaches the edge of a meadow and abruptly bends south-west. The tread isn't always obvious, and if you continue north, you'll cross a low, nearly flat divide and in 0.2 mile from the bend will reach a lakelet. This lakelet, which is just beyond a soggy meadow, has quite a nice campsite beneath north-shore whitebark pines.

Just after the bend the Pacific Crest Trail heads briefly west, then descends north, passing just above two small ponds before reaching a gully above the northeast corner of **Noble Lake.** Camping at this snag-infested lake is second rate, for trees are scarce and the area is often windy. Given a choice, I would certainly choose to camp at Bull Lake rather than in the Noble Lake environs.

HL-9   Highland Lakes to Wolf Creek Pass, Upper Wolf Creek Canyon, East Fork Carson River Canyon, Bull Canyon and Bull Lake

Distances
4.2 miles to junction with Murray Canyon-
    Golden Canyon Trail
4.6 miles to junction with Noble Canyon Trail
5.5 miles to junction with Bull Canyon Trail
6.5 miles to junction with Bull Lake Trail
6.8 miles to Bull Lake
8.8 miles to Falls Meadows in East Fork
    Carson River canyon

Trailhead   See the Route HL-1 trailhead

Introduction   In the past the shortest way in to the middle reaches of the East Fork Carson River canyon has probably been the way least taken. This route, starting from Highland Lakes, is not only the shortest way in, but it also involves the least amount of climbing. Most folks take the Wolf Creek Trail, Chapter 12's Route WC-2, which is about 2¼ miles longer. You can hike down that popular trail a bit, then take the old Noble Canyon Trail up to a spur trail to Bull Lake. Again, this is a shorter way than via the Wolf Creek Trail, though the latter is certainly easier to follow and will probably remain the preferred way in. By continuing west along the old trail to the Pacific Crest Trail, south on it to Wolf Creek Pass, and then back to the trailhead, you can make a fairly scenic, enjoyable 13.3-mile semiloop trip.

Description   Consult the first paragraph of Route HL-6, which guides you east along the first part of the Disaster Creek Trail. This

exists first as a trail and then briefly as a closed jeep road over a gap before returning to a trail. Then consult the first two paragraphs of Route HL-8, which guide you east along the Wolf Creek Trail, which goes through cow-dotted Lower Gardner Meadow before coming to an intersection with the Pacific Crest Trail at Wolf Creek Pass.

Immediately beyond the pass, the Wolf Creek Trail heads north as a road along the west side of a wet meadow. This road quickly diminishes and one can then take a use trail east along the meadow's north edge. This use trail isn't the real route, which isn't at all obvious. To find it, you first follow the road 90 yards north from Wolf Creek Pass, then leave the road where it reaches a gate, and gingerly tiptoe across the spongy meadow to its east side. There, you start north, and very quickly—you hope—find tread, which takes you to a jump-across creeklet—Elder Creek—at the meadow's northeast corner. Here you join the alternate use-trail route and start east down the north bank of Elder Creek.

After several minutes of descent past red firs and lodgepole pines, you veer away from Elder Creek and cross a briskly flowing creek from Asa Lake, then in 200 yards cross a similar creek. Just 50 yards past it you reach a break in the forest, from where you'll see a 40-foot-high lava block which has fallen into the Elder Creek canyon. Due to its many knobs, this block is much easier to climb than one would first expect. Onward, we parallel the creek, crossing to its south bank after ⅓ mile. In early season the crossing could be a 10-foot-wide ford.

Boggy stretches lie ahead, so the trail leaves the creek for a winding traverse east-southeast, then from a creeklet it makes a descent east to a wet meadow and parallels it for 100 yards. Then we cross a low, bedrock ridge and parallel Elder Creek east for ⅓ mile. The creek then veers northeast and quickly so do we. As we descend toward the creek, you may see an old trail branching right, which you'll want to avoid. About a minute past that junction you cross the creek, then climb about 15 feet in elevation to start a momentary traverse east above a willowy flat. You then abruptly drop to the flat and skirt northeast along its edge. Remember the details here, for if you return this way, you'll find the trail harder to follow (unless it is improved in future years).

The creek jogs east, then north, while your sometimes obscure trail through meadowland maintains a northeast course, reaching the creek in ¼ mile. If you're bound for Bull Canyon, don't cross the creek at its ford. Rather, go cross-country about 250 yards north to where you see a jeep road, the Wolf Creek Trail, about to plunge through the creek. If you're bound for the East Fork Carson River canyon, ford the creek and go about 130 yards east-northeast over to a junction with the

Murray Canyon-Golden Canyon Trail, here a jeep road. If you take this trail, consult Chapter 12's Route WC-2, which guides you 4.6 miles to a junction near **Falls Meadows in the East Fork Carson River canyon.**

From the junction, the jeep road goes just 120 yards north before crossing Wolf Creek. Bound for Bull Canyon, you continue north, and in a few minutes bend northwest and cross an area devastated by repeated avalanching. You go briefly north of it, then the road immediately angles northeast, descending in 90 yards to an obvious junction with a spur road east over to a cow camp with a cabin. Where the road angles northeast, you have a junction with the old **Noble Canyon Trail.**

Unless it's been improved, the tread will be invisible to you. However, after about 100 yards of hiking north-northwest, a faint path should begin to appear, which northward becomes an old jeep road. This road traverses about ⅔ mile north before angling west over to nearby Bull Canyon creek, a difficult boulder-hop or possibly a wet ford. Then from its bank you have a steep, minute-long climb north to a junction with a newer trail, the **Bull Canyon Trail.** Chapter 12's Route WC-1 describes the trail up to **Bull Lake** as well as the trail up Bull Canyon and then down to the Pacific Crest Trail, along which you'd do a backtrack of Route HL-8, the previous route, to your trailhead.

HL-10   Highland Lakes to Wolf Creek Pass, Arnot Peak, Golden Canyon and East Fork Carson River Canyon

Distances
2.6 miles to flat saddle on the Sierra crest
4.6 miles (approx.) to Arnot Peak
6.4 miles to junction with Murray Canyon-Golden Canyon Trail
8.6 miles to junction with Paradise Valley and Golden Canyon trails
12.4 miles to junction with East Carson Trail

Trailhead   See the Route HL-1 trailhead

Introduction   Perhaps the easiest way to Arnot Peak's summit is along this route, leaving the PCT at a broad saddle almost 1 mile southeast of Wolf Creek Pass. This in

itself is a fine day hike, though you should expect some snow along the route and wear appropriate boots. Overnight users can continue south on the Pacific Crest Trail to Golden Canyon, then descend through it to the scenic mid-to-upper part of the East Fork Carson River canyon. In it, you are about as isolated as you can get anywhere in the Sierra Nevada—short of going cross-country. Although there are other ways to reach this canyon, notably from the Clark Fork Road, this route offers a minimum amount of climbing.

Folger Peak and Half Moon Lake, from cross-country route to Arnot Peak

Description Consult the first paragraph of Route HL-6, which guides you east along the first part of the Disaster Creek Trail. This exists first as a trail and then briefly as a closed jeep road over a gap before returning to a trail. Then consult the first two paragraphs of Route HL-8, which guide you east along the Wolf Creek Trail, which goes through cow-dotted Lower Gardner Meadow before coming to an intersection with the Pacific Crest Trail at Wolf Creek Pass.

We turn right on the Pacific Crest Trail and climb southeast above a small creek that emanates from a large meadow and cascades down resistant volcanic rocks to a small gorge below. Our trail stays close to a crest as we climb above the cow-dotted meadow, and soon we hike up a small gully to reach a **flat saddle on the Sierra crest.**

Arnot Peak

From the saddle you can start a cross-country route to the top of Arnot Peak, the route being a bit shorter than the standard route in Route HL-7. It does, however, have some snow patches, which in early season are more like snowfields. Start this route by going about ½ mile southwest to a ridge above Half Moon Lake, ideally reaching the ridge at a point where its crest becomes quite steep. You then leave it for gentler, east-facing slopes. The ensuing brushy, though scenic, ascending traverse gets you to a major saddle at the south end of the ridge, where you join the standard route and then follow it to the summit of **Arnot Peak,** whose views are described in Route HL-7.

From the flat saddle we wind down to the headwaters of Wolf Creek. We cross several branches of its west fork in rapid succession,

and one could camp in this vicinity. Check especially by the north edge of a meadow that is just above the trail and is just east of the branch where the trail turns from southeast to east. The east-traversing trail soon turns southeast again and descends to the impressive canyon of the silty, wide middle fork. The canyon can have debris flows when conditions are right: thick snowpack and heavy rains. However, for most summer hikers there is little danger if they camp on the narrow floodplain just below the stream crossing.

After crossing the wide, rocky middle fork of Wolf Creek, we traverse east past caves and fingers, found on a cliff of deeply eroded volcanic deposits above us, and after 0.5 mile from the last fork we arrive at the slightly cloudy, multi-channeled east fork. Here one can camp on a small flat below the trail but above the west bank or perhaps search for secluded spots a few minutes' walk downstream.

Now the Pacific Crest Trail climbs, at first rambling across gullied slopes, then switchbacking up to a northern, high traverse that offers us views of the corrugated, steep north cliffs of the Arnot Peak massif and of glaciated Wolf Creek canyon. Glaciers arose not only from Arnot Peak but also from the Highland Lakes ice cap. The trail curves east around a ridge and then it heads up its east side. Midway up it we pass a small trailside pond on the left. The origin of this pond is worth noting. The spring that flows from the volcanic rocks just below the trail proved to be a reliable source for water-loving plants, particularly willows. A thick cluster of plants developed around the base of the spring, and the plants eventually trapped enough sediments and dead plant matter to form an effective dam, which resulted in the pond. You can see a similar feature, named Davis "Lake," early on this chapter's Route HL-1.

The large, open, glaciated bowl east of us now becomes more gentle-sloped and more wooded, and soon we are hiking along its upper reaches toward a highly fractured, steep-sided volcanic butte. In a gully just below its southwest slope we meet a junction with the **Murray Canyon-Golden Canyon Trail.**

Murray Canyon-Golden Canyon Trail

This northbound trail is a part of the old Murray Canyon-Golden Canyon Trail, which ran from the head of one canyon to the head of the other before the Pacific Crest Trail was completed in these parts back in 1976. South from here, our newer trail more or less follows the abandoned tread of the older trail, though our route is much better graded. From the junction the northbound trail traverses 1.9 miles to a saddle dividing Murray Canyon from Wolf Creek Canyon. This trail is described in a southbound direction from that saddle in Chapter 12's Route WC-2. Northbound, the trail is quite obvious, but not southbound.

Just 80 yards south beyond the junction we reach a fairly open saddle that is immediately south of the previously mentioned volcanic butte. Onward, we wind southeast across the willow-choked headwaters of Murray Canyon.

About ⅓ mile before leaving this glaciated bowl, we encounter a large campsite off to the left, just west of a creeklet. From this vicinity you could descend north into Murray Canyon, where, on gentler slopes, you could locate cow trails that finally fuse into one trail before joining the main trail down Murray Canyon. Be aware that the canyon's creek is off limits to fishing.

We quickly pass a smaller, drier campsite before our trail levels off on a wide saddle above Golden Canyon. On it you'll find two types of volcanic rocks. Most of the dark rocks are composed of andesite—the commonest Sierra Nevada volcanic rock—which you've been seeing in one form or another along most of this hike. The other rocks, which occur in a small, buff-colored outcrop on the right, are composed of rhyolite. Its eruption onto the earth's surface was more violent than the andesite eruptions.

The old Golden Canyon Trail climbed north to the saddle here, and on the way down from the saddle you may still be able to pick it out as you gradually curve west across sagebrush-covered slopes. Along here you have a continuous view of dominating Stanislaus Peak, which is just to the right of a much lower but nevertheless prominent knob of andesite that sits atop the south rim of Golden Canyon. Our trail soon curves from southwest to south, crosses a usually dry gully, and quickly arrives at a junction with the **Paradise Valley and**

An outcrop of rhyolite

Basque carving on a lodgepole pine

Golden Canyon trails. This junction is about 210 yards before you'd reach a lively creek with a fair one-tent site by its north bank. The descending Golden Canyon Trail is fairly obvious, but the ascending Paradise Valley Trail is not. If you plan to take this latter trail, you're best off just heading west up slopes to the lower part of a nearby ridge, where you should find the trail climbing rather steeply southwest up to a nearby pass. To continue south on the Pacific Crest Trail, consult the last part of Chapter 15's Route CF-3.

Golden Canyon Trail

If you start east down the Golden Canyon Trail, you may soon see an old trail that climbs steeply north toward the Pacific Crest Trail. Onward, you descend steeply east, then at a better gradient descend east-northeast for ½ mile to Golden Canyon's creek. Because this stream is part of the habitat of the threatened Lahontan cutthroat trout, no fishing is allowed in it. The same applies to East Fork Carson River above Falls Meadows. The trail crosses the creek by a campsite, continues ¼ mile downstream and recrosses the creek at the highest exposure of granitic rock. The trail, now gravelly rather than dusty, stays on this side of the creek, traversing over granodiorite all the way down to East Fork Carson River. The descent quickly becomes a very steep one, but we are soon rewarded with a view of the creek's 80-foot-high fall.

As we wind down to gentler slopes, the moderate forest cover of red firs, western white pines and lodgepole pines becomes a more open assemblage of junipers and lodgepoles. Enjoying good views down-canyon, we hike along the edge of a band of willows, followed in 100 yards by a cluster of aspens. Within this cluster you'll see initials carved on trunks by Basque sheepherders, and about ½ mile downstream you'll see some more, rather graphic carvings. Here, among aspens, lodgepoles and junipers, is an adequate campsite. Just beyond it our trail veers away from the creek, and then it drops steeply east to the creek again.

After the drop, the trail eases off and quickly reaches the lip of a 50-yard-long gorge. Here the cascading creek is cutting down along a vertical joint—hence the straight, vertical walls. From the brink we leave the creek for a traverse north, then rejoin it after descending short, steep switchbacks down a brushy slope. For the next ½ mile we follow the cavorting creek, then veer north, cross a low saddle, turn east and ford East Fork Carson River. Here you can camp (best on the high east bank). Then, in just 150 yards, this trail ends at a junction with the **East Carson Trail.** Chapter 12's Route WC-5 describes this trail from Falls Meadows 2.2 miles south to this junction, then 5.5 miles beyond it to a junction with the Pacific Crest Trail in the upper part of the river canyon.

Chapter 11   Noble Canyon

NC-1   Pacific Crest Trail to Noble Lake, Peak 10,082, Tryon Peak, Asa Lake and Bull Lake

Distances

2.9 miles to junction with lower Noble
  Canyon Trail
3.8 miles to Noble Lake
4.4 miles to junction with upper Noble
  Canyon Trail
4.9 miles to saddle on the Sierra crest
5.5 miles to Tryon Peak
5.9 miles to Peak 10,082
6.1 miles to junction with Bull Lake Trail
6.4 miles to Bull Lake
6.5 miles to Asa Lake

Trailhead   From Ebbetts Pass drive 0.3 mile northeast down to a spur road to a nearby trailhead parking lot, complete with outhouse. This spur road is 3.9 miles above the Noble Canyon trailhead (next route), which in turn is 1.4 miles above Silver Creek Campground. To reach this campground from east of the Sierra crest, leave Highway 89 about 5 miles south of Markleeville, where the highway starts a climb toward Monitor Pass. On Highway 4 you drive 2.4 miles south up to the Wolf Creek Road junction, which is immediately south of the Centerville Flat Undeveloped Camping Area. From the junction you then drive 5.0 miles southwest up to Silver Creek Campground. If you're driving to the Ebbetts Pass area from the west, the best campground will be Bloomfield Campground, which lies 1.0 mile southeast down Highland Lakes Road 8N01. This road leaves Highway 4 just 1.3 miles west of Ebbetts Pass.

Introduction   It appears that most Pacific Crest Trail users starting from the Ebbetts

Pass trailhead go only as far as Noble Lake. But being subalpine and windswept, it leaves something to be desired, so you can continue south to Asa Lake or east to Bull Lake. The shortest way to Asa Lake, however, is from the Highland Lakes trailhead, and although your route from Ebbetts Pass provides the shortest way to Bull Lake, most folks prefer to start from Wolf Creek Meadows, since from there a lot less climbing is involved. Still, you can set up a base camp at or near Noble Lake and then make day excursions to either Asa or Bull Lake, or to any of several relatively close summits. Then, from just above Noble Lake you can start a loop that includes both Asa and Bull lakes. Bull Lake has the best swimming and fishing, Asa the best camping, Noble the most wildness.

Description   Starting from the south end of the parking lot, you hike almost ¼ mile south up a spur trail to a junction with the Pacific Crest Trail. From here the "PCT" winds west in ⅓ mile to a crossing of Highway 4 just 230 yards northeast of Ebbetts Pass. To continue north through California on this tri-state trail, consult my guidebook *Pacific Crest Trail*, which is cited in this book's "Recommended Reading and Source Materials."

Southbound, we start by first climbing moderately northeast to a low point on a minor ridge, from which we have our first view down into deep, glaciated Noble Canyon. (The name "Noble" has been misspelled as "Nobel" for so many years that the incorrect name still persists, despite a 1979 U.S. Board on

Geographic Names decision against it.) Above the canyon, standing due east of us, is 10,935' Highland Peak—the main destination of Route NC-3—and one of the highest peaks in the Ebbetts Pass-Sonora Pass area. It is also the highest peak you would see, if you were hiking north, until Mt. Shasta, hundreds of miles farther. Just ½ mile south of Highland Peak is unnamed Peak 10,824, which vies with the north summit of Silver Peak—1½ miles north of Highland Peak—as the second-highest peak in the area. Surprisingly, the U.S. Geological Survey determined the elevation of the lower, south summit but not the north, which I estimate at 10,820–25'.

Leaving the ridge above our trailhead, we briefly descend south, then commence a winding, partly meadowy traverse along the base of some impressive, deeply eroded volcanic cliffs, which are remnants of extensive, mostly andesitic lava flows and mudflows that once buried all the granitic terrain we see below. Soon we climb up a small, shady gully, pass through a gap on the south side of a granitic knob, curve northeast down through a small meadow with corn lilies, and then curve northwest down across a ridge. Almost immediately we recross the ridge as we round the north end of a smaller granitic knob before starting a long, winding descent south.

We cross three seasonal creeks, then three lushly lined, more permanent ones, the last one being Noble Creek. Like the creek just before it, this one has a gully choked with enormous volcanic boulders that fell from higher slopes. From this last gully we make a brief climb north up stark slopes, dotted with mule ears and junipers, to the end of a ridge. From this we bend south and in 90 yards come to a junction with the **lower Noble Canyon Trail** (next route).

Our PCT segment switchbacks several times and offers us great vistas before we approach Noble Lake's outlet creek. We parallel it just briefly upstream, then soon arrive at a seeping gully above the outlet of **Noble Lake.** Generally, golden trout can be planted in lakes in this area if they are about 9000 feet or higher in elevation. Noble Lake is at 8870 feet, which is fairly close, so from 1968–75, golden trout were planted. The plantings were unsuccessful at this 4-acre lake, which has a real limiting factor, a shallow depth of only 12 feet. Brook trout have been planted annually since 1975.

You'll find a small campsite wedged between the trail and the lake. However, the best one in the vicinity is among whitebark pines along the north shore of a lakelet above Noble Lake. To reach it, just head up either side of the seeping gully to a nearby spongy meadow and traverse north to the adjacent, waist-deep, willow-lined lakelet. This lakelet lies along the start of Route NC-3's ascent to Highland Peak, and if you're interested in climbing it (but not Silver Peak), then the lakelet's campsite makes an ideal base camp.

Noble Lake, like its satellite, lies in a subalpine environment, which means three things. The lake will be too cool for enjoyable swimming. The campsites will be windy—bring a tent. And, since the lake has a low rate of

Impressive, deeply eroded volcanic-mudflow cliffs near Ebbetts Pass

nutrient production and a high rate of fisher-men visitation, trout can be few and far between. A much better lake for swimming, camping and fishing is Bull Lake, which has a much more hospitable environment despite being barely 200 feet lower than Noble Lake. Some folks also like to visit Asa Lake, which has excellent camping but has cool and over-fished water.

To visit both Bull and Asa, you start a climb south above the shore of Noble Lake, passing two miniscule ponds before shortly veering east. This traverse up along the edge of a wet meadow soon jogs northeast, to where you make a seasonally sloggy crossing in the meadow's neck. At times, the trail here isn't too obvious, but it immediately turns south to start a moderate ⅓-mile climb to a junction with the **upper Noble Canyon Trail.**

Now you have to make a choice. On the Pacific Crest Trail you'd make a scenic, if sometimes soggy, climb southwest 0.5 mile up to a saddle on the **Sierra crest.** From it you could climb cross-country to two summits: either 0.6 mile west to **Tryon Peak** or 1.0 mile east to **Peak 10,082.** Then, too, you could ignore both and follow the PCT about 1.6 miles until you see **Asa Lake,** then leave the trail and descend to its close-by north-shore campsites. All of the above features are elaborated in Chapter 10's Route HL-8, which describes the PCT in the opposite direction.

On the upper Noble Canyon Trail you head over to Bull Lake. You'll appreciate the newer PCT when you start up the old upper part of the Noble Canyon Trail: it is definitely steep. However, after only a 0.3-mile struggle, you reach a scenic saddle, which presents a view east down Bull Canyon.

We make a brief, steep descent past whitebark pines and mountain hemlocks, and then our gradient becomes moderate as we descend past a field of willows and lupines that line the headwaters of Bull Canyon creek. We veer left from the creek and resume a steeper descent, first northeast down in-creasingly open slopes, then southeast more or less along a creeklet. We cross it where the

Peak 10,082, from Bull Canyon saddle

slope's gradient abates, and continue south-east, under forest cover, to the edge of a meadow of willows and corn lilies. The trail can be vague ahead, so don't feel bad if you lose it. Essentially, it continues southeast over to the meadow's creek, follows it briefly east to where it bends north, crosses to the east bank and then continues briefly north to a bend east. Here, at the edge of a conifer forest, you're likely to find a messy cow camp.

A trail tread that may be obvious starts from it, and on it we start a gentle descent east, while Bull Canyon creek, on the left, falls away from us at a steeper gradient. After the gradient begins to steepen as the trail angles east-southeast, we reach, in a minute or two, a junction with a trail, 0.3 mile from the cow camp. This unofficial trail forks right, curving south as it starts a contour toward Bull Lake. However, it very quickly dies out. If you don't mind a ¼-mile cross-country traverse, then take this route. It saves you about 120 feet of elevation loss, which you'd then have to make up.

If you'd rather stick to an official trail, then keep descending the Noble Canyon Trail, now at a moderate gradient, for about 300 yards southeast to a junction with the **Bull Lake Trail.** This junction may be obscure. It's at a spot where you get a view to the east of a corn-lily meadow, in a swale about 150 yards away and below you. Chapter 12's Route WC-1 joins us here.

If you miss the junction, you'll find yourself climbing up the trail to Bull Lake. The trail can be faint, but even if you do lose the tread, the hiking isn't all that bad. Further-more, you can't miss **Bull Lake,** which fills most of a slightly scalloped bench. One camp-site lies at trail's end, by the lake's north tip, while a second shoreline site lies along the south bank of the lake's inlet creek. Be fore-warned that on a typical summer weekend, these two *small* sites can't hold all the back-packers. See the next chapter's Route WC-1 for a description of Bull Lake's fishing opportunities.

Should you wish to make a loop over to Asa Lake, return to the Noble Canyon Trail and continue down it a little over 1.0 mile to a junction, at which the main trail veers left. You angle right, still on a part of the old Noble Canyon Trail, and drop to a nearby creek—the one from Bull Lake. You then follow in reverse the description of Route HL-9 to Wolf Creek Pass, then part of Route HL-8 from that pass to Asa Lake.

NC-2   Noble Canyon Trail to Pacific Crest Trail

Distances
0.9 mile to crossing of Noble Creek
3.0 miles to crossing of Highland Peak
  tributary
3.9 miles to Pacific Crest Trail

Trailhead   See the Route NC-1 trailhead.
Parking at the trailhead (Highway 4's highest
switchback, at mileage post ALP 24^{00}) is
limited to a few cars at best, so head about
280 yards north down Highway 4 to a spur
road, on the east side, which has ample
parking and offers splendid views of the local
terrain.

Introduction   Once the Pacific Crest Trail
was completed to Noble Lake, it shaved off
1.0 mile of distance—compared to the old
Noble Canyon Trail—and it became the
preferred route. Still, the old trail isn't that bad
when you consider the amount of elevation
change you do on a round-trip basis. The
Noble Canyon Trail has only 100 more feet of
gain, round trip. If you head out from Noble
Lake to Ebbetts Pass on the PCT, you lose
hundreds of feet of elevation, and then have to
make almost all of it up. But if you head out
on the Noble Canyon Trail, elevation gain to
Highway 4 is minimal.

Description   From your trailhead you have
an enticing view south up Noble Canyon, and
more views appear along the first part of your
trail, which is across generally open slopes

dotted with some trees. Soon you arrive at the
north edge of a snag-filled swamp, which
likely owes its existence to the resident
beavers. Just past it the trail angles southeast,
and in several minutes we reach the canyon's
creek. This we parallel through a small
meadow upstream, then veer away from it for
a couple of minutes, at first toward some
granitic cliffs that should appeal to technical
rock climbers. Additional cliffs lie about ¼
mile up-canyon. We then face a crossing of
Noble Creek, which for most of the summer is
fortunately only a boulderhop. The creek contains a good population of brook trout, and
you can expect a good catch of 6–9″ fish.

Once on the east bank, we stroll 210 yards
southeast to a cottonwood-lined, dry stream
bed—once an east branch of Noble Creek—
which back in the 1970s was a quite active
stream. However, work by beavers plus
landslides and avalanches down Silver Peak's
steep, unstable slopes have altered the creek's
course. Just beyond the dry stream bed we
diagonal southeast briefly across the south
part of a sagebrush meadow. In it, keen-eyed
hikers might recognize a cattle-drive route
which descends about 3 miles down-canyon to
a cow camp beside where Highway 4 bridges
Silver Creek. Now on a single, merged trail,
we hike upstream, enter a forest of white firs
and Jeffrey pines, and soon arrive at a usually
brisk, alder-lined creeklet that originates just
below Silver Peak's south summit.

Beaver ponds in lower Noble Canyon

Next, we're forced close to Noble Creek by a cliff of andesitic lava. This flow, like many in the area, is one that began to break up as it was solidifying—an autobrecciated lava flow. Differential weathering, due to different rocks' strengths and weaknesses, has created bizarre, interesting forms near the cliff's top. Also interesting is the structure of the volcanic rocks. They are composed of a three-dimensional, brownish-purple, noncrystalline network that surrounds a green, crystalline mush. It was in such hydrothermally-altered rocks in Silver Creek canyon, below your trailhead, that 1860s miners discovered gold and silver, which caused a frantic, though generally unsuccessful and short-lived, rush of mining activity.

In one spot along your low traverse across the volcanic cliff, the trail periodically gets washed out, and if that has happened there is a slight risk of a quick slide down a steep slope into Noble Creek, about 40 feet below. Just beyond this spot we leave the creek and start up a briskly flowing, alder-lined tributary. After a minute or two, we reach a nice one-tent campsite.

We cross the creek immediately past the campsite, and then make a moderately graded, ¼-mile climb southeast up a minor ridge to a gently sloping sagebrush flat that is peppered with junipers. Heading southeast, we see Highland Peak and its nearly equal southern satellite, both towering more than 3000 feet

above us. Our climb quickly tapers off after we turn south, and then we traverse briefly to a crossing of a boggy meadow of grasses and willows before reaching a nearby creek, the third brisk one we've crossed.

Leaving its aspen-lined banks, we climb a bit more, passing more aspens as we traverse almost ½ mile to a crossing of our fourth brisk creek, a **Highland Peak tributary.** If you follow my route up to Highland and Silver peaks (Route NC-3), you'll end your descent at this creek crossing. You could also start an ascent from here, up to a saddle between the two peaks, but such a route is very steep and very taxing.

With just under 1.0 mile and 500 feet of elevation gain before we reach the Pacific Crest Trail, we make a gentle-to-moderate ascent to our fifth and last brisk creek. This one drains not only the slopes of Highland Peak's satellite but also Noble Lake and its satellite lakelet. Ahead, we climb south steeply for about ¼ mile, have a breather up along a gently climbing ridge, and then climb steeply but briefly to a junction with the **Pacific Crest Trail.** To the west this trail winds, climbs and descends 3.0 miles to a crossing of Highway 4. Just 0.3 mile before that crossing is a junction, from which a spur trail leads 0.2 mile north to a large trailhead parking lot. See the previous route for a description of this trail segment plus the 0.9-mile segment up Noble Canyon to Noble Lake.

NC-3   Highland and Silver Peaks

Distances
0.7 mile (approx.) to first crest saddle
1.6 miles (approx.) to Peak 10,824
2.0 miles (approx.) to saddle between Peak
    10,824 and Highland Peak
2.3 miles (approx.) to Highland Peak
3.2 miles (approx.) to saddle between High-
    land and Silver peaks
4.2 miles (approx.) to south summit of Silver
    Peak
4.5 miles (approx.) to north summit of Silver
    Peak
5.8 miles (approx.) back to saddle between
    Highland and Silver peaks
7.5 miles (approx.) to Noble Canyon Trail at
    Highland Peak tributary

Trailhead   None. Start cross-country route from Noble Lake.

Introduction   This route is definitely the most taxing cross-country route in the book. Furthermore, I recommend doing it as a day hike, starting from the Noble Canyon trailhead (previous route). As such, the total route is then 15.3 miles long, making it the book's most taxing day hike. Your other alternative is to set up a base camp near Noble Lake, make the 7.5-mile cross-country jaunt, hike 0.9 mile up the Noble Canyon Trail to the Pacific Crest Trail, and then 0.9 mile up it back to Noble Lake. The choice is yours, depending on what shape you're in. Some people may decide, after conquering Highland Peak, that it's best to backtrack rather than to take the recommended descent route. Obviously, this route is not for everyone, though registers atop Highland and Silver peaks indicate that quite a few people have done it. If you're out for summit views, you'll find the best ones from the first summit, Peak 10,824. Only peak baggers need visit the other three summits, which offer increasingly better views of cultivated Carson Valley, but increasingly poorer views of mountainous Carson-Iceberg Wilderness.

Description Leave the Pacific Crest Trail near the outlet of Noble Lake, and climb east up either side of a seeping gully to a nearby spongy meadow. From it you could traverse north to an adjacent, waist-deep, willow-lined lakelet. This is a suitable base camp.

From the wet meadow just south of the lakelet your cross-country route climbs northeast to a nearby minor gap lying between steep slopes and a low northwest ridge. Just past the gap you quickly reach a talus slope, which gives way to steeper, more solid slopes. Soon you start to curve east, then southeast, climbing steeply up into a minor side canyon. Rock fringe and Sierra primrose, together with mountain hemlocks, let you know you're in a subalpine realm. A short, steep climb south

gets you to your first significant goal, your **first crest saddle.**

Ahead, the route is obvious: follow a ridge northeast up to a summit. Actually, your route will be quite obvious all the way to the north summit of Silver Peak, since you stay on or close to the ridge that is part of the Carson-Iceberg Wilderness boundary. At the midway point along your 1,400-foot climb from the saddle to your first summit, you'll have to leave the ridge momentarily, veering right to get around a small though significant outcrop. Onward, you follow the ridge some more, then about ¾ of the way into your ascent you'll find it convenient to again veer right from the crest. You now climb northeast up steep slopes on loose soil that is somewhat held in place by all the whitebark pines. Finally, you make a short scramble to the crest, then walk a few yards east on it to the actual summit of **Peak 10,824.**

Because the views, in my opinion, are the best from this summit, I'll mention all the prominent peaks *outside the area covered by this book's map* that you can expect to see on a clear day. The views from Highland Peak, about ½ mile north, are quite similar. Because these distant peaks are numerous, I'll mention, for each one, only bearing, distance and elevation. With these statistics, plus a com-

Two-topped Silver Peak, left, and Highland Peak, from Peak 10,824

pass, you should be able to identify all of the following peaks. With the book's map, you should be able to identify at least two dozen closer peaks.

Starting due north and scanning clockwise, these features are:

Tower Peak	156°	29 miles	11,755'
Leavitt Peak	161°	18 miles	11,569'
Granite Dome	176°	22 miles	10,322'
The Three Chimneys	188°	19 miles	9,882'
Mokelumne Peak	271°	18 miles	9,334'
Reynolds Peak	304°	5 miles	9,690'
Round Top	305°	16 miles	10,381'
Elephants Back	310°	16 miles	9,585'
Red Lake Peak	313°	18 miles	10,063'
Stevens Peak	316°	19 miles	10,059'
Raymond Peak	319°	6 miles	10,014'
Luther Pass	330°	20 miles	7,730'
Hawkins Peak	337°	15 miles	10,024'
Armstrong Pass	338°	22 miles	8,710'
Freel Peak	341°	24 miles	10,881'
Jobs Sister	343°	24 miles	10,823'
Jobs Peak	346°	23 miles	10,633'

After you've had your fill of views, start north-northwest along the ridge. Then, about where it turns north, leave the ridge and stay just east of it as you descend to the **saddle between Peak 10,824 and Highland Peak.** You've dropped about 300 feet to it, and by dropping east-southeast another 200 feet, you can reach a snowmelt pond that typically lasts well into August. *It is your only near-route source of water.* To play it safe, you ought to carry your own supply, although if you're hiking before late July, you're very likely to encounter snow patches.

Now you face a 400-foot climb to Highland Peak. As usual, you start up the ridge, which here appears to be slate, but is actually volcanic rock, part of a 4-million-year-old, eroded dacite dome. The three other summits along this route are of similar age and composition. Just after you're halfway up the ridge, you'll have to veer right to get around a small headwall. Ahead, you climb but a few minutes straight up to the top of **Highland Peak.** If the register is still there, you can sign it. Looking north, you see the twin summits of Silver Peak. The ridges up to them, particularly the ridge up to the south summit, can look quite intimidating, but actually, they're quite easy. The same can't be said about your 900-foot descent to the saddle between Highland and Silver peaks.

First you have to get off Highland Peak's summit block, which isn't all that difficult, but

nevertheless you should downclimb it cautiously even though most of the rock is solid. You then walk briefly north along the ridge and stop where it angles northwest. Ahead, the ridge is steep and jagged, and midway down to a gentler gradient you'll have a short stretch of careful downclimbing. I preferred to stick as close to the ridge as possible, though you can drop west down steep slopes if the jagged ridge poses too many problems.

Where the gradient becomes gentler, the ridge descends north-northwest. It is densely covered with shrubby whitebark pines, so you'll want to stay just east of it. After a few minutes of relatively easy descent, the ridge almost levels, and atop it you walk a few minutes more to the **saddle between Highland and Silver peaks.** Surprisingly, this gravelly flat is essentially viewless. Remember this spot, since you'll want to return to it to start your descent into Noble Canyon on your return from Silver Peak. You may be tempted to start elsewhere, but if you do, you'll have a greater chance of encountering overly steep slopes along your descent.

Leaving the saddle, you climb north, soon approaching the ridge. Rather than top it, you keep just east of and below it, more or less contouring over to a small ridge saddle and then over to an even smaller ridge saddle. The steep ridge up to the south summit of Silver Peak lies ahead. This bedrock ridge is somewhat blocky, so you'll want to keep just below and to the right of it. As you climb northeast, you'll eventually reach a sizable headwall and veer to the right along its base, then up its east side. Just above it, maybe still with a register, is the **south summit of Silver Peak.** You have views similar to those seen before, but the north summit, being higher than the south summit, obstructs views to the north-northeast, so you might as well continue on. The north summit, though higher, never had its elevation determined by the U.S. Geological Survey. I put its elevation at about 10,820–25'.

From the south summit, cautiously head north along a blocky ridge. It's really quite easy and safe, but this is no place for a turned ankle. Soon the ridge turns northeast and plunges to the saddle between the two summits. You'll want to leave the ridge immediately before this dropoff and, on its east side, carefully do a bit of relatively unexposed downclimbing to a talus slope. From it you head immediately over to the saddle and then make a very easy ascent, climbing about 200

Carson Valley, from south summit of Silver Peak

feet in a few minutes to the **north summit of Silver Peak.** You now have summit views in all directions, although features to the south are somewhat obstructed by the three summits you've already climbed. In the distant, usually hazy, north lies expansive, agricultural Carson Valley.

One of the higher peaks along the Alpine-Mono county line, which runs from the Nevada border south to Sonora Peak, is worth noting. This is 8968' Leviathan Peak, which is 11½ miles distant and lies on a 45° bearing. This peak, which is the ruins of a volcano that was active a few million years ago, stands directly above and behind Monitor Pass, ¾ mile closer. If you've got sharp eyes, you should be able to see Highway 89 crossing the pass. Actually, what's worth noting is out of sight, the Leviathan Mine, which lies 3 miles northwest below the peak. This mine outproduced all others in Alpine County, and it differed from all the others in its product—sulfur. Over a half million tons were produced before this mine shut down in 1962.

Our return starts from the saddle between the two summits. On a traverse south you'll reach an east-descending ridge, which is best crossed in one fairly obvious spot, and then you'll traverse southwest until you reach your ascent route. Retrace your steps back to the **saddle between Highland and Silver peaks.** From this saddle, which is a gap between two ridges that don't quite meet, resist the temptation to head due west over the adjacent ridge.

Rather, start southwest from the saddle and cross the ridge at a point just before it drops steeply south. Here you start west down a secondary ridge, which is not very prominent and is merely a steep descent at first. Quickly, however, it becomes very steep, and you make a knee-knocking elevation loss of about 900 feet before the gradient starts to taper off at about 9000 feet. The ridge, which has been descending west-southwest, drops about 400 more feet in elevation, then curves right, west, for a brief spell before reaching a split at about 8400 feet. A steep ridge drops west while a gentler one drops southwest. Take the latter, which heads toward a creek. You'll reach gentler slopes and then the creek—the **Highland Peak tributary** of Route NC-2—which you briefly follow to its crossing of the Noble Canyon Trail.

Chapter 12   Wolf Creek

WC-1   Wolf Creek Trail to Bull Lake

Distances
1.4 miles to Dixon Creek
4.8 miles to junction with Bull Canyon Trail
5.7 miles to junction with Noble Canyon Trail
6.7 miles to junction with Bull Lake Trail
7.0 miles to Bull Lake

Trailhead   To reach the Wolf Creek Road junction by driving east on Highway 4, first drive up to Ebbetts Pass and then drop 10.6 miles from it to the junction. If you're coming from the north, you'll follow Highway 89 about 5 miles south from Markleeville to a junction with Highway 4. If you're coming from the east, you'll first leave Highway 395, and climb, usually quite steeply, 9.5 miles up Highway 89 to Monitor Pass, then descend 8.2 miles to the Highway 4 junction. Now you drive 2.4 miles south up to the Wolf Creek Road junction, which is immediately south of the Centerville Flat Undeveloped Camping Area. From the junction you then follow Wolf Creek Road 2.2 miles southwest up-canyon to where the pavement ends and the gradient steepens. Over the next 1.1 miles south you first climb and then gently descend to a junction with a road branching left. Those who will be staying overnight in the wilderness register here.

If you're taking Route WC-3, WC-4 or WC-5, head east on the branching road. This goes ⅓ mile northeast along the north edge of Wolf Creek Meadows, then bends sharply left for a short climb north. In 200 yards, immediately past a low ridge, you make a sharp turn right and follow a poor, narrow road ¼ mile up to its end at a sloping parking area that can hold up to 10 vehicles. In early season you may want to drive only half way up this road and park on a flat, for the last part is rutted and can be muddy.

If you're taking Route WC-1 or WC-2, stay on Wolf Creek Road, which goes 1.6 miles farther south to a primitive road, which descends east into nearby Wolf Creek Meadows Undeveloped Camping Area. The Wolf Creek Trail begins just 50 yards down this road.

Introduction   Perhaps the greatest use of the Wolf Creek Trail—a closed jeep road—is day use by fishermen residing at Wolf Creek Meadows Undeveloped Camping Area. The creek is an excellent cold-water trout stream with many deep pools. But from time to time, summer thunderstorms and near flash floods decimate the fish populations. The long-term situation is one of species diversity, high numbers, and longer-lived trout.

The Wolf Creek Trail leads to other trails that get you to very photogenic Bull Lake, which is an ideal overnight goal. On weekends you'll probably have company at the lake, though on week days you may have the lake all to yourself.

Description   Most of our route is up Wolf Creek canyon along a gated road, which is still used today by local cattlemen who graze herds in the canyon. Starting south, our Wolf Creek Trail immediately crosses a usually flowing creek, which marks our entry into Carson-Iceberg Wilderness. We stroll under a canopy of white firs and Jeffrey pines, and in ¼ mile our closed road is forced against the bank of Wolf Creek by a low, granitic outcrop. The same happens at a second outcrop ¼ mile later, and then in another ¼ mile the road actually goes over a barren outcrop. These outcrops are part of a low ridge, and over the final ¼ mile of its exposure, we walk along its base.

At the end of a nearly vertical cliff, about a mile from the trailhead, the road bends north, and then west, circling a grove of cottonwoods and aspens before heading south through a stand of Jeffrey pines. These grow on a broad alluvial fan that has built up at the mouth of Dixon Creek canyon. Just beyond the stand we reach **Dixon Creek,** crossing it near its union with Wolf Creek. Except for times of high runoff, you can boulderhop the creek without too much difficulty. Continuing south, immediately you pass a challenging granitic cliff, which stands above the east bank of Wolf Creek. Protection appears to be rather minimal on the dozen or so potential routes up the cliff, though climbers could top-rope the shorter ones.

For almost ¾ mile beyond the creek we have an easy ascent as the closed road parallels the edge of a floodplain. By its upper end, the road splits into two branches, which climb quite steeply, and then quickly rejoin. Ahead, we have a short, easy climb to some bedrock ribs, which we cross, the last one having a gate along it. From this spot, about 2½ miles from the trailhead, we make a brief, steep descent almost to Wolf Creek, which we parallel a few minutes upstream. Then, about 2¾ miles from the trailhead, we come to a campsite which lies along the edge of a bouldery floodplain. Young pines and firs are invading the plain, but they are likely to be soon obliterated by a flood or an avalanche.

Now we leave the floodplain, climb briefly along the edge of an escarpment Wolf Creek has cut in loose sediments, and then cross a usually brisk creek. About ¼ mile farther you'll see, just east of Wolf Creek, a grassy pond, and then you have a ⅔-mile, usually gentle climb through a white-fir forest to the base of a cliff of highly broken, autobrecciated lava. It is overly steep, glaciated cliffs such as this one that give rise to mass wasting, avalanching and landsliding to produce sediments that form the alluvial fans and floodplains in this canyon. In the past, such geological processes have altered the course of Wolf Creek and lower Dixon Creek, and these courses will certainly be altered in the future. We immediately cross another brisk creek, then parallel Wolf Creek briefly up-canyon.

Soon we veer west, following the creek, and we have our first view of an enormous lava butte, to the southwest, which stands high above closer-by Bull Canyon. In this vicinity

you'll discover, just south of the trail, a spacious horse camp. Just beyond it, the trail bends south-southwest and leads ⅓ mile along the edge of a brushy flat to a junction with the **Bull Canyon Trail.** Not always signed, this junction lies where the jeep road—the Wolf Creek Trail—angles south-southeast. Route WC-2 continues up the road from this point.

We, however, begin a moderate-to-steep ascent southwest up an old roadbed, crossing a rushing creeklet midway to where our route bends west. The gradient then lessens for a spell, but resumes again just before the roadbed narrows to a trail. Soon we arrive at a junction with the **Noble Canyon Trail.** Chapter 10's Route HL-9, starting from the Highland Lakes, climbs north to this junction from a crossing of nearby Bull Canyon creek.

Now in lower Bull Canyon, we start an easy-to-moderate climb west on the seemingly misnamed Noble Canyon Trail. After a few minutes you'll pass through about a 200-yard-long stretch of downed trees, which are the result of a late-spring 1986 avalanche. The quick melting of the heavy snowpack caused a number of avalanches in and about the Sierra, a notable example being a series of avalanches across a ¾ mile stretch of trail in Wolf Creek Canyon (Chapter 18's Route PM-1).

Above the avalanche damage we traverse briefly west to a boulderhop of refreshing Bull Canyon creek, then resume a moderate climb. Soon we cross a creeklet and then parallel its course for several minutes up to a view of a nearby corn-lily meadow. This is a notable landmark for folks *descending* our trail, and it alerts us to an upcoming junction. We're now atop a very minor ridge, which we momentarily leave for a brief, moderate climb west to what can sometimes be an obscure junction with the **Bull Lake Trail.** Continuing up-canyon, the occasionally hard-to-follow Noble Canyon Trail climbs 1.4 miles up to a saddle before making a steep, obvious, 0.3-mile descent to the Pacific Crest Trail in upper Noble Canyon. This 1.7-mile stretch is described in the opposite direction at the end of the previous chapter's Route NC-1.

On the Bull Lake Trail we climb south, rather steeply at first, up a narrow tread through a shady forest. After several minutes we reach a broad bench and then quickly arrive at the north tip of **Bull Lake.** Here there

Bull Lake and a dominating lava butte

are only two small campsites—both too close to the lake for ecologically sound camping—so you could find yourself without a campsite on a typical, popular summer weekend. You might have to camp on the low ridge above the lake's east shore.

At about 8635 feet and covering 6 acres, Bull Lake is one of a few lakes which contain Lahontan cutthroat trout that are maintained by natural reproduction. Cutthroat are good looking, good eating and easy to catch, but please show restraint in catching and keeping them. Catch them and release them unharmed for others to enjoy in the same way. The outlet stream also contains a few fish. Following it down to Wolf Creek may produce some nice brooks, rainbows and browns of pan size. Wolf Creek also contains a sizable population of Rocky Mountain whitefish, which are native to the Lahontan Basin. With a bony system identical to trout and with similar food preferences, whitefish are excellent fighters and make excellent eating. They readily rise to a dry fly, but are more commonly caught on nymphs.

The lake's south shore is fringed by a boggy meadow, which nevertheless is worth a visit, since from that vicinity you have an inspiring view to the north of pyramidal Peak 10,824, which rises gracefully over the lake. You may want to climb the dominating lava butte that stands above the lake's south shore. If you do make the nearly 1000-foot climb up to its broad summit, you'll have a commanding view of the upper Wolf Creek canyon's landscape. Of prime interest is the summit's "patterned ground." This summit was just above a former glacier 20,000 years ago, and was in a cold environment. Blocks of lava were heaved up by subsurface ice that was experiencing alternating freeze and thaw. This is the only patterned-ground locality I know of in the wilderness.

WC-2 Wolf Creek and Murray Canyon-Golden Canyon Trails to Falls Meadows in East Fork Carson River Canyon

Distances
5.9 miles to junction with spur road to cow camp
6.4 miles to junction with Asa Lake Trail
8.0 miles to junction with Murray Canyon Trail
11.1 miles to junction with East Carson Trail

Trailhead Same as the Route WC-1 trailhead

Introduction This route provides a relatively easy way in to the heart of the longest, deepest canyon east of the Sierra crest—the East Carson River canyon. There is only one long climb, a scenic, 1100-foot ascent to a saddle between Wolf Creek and Murray canyons. The 1850-foot descent through Murray Canyon down to the East Carson Trail at Falls Meadows is generally a well-graded, rather pleasant descent, but it can in the opposite direction be quite a struggle, particularly on a hot day. But rather than backtrack, you can make a loop trip by first taking the East Carson Trail down-canyon to its trailhead,

then following roads for 2.2 miles back to your
original trailhead. The heart of the East
Carson River canyon contains Carson Falls,
which is certainly a worthy goal. The shortest
way to it, however, is by starting from
Highland Lakes and following Chapter 10's
Route HL-9, which is 2¼ miles shorter than
the following route. With a total round-trip
distance to and from the falls of 19.6 miles,
that route is within relatively easy reach of
conditioned hikers. (On my strenuous hik-
ing/mapping schedule, any day hike under 20
miles in length and under 4000 feet of elevation change was considered easy.)

Description   First, follow the previous route
4.8 miles to a junction with the Bull Canyon
Trail. From it you stay on the Wolf Creek
Trail—a closed jeep road—which immediately enters a well-watered aspen grove. Just
beyond, you cross a minor creek, and beside
its union with adjacent Wolf Creek lies a
spacious campsite. From it you go but ¼ mile
up the road before reaching a crossing of
alder-lined Bull Canyon creek beside its confluence with Wolf Creek. In early season Bull
Canyon creek can be 20 feet wide.

Once across, you parallel the creek west on
a steep, but thankfully short, ascent to a gate
atop a minor volcanic ridge. Your efforts are
rewarded by a view of the massive volcanic
butte you saw earlier, which will be a landmark to measure your progress all the way up
to the saddle at the head of Murray Canyon.
Below, you see a series of Wolf Creek falls and
cascades, which drop through an inner gorge.

Continuing up-canyon, your road approaches Wolf Creek, which here consists of a
pleasing sequence of cascades, pools and
rapids. Your ascent south is generally easy, but
then you turn southwest and make a brief
moderate climb up beside a tributary to a junction with a **spur road to a cow camp.** The
camp is of no interest to us, but the junction is
a useful point from which to determine the
start of the old Noble Canyon Trail. Just 90
yards up your road, at a point where it bends
from southwest to south, this old trail once
started a climb north-northwest. Actually, it
still does, but the first 100 or so yards are
basically invisible.

From this unseen junction you start south
and after a minute's time begin a traverse
across the lower part of an unmistakable
snow-avalanche path, which originates high on
the slopes below the lava butte. You then veer

Lava butte above Wolf Creek falls

southeast along a fenced-in pasture before
heading south along a lodgepole-pine flat to a
crossing of Wolf Creek. Without a fallen tree,
you'll have to get your feet wet. If you're
heading up toward the Gardner Meadows or
the Highland Lakes, then don't cross, since
you'll only have to recross at a spot that is
almost always a ford, due to lack of suitable
downed trees. Just stay above the creek, and
go about 300 yards cross country until you
find the trail.

Bound for the Murray Canyon saddle, you
continue along the jeep road, and in 120 yards
reach a junction with the **Asa Lake Trail.**
Heading southwest, this trail recrosses Wolf
Creek in 130 yards. See Chapter 10's Route
HL-9 if you're interested in following it.

Ahead, our jeep road now becomes Murray
Canyon-Golden Canyon Trail 1015. In a
minute's time we reach a junction with a spur
road south, which goes to a nearby cow camp.
Straight ahead, our jeep road quickly becomes
a trail, which climbs rather steeply east up to a
nearby fence and gate. Our route, which has
largely been forested, is now on generally open
terrain that supports sagebrush, other shrubs,
and scattered junipers. The trail's gradient is

Panorama: Hiram Peak, Folger Peak, lava butte, Highland Peak massif

usually moderate or moderate-to-steep, and with a pack on your back you'll appreciate the opportunity to stop almost anywhere and enjoy a fine panorama of upper Wolf Creek canyon and its surrounding peaks.

About midway up your climb the trail, which has been switchbacking eastward, turns south and goes along a minor divide. Just east of it lies an unseen creek, which is your only reliable source of water along this ascent. You continue south, climb moderately up past two snowmelt creeklets, and switchback some 200 feet higher to a nearly flat spot, which is a particularly fine spot to enjoy views. Rested, we make a short, level traverse east, then climb briefly south to a saddle and a junction with the **Murray Canyon Trail.** This trail, our route, is the main trail straight ahead, down Murray Canyon. Another trail, which is a part of the old Murray Canyon-Golden Canyon Trail, starts south here, and will be described first.

Murray Canyon-Golden Canyon Trail

Before the construction of the Pacific Crest Trail through this area in the mid-'70s, the Murray Canyon-Golden Canyon Trail climbed out of Wolf Creek canyon, as it does today, but then continued first south, then east, to the upper reaches of Golden Canyon. Today, it just traverses 1.9 miles south up to the Pacific Crest Trail, which then makes a better-graded traverse south to upper Golden Canyon. In the past, this trail has led unsuspecting users astray, for its name suggests that it visits Murray Canyon. It doesn't.

This trail first traverses south to a nearby flat bench, where most people realize their mistake and drop east into Murray Canyon, as footprints and hoofprints attest. It then swings west over to the nearby crest and heads up it. Between trees you can occasionally look northwest across the canyon and see the lava butte you've seen so many times along your route. To its north stands Peak 10,824, beyond which pokes Highland Peak, the highest summit in this vicinity. Arnot Peak and its

monolithic "north pinnacle" stand out in the southwest.

As the forest cover ends, the trail, rather than hugging the crest, contours south across a sagebrush slope and then, just north of an obvious crest knoll, bends southeast through a saddle. You continue south ¼ mile down to a seasonal creeklet, cross it, and traverse an equal distance southwest to the east edge of a grassy crest meadow. Although the trail tends to disappear through it, you'll have no trouble finding it again, for large blazes are found on trees at both the west and east ends of the meadow. You then traverse south along the west base of a steep-sided volcanic butte and reach the Pacific Crest Trail. See Chapter 10's Route HL-10 for a description of this trail from Wolf Creek Pass south to Golden Canyon, and a description of the Golden Canyon Trail east down that canyon.

At the crest saddle separating Wolf Creek canyon from Murray Canyon, you enter an area closed to fishing, since it is the home of native, threatened Lahontan cutthroat trout. This area includes the drainages in Murray and Golden canyons plus East Fork Carson River above our destination, Falls Meadows.

Our Murray Canyon Trail initially starts east-southeast, but quickly bends south to descend along a minor creek. In ½ mile we encounter an adequate campsite, then in 70 yards cross the creek. Now we descend east on a moderate-to-steep grade, which slackens in almost ½ mile, where we cross a trickling tributary. We continue ½ mile farther, first crossing a springy meadow before traversing slopes of white firs, lodgepoles and Jeffrey pines to a junction in Murray Canyon proper. From the junction a minor trail departs southwest to quickly cross the creek we've been paralleling and then it ascends the floor of upper Murray Canyon. The trail can be hard to follow in spots, due to numerous meadows and distracting cow paths. Eventually the trail dies out on the canyon's headwall.

You'll want to continue down the lower half of Murray Canyon. Keeping to the main trail, you stay just north of and above the creek, being able to drop to it from almost any spot along the trail. In ¼ mile you pass through a meadow, where cows have muddied the environs and obscured the trail. Just maintain your northeast bearing across a bench and soon you should be dropping moderately on an obvious tread. Over the next ½ mile your trail crosses over half a dozen minor rivulets, then it bends east for a short, moderate-to-steep descent to a rockhop across the canyon's creek. By the southeast bank you'll find an adequate campsite, though better camps lie in the Falls Meadows environs.

With that goal in mind, we start a traverse east, which quickly ends where the lower part of Murray Canyon has been left high above the floor of the 700-foot-deeper East Fork Carson River canyon. From a minor ridge we pass through a gate and leave the hanging canyon behind as we start a brushy descent into the more severely glaciated trunk canyon. About 15 switchback legs guide us down the west wall of the trunk canyon, and from one switchback midway down this stretch, we have a picture-perfect view south up-canyon toward an inner gorge that hides Carson Falls. The 0.6-mile-long, switchbacking descent ends as abruptly as it began, reaching a junction with the **East Carson Trail** near the west edge of Falls Meadows. This junction is immediately south of Murray Canyon's creek. Look for suitable campsites either among the cottonwoods in this vicinity, or just north of it, on a flat shaded by mature Jeffrey pines. To continue onward, see Route WC-4, which describes the East Carson Trail south to the Soda Springs Guard Station, and Route WC-5, which describes it south from that station to our vicinity and beyond it all the way up the canyon to a junction with the Pacific Crest Trail.

Descending into the East Carson canyon

The East Carson River below Carson Falls has a mixed population of naturally reproducing rainbow, brown, brook, cutthroat and whitefish. The population extends downstream all the way to Wolf Creek. However, in the stretch from Soda Springs Guard Station down to Silver King Creek, there are several long stretches of shallow flats that have few fish. In the East Carson canyon, individual brown trout have been recorded up to 20″, but the average is in the range of 9–12″. Whitefish average 14″ and weigh one pound. All the other species average 7–12″, which is typical for most wilderness stream populations. Anglers hungry for fish should stalk deep pools for wary bottom-hugging whitefish. Small dark flies and nymphs fished deep produce delicious rewards.

WC-3   High Trail to East Carson Trail

Distances
6.6 miles to East Carson Trail
9.1 miles to Soda Springs Guard Station

Trailhead   See the Route WC-1 trailhead

Introduction   From the Wolf Creek Meadows area you have two main routes leading

over to the northern part of the giant East Fork Carson River canyon: the High Trail and the East Carson Trail. Each has its assets and its liabilities. The High Trail is about a mile shorter, but it climbs about 1000 feet more. It offers some very pleasing views, but it is short on water and campsites. Finally, along the

High Trail, hikers have to ford the Carson River just once, versus five or three times, respectively, for the Carson River Trail or the river trail with its shortcut variant. (If you're willing to do 2½ miles of cross-country hiking, you'll have only one ford.) So, which route should you take? Before mid-July take the High Trail, for then the Carson River is too deep, swift and cold for enjoyable fording. If you take the river trail in early summer and find the river ford too dangerous, you can find plenty of camping space on flat lands near the ford.

However, most folks will want to continue at least to the forested lands in the Dumonts Meadows area, where Soda Springs Guard Station—the only such station within the wilderness—is located. Although camping isn't allowed at the guard station, it is allowed at the many forested sites both up- and down-canyon from it.

If you're looking for the easiest route to Soda Springs Guard Station, neither the High Trail nor the East Carson Trail is it. Instead, you'll want Chapter 13's Route RF-1, which is not only the shortest, but is also mostly downhill. However, many folks don't like driving all the way to Highway 395, then west up the steep road to the trailhead at Rodriguez Flat. If you take that road, be sure your brakes are good.

Description   From the trailhead parking area you go 50 yards northeast up a narrow road to the start of the conspicuous High Trail, which branches right, south. The trail is well graded, maintaining a fairly constant, moderate gradient both up to the route's high point and down from it to the river. At first the trail goes across open slopes of sagebrush and mountain mahogany, so you have views west down at Wolf Creek Meadows. Quickly, however, you reach forest cover, and views all but disappear as you enter Carson-Iceberg Wilderness before you arrive at a gate on a minor ridge 0.6 mile from your trailhead parking area. Through an open Jeffrey-pine forest you continue climbing 0.4 mile more through the thinning forest to a sagebrush saddle on a volcanic crest.

Here, you have a view east down to the Carson River environs and beyond, plus a view northwest, which includes butte-capped Hawkins Peak, 14½ miles away. Only a few yards down the trail from the saddle is another interesting sight—a tremendously large granitic boulder that has split in two. Since it lies on a volcanic slope, it probably got here on a giant glacier descending through Wolf Creek canyon. If you climb up on the lower half, which has fallen flat, you can see the surface along which the boulder cracked. It is well weathered, and in places is pitted up to 3 inches deep. Such weathering in granitic rocks takes a long time, perhaps more than 100,000 years.

From the saddle near the split boulder, High Trail 1016 first traverses along a view-packed, well-defined crest, then leaves it for a climb through a pine-and-fir forest. It crosses the now broader crest near a small, grassy flat, then climbs south up to a larger expanse of meadow on gently sloping land. A fair campsite could be established here, and you could get water from a spring near the meadow's head, or from Railroad Canyon creek, immediately past it. These are your only reliable sources of water along the High Trail.

From roughly the boundary between granitic rocks and overlying volcanic rocks, we start another round of ascents. We climb moderately but briefly east to a snowmelt creeklet, then head south along it up a steeper grade to its headwaters. From there, we climb briefly east to round a minor ridge and essentially end our ascent. Now in forest, we have a view or two before we round a nearby minor ridge and have our first really good view. You see Bagley Valley, with Heenan Lake just beyond it, to the north, and Silver King Valley, with its Vaquero Camp, to the east. Soon we climb past blocky lava, then climb to a ridge of fractured lava, which has a third good view.

The best viewpoint, however, lies about ¼ mile ahead. From a minor gap walk 60 yards northeast out to a small point that is 5 feet higher than the trail. Not only do you see Bagley and Silver King valleys, both formed in part by faulting, but you see features way beyond them. To the northwest you see, above the Carson River canyon, pointed, volcanic 10,024′ Hawkins Peak and distant, granitic 10,881′ Freel Peak. In the east-southeast, poking above the upper end of Silver King Valley, are some high summits of the Sweetwater Range, about 22 miles away.

Your trail, which has recently flirted with the idea, now decides to descend in earnest. For the first 0.4 mile, the descent is gentle through a fir forest; then the trail turns east

Silver King Valley, from the High Trail

and briefly descends along a ridge to a switch-back. Ahead, the moderate grade continues as we descend south, to cross the two gullies of Snowslide Canyon, the second one avalanche prone. Just a few minutes beyond the canyon, among white firs and Jeffrey pines, we cross another avalanche gully. Soon we round a granitic ridge, leave the unstable volcanic slopes behind, and descend briefly but moder-ately south-southwest to a broad, shallow gully with a snowmelt creeklet. Up it we maintain our bearing past Jeffrey pines, white firs and aromatic tobacco brush to a notch in a granitic ridge.

The trail then makes a switchbacking descent, dropping more than 200 feet closer to the canyon floor. Next it arcs southwest for ½ mile, first descending across brushy slopes and

then traversing a Jeffrey-pine flat to Bryant Creek. If, just before you reached this creek, you were to head due east, you'd reach East Carson River Trail 1011-1 in ¼ mile, at a river ford. Keeping to the High Trail, we reach the river in 200 yards. You'll find, on the trail's upstream side, a small campsite nestled among lodgepole pines. Flat lands border the river's edge for a full ½ mile upstream and for more than a mile downstream, so if you can't con-tinue any farther, due to high water, you're bound to find a suitable campsite here.

If you do ford the river, which generally is little more than knee deep, you'll reach the **East Carson Trail** in only 70 yards. Consult the last part of the following route for the next 2.5 miles of nearly level route, to **Soda Springs Guard Station.**

WC-4   East Carson Trail to Soda Springs Guard Station

Distances
2.3 miles to Grays Crossing
4.2 miles to second crossing
4.9 miles to junction with cutoff trail
5.2 miles to third crossing
6.6 miles to fourth crossing and reunion with cutoff trail
7.0 miles to fifth crossing

7.4 miles to junction with High Trail
8.4 miles to junction with horse trail
9.6 miles to junction with Poison Flat Trail
9.9 miles to Soda Springs Guard Station

Trailhead   See the Route WC-1 trailhead

Introduction   First, read the introduction to the previous route to see whether the East

Carson Trail to Soda Springs appeals to you. If it does, you have three variations to consider: a cross-country route, a shortcut trail and a horse trail. By using the first two in combination, you can reach Soda Springs Guard Station with only one ford. However, by using the main trail and then the horse trail, you'll have seven fords. Other combinations have intermediate numbers. The combination using the minimum of effort—the main trail and the shortcut trail—requires three fords. On horseback, you don't have to worry about fords slowing you down. But if you're on foot and you remove and then put on your boots at every ford, allow about 20 minutes per crossing—more, if you're not in a hurry. I met one backpacker who, after each crossing, pulled out a paperback novel and read it till his feet dried. Now, that's relaxation!

Description   From the trailhead parking area you go 50 yards northeast up a narrow road to the start of the conspicuous High Trail, which branches right, south, and then continue a fairly steep climb 70 more yards to a crest. Here you'll note erratics—boulders left by a Wolf Creek canyon glacier that has long since retreated. These light-gray, granitic boulders are easily identifiable, for they strongly contrast with the dark, brownish volcanic bedrock. Onward, we continue 120 yards east up the road to its end at a gate on a minor ridge, where we see more erratics. Here we enter Carson-Iceberg Wilderness as we start a descent along East Carson Trail 1011-1. At first we pass some scrubby mountain mahoganies and occasional pinyon pines, but where we reach Wolf Creek Lake, 0.7 mile down the trail, the trees are mostly Jeffrey pines and white firs.

On your moderate descent to this lake, you traverse across some clay-rich slopes. If you've ever hiked on any volcanic soils, such as here, when they were wet, you'll know just how slippery these clay-rich soils can be. The overly steep slopes west of Wolf Creek Lake contain volcanic sediments that perhaps about 10 million years ago were deposited by streams on top of a resistant lava flow. These clay-rich sediments, in turn, were subsequently buried under successive lava flows. During the last million years, East Fork Carson River cut the gorge we're hiking through, and in doing so it cut a relatively flat bench that today holds Wolf Creek Lake. But by cutting this gorge, the river exposed the weak, clay-rich sediments just west of and above the bench, and these sediments, when they became wet, failed to stay put, collapsing as a massive landslide. Some of the sediments, together with some of the overlying lava flows, slid hundreds of feet down to the river, but much of them settled on the edge of the bench, forming a dam that blocked drainage behind it. Water is retained quite effectively by a clay dam. Take a short walk around the lake and note the expansion cracks in dry mud, which are so typical of clay-rich soils.

From the southeast corner of this lake, which can be only knee-deep in late season, we traverse ⅓ mile east to a gully. Now we round a flat-topped *autobrecciated* lava flow, which is a stiff, viscous flow that broke up by itself as it slowly advanced downslope. Note its blocky, loose character, which contrasts with other lava flows you'll see up-canyon. Just after circling the edge of the flow, we reach a never-failing creeklet that drains Railroad Canyon. Here, you may want to stock up on water, for East Fork Carson River up to Soda Springs is known to carry *Giardia*

Wolf Creek Lake

lamblia. (I, however, have drunk the river water on several occasions, and never came down with giardiasis. You decide whether you want to play it safe or take a chance. Usually, the tributary streams you encounter in an area are less likely to contain giardia than the main stream.)

Our trail starts down lower Railroad Canyon, then curves southeast and traverses benches for ½ mile, passing through a gate and entering private property. Soon the trail makes a quick jog left down to **Grays Crossing** on East Fork Carson River. From at least the river's union with Wolf Creek, about 3 miles downstream, up to Carson Falls, a 2-day hike away, the "East Carson" supports a naturally reproducing mixed population of rainbow, brown, brook, cutthroat and whitefish. Brown trout are typically 9–12″, but have ranged up to 20″. Whitefish average 14″, and the other trout average 7–12″. Try stalking deep pools for wary whitefish, which hug the bottom. Use small, dark flies and nymphs for best results.

Here, across from a gap that drains Bagley Valley, the hiker has two choices. The safer and easier route is to continue on the East Carson Trail by first fording the East Fork, which from late July onward is usually knee-deep or less. Up through mid-July, it can be thigh-deep and dangerously swift, at least for hikers. Equestrians probably won't have a problem fording this broad, mossy-bouldered stretch. The second choice, which is not a viable option for equestrians, is to keep to the river's southwest bank and hike cross-country up-canyon. It will be described first.

Cross-Country Route

This route is recommended for experienced hikers only. In late season, after Labor Day, you'll be able to hike mostly along the river bed, but before then you may have to make a number of short detours up and around low cliffs. By not having to make two fords, you would save up to an hour's time—other things being equal. However, this 2.5-mile route is 0.4 mile longer than the very easy, fast East Carson Trail route, which is mostly a level road. Furthermore, cross-country hiking is never fast, so don't expect to save any time.

The route starts out easily enough across a sagebrush flat that has several fair campsites under lodgepoles. You'll probably leave all the cows, if any, behind as you enter Bureau of Land Management land at the mouth of a straight, narrow, southeast-bearing gorge, which has extensive talus slopes on the far bank, derived from the loose, pinkish-brown volcanic cliffs above. Midway up the gorge these slopes are replaced by a wide bank on which you'll find, if you wade across, many shady campsites. Few campsites are found on our side, and the last mile of gorge forces us many times to briefly climb above the river. Along this tiring stretch you'll pass columnar lava flows, and then impressive cliffs on the opposite side, which are composed of thick, blocky, autobrecciated flows. The gorge ends at the west edge of Silver King Valley, where once again you are on private land. Walk east a couple of hundred yards until you spy the conspicuous East Carson Trail, which climbs moderately south from the meadow's edge up to a gate and Forest Service land.

On private land on the east bank at Grays Crossing, our public East Carson Trail climbs 220 yards along Bagley Valley's creek, then crosses and immediately recrosses it at a bend. Next it climbs an additional 220 yards east up to a junction with an abandoned road, which heads north to cross the nearby creek. Now we're on a road, which immediately passes a small pool that seasonally turns pink with blossoms of water smartweed. Our road then climbs gently as it gradually curves southeast ¼ mile over to a junction with the main Bagley Valley road.

On the main road we hike southeast, mostly on BLM land, paralleling the rather straight base of some hills on our right. We're also paralleling an unseen fault that runs the length of Bagley and Silver King valleys. Precisely midway along our stretch of road to another junction, we cross a barely detected watershed divide, which theoretically separates the two valleys. At the junction, which is just inside private land, the main road branches left, east, over to open, visible Vaquero (Spanish for "cowboy") Camp.

We take the less-used road, and continue southeast along the east base of the hills, passing through two gates. At the second, which is ½ mile beyond the junction, the road ends, and from it a conspicuous path curves southwest along the hills' base to the mouth of the East Fork Carson River canyon—the end of the cross-country route. This path is not your route. Rather, you continue more or less straight ahead, roughly east-southeast, through a grassy meadow, to a meander in the East

Carson, your **second crossing.** If you're on horseback, you'll probably cross here and then maintain your bearing to the meadow's edge, by which time the trail should once again be obvious. If you're on foot, you may find the ford too deep for your liking. If so, go 200–300 yards upstream to where it is much shallower. Then head south or southwest to a trail you see climbing south from the meadow's edge. From about this area up to Soda Springs Guard Station, there are several long stretches in the East Carson that are very shallow and have few fish.

You leave the herds of cows behind as you make a brief, moderate climb among Jeffrey pines, first south and then west, to a gate by an enormous, 25-foot-long granitic boulder. This boulder is one of many in the area that lie exposed, and they likely are erratics pushed or carried here by a former East Fork glacier. If you try climbing to the top of the enormous boulder, you'll see it has two deep, weathered pits, which may have taken several hundred thousand years to form. This glacier was very old indeed, though in more recent times the East Fork canyon has been invaded by smaller glaciers.

In its day the ancient glacier stretched a full 18 miles from the saddle above Wolf Creek Lake (the one near Sonora Peak) down the East Carson canyon to here, where it dumped the sediments it carried and formed the terminal moraine you're standing on. In contrast, the glacier flowing down Silver King canyon never made it to Silver King Valley; rather, it stopped near the Poison Lake Trail junction, only 8 miles north of its source. The East Carson glacier, on the other hand, was dwarfed by the mighty glacier that flowed west from the Sierra crest near Sonora Pass down

the Stanislaus drainage. The difference in these lengths is due mainly to the *rain shadow* cast by the high ridges that separate the canyons—eastward, the precipitation greatly decreases.

From the gate by the enormous boulder, we ramble southeast on Forest Service land, which quickly becomes a gentle landscape with sagebrush and scattered Jeffrey pines. In 0.4 mile we again enter private land, and immediately we reach an often obscure junction with a **cutoff trail.** This spot is about 70 yards north-northwest of a large, solitary, lightning-zapped Jeffrey pine. Most folks will take this trail, since it doesn't cross the river and it is also ¼ mile shorter than the equivalent segment of the East Carson Trail. Both trails start across private land, which extends only to the wilderness boundary (south edge of Section 1 on the map). The shorter trail will be described first.

Cutoff Trail

We start south across a gentle slope that is dominated by aromatic sagebrush, but also includes large-leaved, scented mule ears and scattered Jeffrey pines, whose bark emits a fragrant butterscotch odor (stick your nose in a bark furrow and smell it). Soon we enter a low gorge that is being cut by the East Fork. Above its east bank is an Ice Age lava flow, composed of basalt, which while cooling and solidifying, contracted and broke into columns. After about ½ mile, the trail momentarily veers up along a seasonal creeklet. Cross it and then climb southwest up over the crest of a low ridge. Soon the southbound trail crosses a similar ridge and then gradually approaches the East Fork. We round a bend, spy a good campsite among lodgepoles on a riverside flat,

View north across Silver King Valley and the second crossing of the East Carson River

and then in 0.2 mile descend to trail's end at a barbed-wire gate between two closely spaced Jeffrey pines. Here, at the east edge of a meadow, we rejoin the East Carson Trail, which fords the river westward at this spot.

If you're on horseback, you won't mind the East Carson Trail's extra ¼-mile length, and you won't have to worry about the two fords that lie ahead. From the cutoff junction the East Carson Trail angles southeast and descends ¼ mile to a ford, your **third crossing,** at a prominent bend in the East Fork. Once across the river and in a meadow, you may lose the tread. Actually, there are two treads, and neither is obvious. Both begin at the base of a slope at the meadow's edge. The path that seems to be used most by those climbing south has a south-southwest bearing, while the one used most by those descending north runs due south. The two paths converge in about ¼ mile, at the end of your moderate ascent.

Now you walk along the top of an Ice Age basalt flow. About ¾ mile from the last ford you reach the north edge of a wet, sloping meadow, in which you may lose the tread. A creeklet flows down the meadow's edge, and you cross two more as you head southwest across soggy ground. After the third, about 150 yards past the first, your route becomes a broad, sandy trail—a former jeep road. On it you hike first through a Jeffrey-pine forest, then across a sagebrush flat, before re-entering

forest and quickly reaching a gate. From it you descend 180 yards to the East Carson for a **fourth crossing and a reunion with the cutoff trail.** You'll find lodgepole-shaded campsites on each bank immediately upstream from the crossing.

Ahead, the East Carson Trail may at first be vague as it heads up-canyon through a meadow. You stay close to its north edge as you head ⅓ mile west over to a river meander, then a similar distance west-southwest across a sagebrush flat to your **fifth crossing.** If you were to walk northwest 0.2 mile from this spot, or a similar distance west, you'd hit this book's previous route, the High Trail. The ford is just a knee-deep wade by late season, but it can be a raging, 20-yard-wide traverse before late July.

Once across, we follow the tread southwest to a bank above an open, sometimes damp flat, which we cross in the same direction. Then, from a gap in a low granitic outlier, we go 110 yards to a junction with the **High Trail.** Folks taking that route to Soda Springs Guard Station or beyond join us here.

On the broad, gravelly East Carson Trail we parallel the river upstream to the north edge of a sagebrush flat. Here, the river veers briefly west, but our tracks head south. By continuing west 100 yards along the river, you could find small, suitable campsites in a stand of lodgepoles. Following our route south through sagebrush, we briefly touch upon the river's edge, at a point about ½ mile beyond

A pleasant view up-canyon just before reaching the Horse Trail

the High Trail junction. Here you'll spy a good, cattle-free campsite among lodgepoles on the west bank of East Fork Carson River.

Continuing south past thick sagebrush, we come to a dry wash that emerges from a small, very bouldery, granitic gorge. We hike up the west side of the wash to a low, bedrock saddle, make a short descent—with a pleasant view up-canyon—past a small, steep cliff, and then reach a larger, longer, steeper one. Here, we are again beside the East Fork and an obscure junction with an alternate route, a **horse trail.** This variation of the East Carson Trail will be described first.

Horse Trail

At first this route is just a southward saunter along the river's east bank. The tread is not obvious. Soon the river bends west, but you continue 90 yards south to a reunion with the east bank at a bend in the river. Cross here, parallel the river briefly south to where it curves east, and continue south on what should by now be very distinct tread. Your trail is multitracked in spots, and ½ mile from your ford it splits into two distinct paths. The left path heads 0.2 mile past Jeffrey pines and sagebrush to a meadow, where the tread becomes indistinct. From here, you could head east over to the nearby riverbank, which has spacious campsites typically used by those on horseback. You could also continue south through the meadow to where you would meet the river where it bends east. Continue south along its west bank about 50 yards, then look for a crossing.

The right path heads ⅓ mile south through an open forest to a clearing, from which you can go about 30 yards east to the crossing referred to just above, which is immediately upstream from where the river bends east. From the crossing a vague tread, obscured by cattle paths, leads 110 yards among willows and brush to a meeting of the footpath, which is described below. Be aware that you don't have to cross in this spot, for from the clearing the right path continues 180 yards south to a major river meander. You'll find a large packer's site on the west side of the trail. Once you cross to the south bank, you can continue along the horse trail for about ¾ mile, to where it comes within 20 yards of the main East Carson Trail about ½ mile west of Soda Springs Guard Station. The main trail may not be obvious, even though it is close by, but if you try to continue much farther west on the

horse trail, you'll find it deteriorates very quickly.

Back at the steep cliff by the riverbank, the foot-trail variation of the East Carson Trail heads about 140 yards southeast to three closely spaced Jeffrey pines in a sagebrush flat. Any other trail you may see is likely one of many cattle paths made by the myriad animals grazing the canyon floor. Leaving between the south and east pines, follow a path that curves from southeast to south, and soon you'll be paralleling the east side of a dry, abandoned meander of the East Fork. If you're on the right path, it will soon reach a granitic cliff that plunges down to the bank of the East Fork. Here you scramble across boulders at the cliff's base, which are the only obstacle along this route for equestrians.

Ahead, you have an easy, open walk southward, mostly through sagebrush, that parallels the East Fork. Near the end of your traverse you may identify the Poison Flat Trail, descending south, about 200 yards east of and above you. About ¾ mile beyond the small cliff, the river bends west and you go about 90 yards southwest to where you should meet a trail from a crossing mentioned in the horse-trail route. If you miss it, due to all the cattle paths, you'll momentarily reach the riverbank and make a quick curve south, then west, along it to the main horse trail, where you'll see a large packer site on the river's north bank. Backtrack about 200 yards, look for a tread southeast, which will lead you 260 yards, first through willows and then up through sagebrush, to a junction with the **Poison Flat Trail.** This junction is among Jeffrey pines near the base of a slope.

Staying close to the base, we now head south 230 yards through an open forest to the first of several Poison Creek distributaries. You might plan to camp in this area for two reasons. First, the water is supposed to be giardia-free, while the beaver-inhabited East Fork is not. (However, there are no guarantees about the presence or absence in either.) Second, camping is not allowed on the fenced-in Soda Springs Guard Station land. (In earlier days, it had a nice, unofficial campground, but visitors' horses competed with the government's stock animals for the limited forage in the enclosure.) After crossing as many as five flowing distributaries, we arrive at **Soda Springs Guard Station.** You can expect it to be manned on a ten-days-on, four-days-off basis (off every other weekend) from

Soda Springs Guard Station

about mid-June through mid-October. So, if you're passing through on a weekend, you may not see a ranger. Since you're in the wilderness and should take personal responsibility, don't expect to get any help, medical or otherwise, at this station; it wasn't set up for that purpose. You can camp just about anywhere near the guard station outside its fenced area, and if you want safe water, take if from the station's tap. Immediately south of the station is a gate, and if you want to continue farther up-canyon, read the following route description.

WC-5   East Carson Trail from Soda Springs Guard Station to Pacific Crest Trail

Distances
2.2 miles to junction with Murray Canyon Trail
3.2 miles to Carson Falls
4.4 miles to junction with Golden Canyon Trail
9.9 miles to junction with Pacific Crest Trail

Trailhead   See the Route WC-1 trailhead

Introduction   Whether they start from Wolf Creek Meadows or Rodriguez Flat, most visitors to the Soda Springs environs travel no farther up-canyon. The following route is for those who want to go farther. It takes you to the upper part of the canyon, where you meet the Pacific Crest Trail, which provides access up the last part of the canyon. I highly recommend this trip, for a journey up the long, deep Carson River canyon is one of the Sierra's more memorable, though certainly challenging, routes.

Description   From a gate immediately south of Soda Springs Guard Station we start west, the Jeffrey pines and other conifers quickly yielding to sagebrush. The mostly open stretch ahead constitutes the southern part of ill-defined Dumonts Meadows. These meadows were named for a woodcutter, who along with other French Canadians in the 1870s razed large stands of conifers in eastern Alpine County, the logs being used for timbers in a vast network of tunnels in the Comstock Lode beneath Virginia City.

Fishing is generally better in the East Carson River above the Guard Station than

below it, since the lower part of the river has several long, shallow stretches that aren't conducive to supporting fish. Upstream to Carson Falls, expect to catch rainbow, brown, brook, cutthroat and whitefish.

In ⅓ mile we cross a spring-fed creeklet, just beyond which you should find a well-used campsite under lodgepole pines, only 20 yards downslope. Immediately below it is the horse trail mentioned in the previous route, and it briefly parallels our trail before dying out. In ½ mile we reach a grassy meadow, and here the trail can be quite obscure. If you lose it, continue through the meadow to its northwest end, where the trail should reappear and take you 200 yards northwest to a wide ford of East Fork Carson River.

Continuing northwest from the ford, we arrive at an unsigned trail junction only 20 yards east of a large, trailside Jeffrey pine that is marked with a conspicuous blaze. The blazed, eastbound trail goes along the base of the canyon's north wall before fording the East Carson. Our easy trail starts west through a meadow and then gradually curves south, crossing one permanent and several seasonal creeks and skirting the edge of spreading Falls Meadows before it reaches wide, refreshing Murray Canyon creek. Just beyond it you'll find campsites near a junction with the **Murray Canyon Trail.** Most of the Falls Meadows environs, like the extensive inholdings south up the canyon to Dumonts Meadows, was a private inholding in the wilderness until it was purchased by the Forest Service in 1990–91. Fishermen can leave their rods behind, for from this point onward, fishing in the river or in any of its tributaries, including Murray Canyon creek, is strictly prohibited, due to an extinction threat that the population of native Lahontan cutthroat trout faces.

Ahead, the route through Falls Meadows can be vague, due to cattle tracks, thick grass, and detours that hikers take when the water table is high in early season. You start out by following Murray Canyon creek about 200 yards south, to where it starts to curve over to the East Fork. You then stay close to the base of the canyon's west slopes. The trail is quite obvious to a point about ⅔ mile from the junction, where we come to a creek bed. Hike 60 yards directly up it before veering left. It appears that due to continued use across fragile meadow soils, the trail gradually cut deeper, and a seasonal creek then altered its course along this stretch. Trails through meadows are always a bad idea, though to reroute the trail in the Falls Meadows area would take a great deal of work.

The East Carson Trail curves east over a low granitic ridge, and then you climb very steeply for about 50 yards up a granitic outcrop. It is through this resistant mass of granitic rock that nearby Carson Falls has cut an impressive gorge. Your grade lessens and in about 50 more yards you may see where a horse trail starts a winding route south. Unless you're really looking for this trail, which bypasses the falls, you probably won't see it.

In a minute or two you climb up to a shallow notch, and then traverse east about 70 yards more, to where it's quite obvious you can leave the trail and head over to an adjacent brink overlooking **Carson Falls.** The best viewpoint is an isolated mass of bedrock just below the main fall. Be careful getting out to it, since a slip could be fatal. There are several small falls above the main fall, which is two-tiered, separated by a frothy punchbowl. Here you can note the importance that joints have played in determining the local landscape. Joints are fractures in the granitic rock, and the river has taken advantage of them, carving out an angular gorge.

After taking in the sights and sounds of Carson Falls, return to the trail, which momentarily heads east over to quiet water above the falls. You briefly tarry along the river's edge, then leave it for a short traverse south to a junction with the horse trail. This junction may be indistinct, but from it you'll traverse 110 yards east to a small but prominent bedrock point. We round it, almost touching a river meander as we start south, then curve ¼ mile southeast over to a ford of the Carson River. You may note along this stretch some signs of beavers, which have logged some aspens in this sometimes swampy flat.

Once across the river, we have a short ½ mile walk that stays just above its rocky east bank. Where the river turns abruptly west, we leave it and continue up-canyon ¼ mile, almost touching the river again just before a junction with the **Golden Canyon Trail.** This 3.8-mile-long trail is described in a descending direction at the end of Chapter 10's Route HL-10. If you walk southwest just 150 yards on this trail, you'll reach the Carson River, which has a very good campsite on its high east bank.

The next 5.5-mile stretch of route, between the Golden Canyon and Pacific Crest trails, is, as of the early 1990s, unmaintained. Therefore, the description that follows, which was based on conditions that existed while the trail was maintained, will become increasingly dated with time. You can expect downed trees, discontinuous tread, and even trail burial beneath avalanche debris. On the other hand, you'll be in one of the most primitive, least visited stretches of canyon in the Sierra Nevada.

From the junction, the hike up-canyon curves southeast and quickly becomes a steep, brushy climb up 400 vertical feet to the top of a granitic mass that has withstood repeated efforts by past glaciers to eradicate it. Leaving its southeast end, the route rollercoasters for ½ mile, then touches upon a river meander just before it starts a fairly long climb. A 100-foot-high lodgepole at the tip of the meander indicates that the eastward-working sand spit on which the pine grows has been around for quite some time. Eventually the river will, probably in time of flood, cut a course straight north and leave this eastward-looping curve high and dry.

Our climb from the meander is a winding one that crosses a few creek beds before going south up the gully of a seasonal creek. In the East Carson canyon—called White Canyon in the section we're now entering—major north-south joints, or fractures, break up the granitic

Pinnacles and cliffs just north of the Pacific Crest Trail junction

bedrock, forming gullies and ridges that are oriented north-south. Our one-mile climb from East Fork Carson River eventually ends at the top of the easternmost north-south gully.

Beyond the top, junipers and pines are momentarily left behind as we descend into a shady red-fir forest. Our path levels off at a year-round creek, and beyond it we parallel the Carson River 3 miles upstream. Our shady path crosses many creeklets as it progresses gently to moderately up-canyon, and along here one has glimpses of the high cliffs along the canyon's east side. Large, granitic summit pinnacles and deep, enormous chimneys will beckon climbers to stay for days or weeks. A 900-foot-high face on the canyon's west side adds to the enticement.

At the south end of the cliffs, a descending ridge forces our route across the river, which can be a slippery and wet crossing in early and mid-season. Once on the west bank, we hike south, and in about 150 yards arrive at a junction with the **Pacific Crest Trail.** If you continue 5.2 miles up-canyon to its head at a saddle, you'll follow this trail, which in the mid-70s replaced the old upper stretch of the East Carson Trail. This stretch is described in the opposite (down-canyon) direction as Chapter 17's Route SP-4.

If you've followed the East Carson Trail since its start, you owe it to yourself to continue up the canyon to its head, for there are few trails in the Sierra Nevada (no other east of the crest) in which you can make such a lengthy hike up through a single canyon. You start in the canyon's lower parts among Jeffrey pines, sagebrush and mountain mahogany, and end at its head among whitebark pines and mountain hemlocks. The scenery, too, changes dramatically.

If you make this lengthy trek to the saddle at the canyon's head on foot, then I suggest the following route back. Rather than back-track, something I avoid wherever possible, climb cross-country east from the saddle. The gradient is fairly steep and the air is thin, but this ridge route up the south boundary of Carson-Iceberg Wilderness is safe and obvious. After about 600 feet of elevation gain the ridge gradient eases, and you can turn north for an ascending traverse to 11,398′ White Mountain. Though you could skirt past its summit block, you'd then miss topping the second highest peak in the area; only nearby Sonora Peak is higher.

From the summit, continue north down the ridge for about one mile, to where it splits. You could follow the northeast ridge about another mile to your next goal, a saddle, but the going gets pretty steep as you approach it. Rather, from the split, descend about a mile east down slopes until you reach Silver Creek, then climb northwest, gaining back 600 feet, to a saddle. From it you descend into the Silver King headwaters, following Chapter 13's Route RF-7 in the reverse direction down to Upper Fish Valley. Here you take Silver King Trail 1017-1 north down to Poison Flat Trail 1018, which you take west down to Dumonts Meadows and the East Carson Trail.

If you're on horseback, you won't want to take the cross-country route starting from the saddle at the canyon's head. Instead, you'll have to follow Chapter 18's Route PM-1 in reverse, down Wolf Creek canyon. Then take the trailhead road 1½ miles down the lower part of the canyon to a main road. Follow it first east, then northeast, almost 1½ miles to a junction with Silver Creek Road. Follow this ¾ mile up along the creek to a junction with a road to Summit Meadow, which branches right, then continue one mile farther up your road to its end, the start of Route PM-2. This will take you up Silver Creek canyon to the saddle above Silver Creek, from which you descend into the Silver King headwaters.

Chapter 13 Rodriguez Flat

RF-1 Rodriguez Flat to Soda Springs Guard Station

Distances
1.0 mile to junction with Driveway Trail
3.3 miles to junction with Silver King Trail
3.4 miles to junction with Poison Lake Trail
4.0 miles to junction with Poison Flat Trail
5.1 miles to junction with Soda Cone Trail
5.2 miles to Soda Cone
6.9 miles to junction with East Carson Trail
7.2 miles to Soda Springs Guard Station

Trailhead Leave Highway 395 either 7.7 miles south of its junction with Highway 89 or 15.7 miles north of its junction with Highway 108, start up Mill Canyon Road, then follow Golden Gate Road to its end. However, the start of Mill Canyon Road is easily missed if you're driving fast or at night. It lies roughly midway between the towns of Coleville, north of the road junction, and Walker, south of it. Coleville has few services, whereas Walker has gas stations, motels and cafes. In my opinion, the most notable landmark in Walker is the K & M Restaurant (the sign also says AMERICAN-BASQUE DINNERS). After several days of 20+ mile hikes with very little lunch, I can really work up an appetite, and this restaurant is one of few in the Sierra Nevada where you can absolutely stuff yourself on fairly good food at only a modest cost. From that restaurant drive 2.2 miles north to the Mill Canyon Road junction.

There is *de facto* camping near your trailhead, but if you want to stay at a real campground, you'll have to stay at one of three that are south of Walker. South from the K & M Restaurant in "downtown" Walker, these are: Shingle Mill Flat Campground (private, reached in 3.2 miles), Bootleg Campground (8.4 miles) and Chris Flat Campground (10.0 miles), this last one being 3.5 miles north of the Highway 108 junction.

Once you turn off Highway 395 onto Mill Canyon Road, you drive only ⅓ mile southeast up it, to where it veers left. You keep to the right on Golden Gate Road, climb west across fault-formed Little Antelope Valley, and then climb up an increasingly steep gradient. You cross a creek, then bend north and climb steeply ½ mile up to a creek recrossing—the spot to get water if you plan to camp near the dry trailhead. Here you're 3.8 miles from the highway, and you now climb at an easier gradient 2.5 miles to a junction on shrubby Rodriguez Flat. Here you'll find a bulletin board with self-registration wilderness permits. Fill out one of these if you plan to stay overnight in the wilderness. For all routes but Route RF-2, you turn left here and take a narrow, rocky road ½ mile to its end. Just 100 yards before its end, a spur road juts left to an adjacent dry-camp area. This is not an official campsite, so haul out any trash you create.

The main road continues southwest ¼ mile across Rodriguez Flat to a second junction, and for Route RF-2, park where the road is blocked off, 0.1 mile straight ahead from the junction. Most traffic turns left at this junction, going ⅓ mile south to Little Antelope Pack Station. The parking space there is *reserved solely for the station's clients.*

Introduction The Soda Springs area in the East Fork Carson River canyon offers abundant camping in a setting that is reminiscent of the Sierra's largest west-slope canyons, such as Kings Canyon and Yosemite Valley, but

Crest view toward Highland and Silver peaks and Silver King and Bagley valleys

sans people. The shortest and easiest way in to the Soda Springs area is along Route RF-1. Except for the first ¾ mile, the route is almost all downhill. Of course, this means that the way out is almost all uphill—over 2000 feet of climbing. Still, this amount of elevation gain is only a little more than that of a longer, popular route, Chapter 12's High Trail. And with a lighter pack and after a bit of acclimatizing, the return route shouldn't be that bad, particularly since you can cool off in refreshing Silver King Creek, which you encounter after you've done most of the climbing. Near the creek, Route RF-1 meets the Poison Lake Trail, described in Route RF-3. Also along Route RF-1 you have the opportunity to visit the Soda Cone, which is probably the largest tufa formation in the Sierra Nevada proper.

Description From the end of the rocky road, you traverse southwest for several minutes to a junction with Snodgrass Canyon-Fish Valley Trail 1020. Northwest, this drops ¼ mile under forest cover to Little Antelope Pack Station, then continues northwest over to the nearby trailhead of Route RF-2, by the headwaters of Snodgrass Creek. Continuing southwest, we immediately enter Carson-Iceberg Wilderness, and then climb through a forest of white fir, red fir, lodgepole pine and western white pine. Beyond ⅓ mile of moderate-to-steep ascent, we encounter open country, the trees yielding to sagebrush and some rabbitbrush, bitterbrush (antelope bush) and mountain mahogany. Mountain snowberry is also present, though it usually goes unnoticed when its white berries are absent.

The ancient, Jurassic-age metamorphosed sediments of Rodriguez Flat are now replaced by youthful volcanic rocks and sediments, and views steadily improve as we climb to a crest. On clear days the views are spectacular, and one can see desert ranges northeast well beyond broad, open Rodriguez Flat. One also has views northwest down forested Snodgrass

Creek canyon and beyond it to open Silver King and Bagley valleys, and views west of Highland and Silver peaks. To the southwest you see a rugged crest, which includes one summit with a precipitous east side—Whitecliff Peak.

Our crest is a broad, nearly level one, and once you reach it, only about ¾ mile from your trailhead, your route to Soda Springs Guard Station is mostly downhill, with only a minimum of short, uphill stretches. Across the crest we traverse ¼ mile south before reaching a conspicuous junction with the **Driveway Trail.** Route RF-5 keeps left, south, on the Snodgrass Canyon-Fish Valley Trail, while Route RF-1 branches right, southwest, on Driveway Trail 1019.

Starting down the Driveway Trail, we quickly pass an obvious, oversized cairn, which lies off to our right just past the junction. Built 7 feet high by careful, foreign hands, this cairn stands as a monument to the loneliness of the Basque shepherds who once tended flocks in this area. Called *arri mutillak,* or *"stone boys,"* monuments like this one were built by lonely shepherds to pass the time. Today, hikers seek to be alone and look for places of solitude within this east Sierra landscape.

Most of the Driveway Trail consists of a gentle-to-moderate descent across slopes of low brush. After about 1 ¾ view-filled miles the gradient becomes moderate to steep, and juniper begin to dot the slopes. This gradient continues for about ½ mile, almost to a ford of grass-lined Silver King Creek. Even at the driest times in the driest years you'll get your feet wet unless you're on horseback.

Fishing in this creek is allowed here and for about 4 miles upstream, as far as Llewellyn Falls. Above the falls, the stream and its tributaries are closed to fishing in order to protect threatened populations of native Paiute cutthroat trout. Silver King Creek from

Llewellyn Falls downstream to its confluence with the East Carson River near Vaquero Camp is one of the most productive rainbow streams in California. Anglers often catch around five fish per hour. This is a phenomenal rate for 7–12″ fish. Fish hit well on flies, lures or baits such as worms and salmon eggs. Lower reaches of the stream contain brown trout and whitefish in addition to rainbow. A rumored waterfall in the area between Snodgrass Creek and our creek ford may isolate the upper stream from migrants heading upstream. This reach of stream is so rugged and difficult to traverse that few if any persons have gone through the gorge. The Department of Fish and Game would like to hear from anyone who has made this journey.

Once on the far bank of Silver King Creek, you climb about 80 yards, passing through a gate before reaching a junction with the **Silver King Trail.** Actually, just past the gate, the Driveway Trail splits, and westbound people take the short right fork to the Silver King Trail, while southbound people take the slightly longer left fork to it. From the south junction Route RF-4 heads south, upstream, bound for Long Valley, Commissioners Camp and Tamarack Lake. From the north junction with the Silver King Trail we climb northwest about 70 yards to a junction with the **Poison Lake Trail,** the popular path described in Route RF-3. Bound for the East Fork Carson River canyon, we keep to the main trail, hiking north 35 yards to a second gate. Beyond it we soon pass through an aspen grove and then

climb slightly to the eastern outskirts of spacious, but ill-defined Poison Flat. Exactly why it's called Poison Flat is somewhat of a mystery, for the large herd of grazing cattle seems quite healthy. A clue to the name lies ahead, at Soda Cone.

On Silver King Trail 1017 we head generally northeast across the east part of meadowy Poison Flat, crossing a broad, very low divide about midway to the edge of a lodgepole-pine forest. About here you reach an obscure junction with the **Poison Flat Trail,** this trail appearing to all but the sharpest-eyed to be a continuation of the Silver King Trail. That trail actually cuts north across a meadow to a post (if it is still standing and visible when you arrive here), the tread across the meadow being largely indistinct. Route RF-2, first down the Snodgrass Trail and then up the Silver King Trail, ends at our junction.

Now on Poison Flat Trail 1018, we skirt west past lodgepole pines along the south edge of Poison Flat's expansive east meadow. Grass soon yields mostly to sagebrush, and in a few minutes we turn northwest for a brief climb to a low divide above the head of the meadow. This low divide, is actually the toe of a large lateral moraine that rises to the west-southwest. The part of the moraine directly above unseen Soda Springs Guard Station stands a full 1500 feet above the floor of the East Carson canyon, and the glacier that gave rise to that moraine may have been as thick or thicker. However, the moraine could be quite old, and therefore the glacier could have

Descending the Driveway Trail toward Silver King Creek

flowed down the East Carson canyon at a time when it was hundreds of feet shallower. Still, it must have been an impressive glacier.

Bound for the route's next attraction, Soda Cone, we start down through a series of wet, grassy meadows. The gently descending route is generally easy to follow, though cow paths may momentarily lead you astray. After a 0.6-mile walk from the low divide, and just before we leave the last of the meadows to start a major descent, we reach a junction with the **Soda Cone Trail.**

Soda Cone

If you haven't visited the Soda Cone, don't pass it up. The trail to it can be in various states of disrepair, and several parallel routes may be found. Essentially you head over to the adjacent creek, diagonal west up an adjacent bluff, and in about 220 yards arrive at the **Soda Cone.** You can't miss it. What hikers and equestrians who view the cone from below can't see is a picturesque summit pool, about 12 yards across, filled with bubbling, milky green, algae-rich water. This water, in contrast to the warm water from springs at the cone's base, is quite cold.

Its name, however, is a misnomer: Soda Cone it is not. Rather, it should have been named Tufa Cone. *Soda* implies that its composition is sodium carbonate, though in the vernacular sense, soda is usually taken to mean sodium bicarbonate—baking soda. But in reality, the cone is largely a deposit of calcium carbonate. It began to form as subterranean water, heated by a nearby body of magma, rose to the surface, carrying calcium in solution. At the surface the calcium mixed with carbonate to form calcium carbonate.

In addition to calcium, other elements are transported in the spring water, including uranium, manganese and arsenic. The first two are present only in trace amounts, but the arsenic, measured in one rock sample, makes up 2.3% of the rock. And perhaps this explains how our local area got the name *poison*—Poison Flat, Poison Lake, Poison

Creek. Perhaps grazing animals in the area were poisoned by drinking the tainted water. If you know of a better reason, please let me know. (By the way, Poison Lake and its outlet, Poison Creek, are safe to drink.)

Back on Poison Flat Trail 1018, we start a descent through a forest of aspens, white firs and Jeffrey and lodgepole pines, and the trail's gradient quickly becomes moderate. The shady cover, however, is soon left behind, and westward we have a mostly brush-lined path that leads moderately down to a broad, granitic ridge covered with a veneer of volcanic boulders. Here you have a fine view of Soda Cone, the cone looking like a dome transplant from Yosemite National Park.

Now you have a moderate descent that generally trends northwest. Roughly halfway down this 500-foot drop you pass one large spring and its tufa deposit. Smaller ones are nearby, and elsewhere in this general area. From a gully we now turn south, and wind down almost ½ mile to a junction with the **East Carson Trail**—Chapter 12's Route WC-4. This junction lies among Jeffrey pines near the base of a slope.

Staying close to the base, we now head south 230 yards through an open forest to the first of several Poison Creek distributaries. You might plan to camp in this area for two reasons. First, the water is reputed to be giardia-free, whereas the beaver-inhabited East Fork is not. (However, there are no guarantees about the presence or absence in either.) Second, camping is not allowed at the fenced-in Soda Springs Guard Station land. (In earlier days, it had a nice, unofficial campground, but visitors' horses competed with the government's stock animals for limited forage, so camping was prohibited.) After crossing as many as five flowing distributaries, we arrive at **Soda Springs Guard Station.** You can expect it to be manned on a ten-days-on, four-days-off basis (off every other weekend) from about mid-June through mid-October. So if you're passing through on a weekend, you may not see a ranger. Since you're in the wilderness and should take personal responsibility, don't expect to get any help, medical or otherwise, at this station; it wasn't set up for that purpose. You can camp just about anywhere near the guard station outside its fenced-in area, and if you want safe water, take it from the station's tap. Immediately south of the station is a gate, and if you want to continue farther up-canyon, consult Chapter 12's Route WC-5.

Soda Cone

RF-2 Snodgrass and Silver King Trails to Poison Flat

Distances
2.4 miles to junction with cutoff trail
2.6 miles to Silver King Creek
4.2 miles to "granite gateway"
5.5 miles to junction with Poison Flat Trail

Trailhead See the Route RF-1 trailhead

Introduction This route is a variation of the previous route to the Soda Springs area. Since it is 1½ miles longer and has more climbing, some of it very steep, it is a hard route to justify taking on foot. However, it should appeal to two kinds of hikers: those interested in mining history and those interested in technical rock climbing. The route passes through the heart of the Silver King mining district, which has about two dozen digs in the form of pits, trenches, adits (horizontal shafts) and mines. Past these digs, between miles 4.0 and 4.3, stands a collection of granitic rocks resembling those found in Joshua Tree National Monument's Hidden Valley area—Southern Californians will feel right at home.

Description From where the road is blocked off, we start southwest down it, reaching a fork in 280 yards. On the right branch we descend on Snodgrass Trail 1020, soon exchanging the sagebrush of Rodriguez Flat for mountain mahogany, Jeffrey pine, aspen and willow. Now beside the upper part of Snodgrass Creek, we descend west for several minutes, then both creek and trail bend northwest and we enter Carson-Iceberg Wilderness.

About ¼ mile north of this bend lies the Hilltop prospect. Like other prospects in the area, this one was mined for gold and silver in the 1860s. And like other prospects, it yielded very little precious metal. There may be over 3½ tons of gold at the prospect, but to blast away the rock and process it would require far more money than the gold was worth. The Hilltop prospect also contains iron, lead, molybdenum and tungsten, but again in quantities unprofitable to mine. This is the first prospect near your route, though you drove by another one near the wilderness-permit bulletin board on Rodriguez Flat. That prospect has no economic worth at all.

Onward, you stay quite close to the creek, and you'll note where beavers have leveled stands of creekside aspens. About 2 miles from the trailhead the Snodgrass Trail curves west, then soon passes through a creekside gate and reaches a junction with a **cutoff trail.** This trail drops ¾ mile north to a junction with the Silver King Trail, which from there goes 1.1 miles to the outskirts of the large private rangelands of Silver King Valley. We go left, on the less-used tread, and descend fairly steeply for a couple of minutes to where our trail and Snodgrass Creek meet **Silver King Creek.** This creek can be a treacherous ford before mid-July, and even after that, this swift, slippery-boulder-bottomed stream still deserves respect.

This stretch of Silver King Creek near the confluence of Snodgrass Creek, together with Snodgrass Creek itself, is an excellent place for rainbow trout. During much of the year this stretch of Silver King Creek is quite high and icy cold. Thick willows and alders deter all but the most determined anglers. Trout are abundant and somewhat larger than in the area above an upstream gorge.

Once across, you'll find yourself in a small, grassy, log-strewn meadow. The junction of your trail with the Silver King Trail can be obscure. However, since Silver King Trail 1017 hugs its namesake creek both above and below the meadow, you can't get lost. From the meadow, this trail goes ⅓ mile downstream to a ford, then ¼ mile farther to an obscure junction—at the south end of a grassy flat—with the cutoff trail. There is some potential camping along the Silver King Trail between Snodgrass Creek and Silver King Valley, which through about 1991 was privately owned. Now that it's public land, I can recommend camping there.

The Snodgrass-Silver King confluence lies in the heart of the Silver King mining district. Just up Silver King Creek lie the Mineral Mountain and Silver King prospects, above the west and east banks respectively. Just down the Silver King, by the lower ford, lies an unnamed prospect. In this vicinity miners have found gold, silver, copper, lead and zinc in nearby schist outcrops, quartz veins and placers. However, mining here is definitely not profitable.

From the former mining area, we parallel alder- and cottonwood-lined Silver King Creek upstream. Our trail keeps above the dense

Poison Flat and peaks on the west rim of the East Carson canyon

creekside vegetation. In ½ mile we pass through a gate, then quickly start a steepening ascent west away from the creek, leaving the last source of reliable trailside water behind.

You'll huff and puff as you struggle up along the base of some granitic cliffs, which are bound to tempt climbers. Paralleling a seasonal creeklet near our feet, the climb west soon slackens to a gentle grade. Then the trail turns southwest and leaves the last of the cottonwoods behind for a moderate ¼-mile climb to what can be an easily missed junction in a small opening among aspens. If you're unwary, you just might continue southwest up the old, abandoned Silver King Trail. The newer trail turns south to climb up a gully.

A good outcrop for rock climbing

Before leaving this spot, mining buffs should note that a large prospector's trench lies just to the north, in a migmatite zone with granitic rocks and biotite schist. Typically, it has no economically significant assays.

Our trail south up the gully gets us, in ¼ mile, to a **granite gateway,** through which we pass to enter rock climbers' heaven. On your right stretches a ¼-mile-long cluster of granitic outcrops that offer hundreds of boulder routes and at least dozens of one-pitch roped climbs. Climbers will want to camp nearby, and the best area is to the east of the trail, close to Silver King Creek canyon's brink, which is about ¼ mile from the trail. The creek is your only source of water.

Beyond the granitic outcrops the Silver King Trail makes a rambling traverse across granitic slopes and benches, then in ¾ mile reaches a gully that separates granitic rock on the east from volcanic rock on the west. The trail can be a bit vague immediately before you cross the gully, but you shouldn't have trouble finding the trail south down the gully's west side. It soon leaves the gully for a brushy, scenic traverse west-southwest down to the north edge of a linear meadow in expansive Poison Flat. A post may still be standing to mark this spot. If so, head south from it, essentially cross-country, across the cow-grazed meadow to lodgepole pines along its south edge. Here, with a little bit of scouting, you'll find a junction with the **Poison Flat Trail.** Actually, finding the junction is unnecessary, for the trail is perfectly obvious, and on it you can follow the previous route west to the Soda Cone or beyond it to the Soda Springs Guard Station.

RF-3   Rodriguez Flat to Poison Lake

Distances
3.4 miles to junction with Poison Lake Trail
7.1 miles to Poison Lake

Trailhead   Same as the Route RF-1 trailhead

Introduction   Poison Lake, which despite its name has safe drinking water, is a fairly popular goal because it is the most easily reached of three lakes one can visit from Rodriguez Flat. It is also the only one with trout. The route to Poison Lake is a mostly open one, providing the visitor with a harvest of diverse views. The route is also fairly easy, having in either direction about as much elevation loss as elevation gain.

Description   First, follow roughly the first half of Route RF-1 3.4 miles to the start of the Poison Lake Trail, this spot being just a few minutes' walk past a ford of Silver King Creek. On Poison Lake Trail 1051, you start with a short ascent, and then climb at a lesser grade to a bedrock ridgecrest, met about ¼ mile along the trail. Here, on your left, you'll see an old juniper growing against well-weathered granitic boulders. These boulders at one time were quite jagged, but their corners have been rounded down over tens of millenia, and they have taken on the shape of rounded glacial erratics. Thirty yards up from these boulders you'll see a real erratic, a four-foot-diameter, dark volcanic boulder whose presence in this granitic terrain can be explained only if an ancient glacier deposited it on this ridge—perhaps 150,000 years ago or even earlier. Had a more recent glacier come along after that one and scraped rocks smooth, the weathered surfaces of nearby granitic bedrock would look much less worn.

The trail stays on or near the ridgecrest for about a mile, and some shade is provided by an open forest. Along the trail you're likely to find an assortment of shrubs and herbs with varying degrees of pungency: bitterbrush, sagebrush, mule ears, lupine and coyote mint. The crest route and the forest path give way where the ridge deadends at the base of a steep volcanic slope, and now we climb moderately southwest up a brushy slope to a picturesque granitic outcrop. This provides a major, sweeping view of rounded hills in the north, granitic cliffs in the east, Lower and Upper Fish Valleys in the south, and a ragged crest in the southwest.

Now midway along the Poison Lake Trail, over half of the climbing is done. We continue briefly climbing through thick brush, then ascend several short, steep switchbacks, which deliver us into the forest's shade once again—temporarily, for soon we climb up to a small sagebrush-covered flat with a nearby blocky viewpoint.

From the flat our trail goes west toward a shallow bowl that feeds a tributary of audible Tamarack Creek, then curves gradually west-northwest and climbs very gently past a couple of meadows before topping a broad, viewless ridge above Poison Lake. From here almost everyone heads down to the lake, but if you love summit views, you can head ½ mile along the ridge to the top of a nearby ridgecrest, and from there get a fine view down into 2000-foot-deep East Carson canyon and across it up Golden Canyon to volcanic-tipped Disaster Peak.

From the low point on the viewless ridge you descend steeply but briefly through forest

View toward Lower and Upper Fish Valleys

Poison Lake

down to hemmed-in **Poison Lake.** A few mountain hemlocks here tell you that in most years snow piles deep and lasts long in this 9200-foot-high glacial cirque. Campsites are reached by taking one of two paths. The main one heads west past willows and corn lilies to end at a fairly large packer's camp above the lake's south shore. Just west of the camp you'll find a flowing spring, which waters a profusion of saxifrages and monkey flowers. Drink from the spring, if the thought of drinking from *Poison* Lake intimidates you (it isn't poisonous). The other path heads north across a brushy morainal slope, staying just above the lake's east shore. The lake bottom drops off so quickly here that one could easily dive into the lake without injury (though *not* without a chill).

Poison Lake, lying just outside the Silver King drainage, is open to fishing. This 4.5-acre, 60-foot-deep lake was planted annually from at least 1950 throuth 1974 with 2000 Lahontan cutthroat fingerlings. In 1964, the planting switched to brook trout, occasionally golden trout, and then more cutthroat. Since 1988 brook trout and Lahontan cutthroat have been planted on an alternate-year basis. Fishing is generally good from inflatables.

Shore fishing is good in the early season before the brook trout seek deeper water. The lake is heavily fished by backpackers and by guided parties from Little Antelope Pack Station. Cutthroat trout and some brook are also common in Poison Creek down to the confluence with the East Carson River.

From a north-shore campsite, which is just east of the lake's outlet—nonpoisonous Poison Creek—a conspicuous trail starts north. Hiking on it, however, I found both horseshoe prints and boot prints, though the trail basically died out after about ⅓ mile. It wasn't obvious just how much farther down-canyon the hikers and the riders traveled. From about ½ mile to 1½ miles down from the lake, the floor of Poison Creek canyon has a gentle gradient, and it can offer some truly isolated camping. However, from where the creek changes its course from northeast to north, the gradient becomes very steep, and for horses it soon becomes suicidal. And for all but the most stout-hearted mountaineers, a descent all the way to the floor of the East Carson canyon would be an exhausting, nerve-wracking trek. Having made this slipping, sliding descent, I strongly recommend against it.

RF-4 Rodriguez Flat to Lower Fish Valley and Tamarack Lake

Distances
3.3 miles to junction with Silver King Trail
4.0 miles to mouth of Tamarack Creek canyon
6.3 miles to Commissioners Camp in Lower Fish Valley
6.8 miles to Llewellyn Falls
8.3 miles to southwest corner of Tamarack Lake

Trailhead Same as the Route RF-1 trailhead

Introduction Though it lies deep in the eastern part of the wilderness, Commissioners Camp in Lower Fish Valley is relatively easy to reach. After an initial climb of ¾ mile, you descend to Silver King Creek, which you follow leisurely upstream to the camp. For many, particularly those on horseback, Commissioners Camp is the farthest they'll want to travel, except perhaps for a short excursion to nearby Llewellyn Falls. However, for others, Tamarack Lake will be the prime goal, if only to rise above the cow country. They'll have to work to reach the lake, but it certainly justifies the sweat one expends in the process. Finally, the strongest of the strong can go cross-country from this lake to chilly Whitecliff Lake, though this goal is more easily reached by following Routes RF-5 and RF-6.

Description   First, consult Route RF-1 for a mostly downhill jaunt to an always wet crossing of Silver King Creek. Just beyond it you pass through a gate, and here the Driveway Trail quickly forks, the right branch climbing west momentarily to a junction with the Silver King Trail, while the left branch traverses briefly south, upstream, to another junction with the same trail. Since we're heading upstream, we take the left branch. On Silver King Trail 1017, we now have a pleasant 350-yard walk past grassy, shaded, creekside campsites, which are among the best you'll find anywhere in Carson-Iceberg Wilderness. Then, with our feet barely dry from the Silver King Creek ford, we must ford the creek again. Fortunately, grassy banks on both sides help make the knee-deep, 10-yard-wide ford a pleasant one. Before mid-July, expect a more challenging ford. You have to make these two fords because a photogenic, granitic pinnacle and its adjacent cliffs prevent the Silver King Trail from continuing along the east bank all the way down to the Driveway Trail.

Now on the east bank, we leave the base of the pinnacle and parallel Silver King Creek ⅓ mile upstream to the toe of a granitic mass, around which our trail heads northeast. From the toe you'll note, just to the west, the **mouth of Tamarack Creek canyon,** where Tamarack Creek joins much larger Silver King Creek. The original trail to Poison Lake headed up Tamarack Creek's canyon, but the tread faded into oblivion before the 1970s. You can camp along Tamarack Creek, which has an excellent population of small rainbow. These inhabit a stairstep of old beaver dams upstream from the confluence. The dams are interesting, but to anglers, Silver King Creek may be more appealing, for it provides extremely good fishing for slightly larger rainbow.

From the toe of the granitic mass we make a ¼-mile contour to the north end of aptly named Long Valley. Silver King Creek meanders lazily through the glacial sediments that long ago buried the canyon's bedrock floor, and our trail approaches several of these meanders before reaching, about midway through the valley, a spot from where you'll see a good campsite on the west bank of the creek.

The nearly level trek south through Long Valley is usually a pleasant one, though in early season the ground can be quite boggy. To the west rises an island of granitic rock, which is bounded by Tamarack and Silver King creeks. From the valley's south end one climbs briefly southwest up the now-shaded trail to a granitic saddle, then makes an even briefer descent to the north end of open, spacious Lower Fish Valley. In it, we first contour southwest, then start to curve south. At this curve you'll note a small campsite and, to the west, a low gap, which provides the hiker with ready access to the upper part of Tamarack Creek canyon.

In Lower Fish Valley we head southeast, generally at a distance from Silver King Creek, but in about ½ mile we come to a spot where a large, laterally migrating creek meander has cut into the trail, forcing a relocation of it. If you walk along the north edge of the meander and balance on a log across Silver King Creek (ford it if there is no log), you'll find yourself by **Commissioners Camp,** whose most frequent guests are the valley's cows. Here you'll find a large packer campsite. The camp was once known as Governors Camp. Located on a lodgepole flat immediately south of Tamarack Lake creek, it was formerly named after then-Governor Edmund G. Brown, Sr., who liked to stay there while deer hunting each year. At Commissioners Camp and in the vicinity you can legally fish for trout. But above **Llewellyn Falls,** which are about ½ mile southeast, at the far end of Lower Fish Valley, all creeks are closed to fishing in order to protect a threatened population of native Paiute cutthroat trout. (Note: to reach Llewellyn Falls along the Silver King Trail, you continue about ½ mile southeast to the end of the valley, start a climb, and quickly reach a sign that directs you to the photogenic, 20-foot-high cascade. Should the sign be missing, simply let your ears lead the way.)

From the camp you can make a moderate-to-steep 2-mile climb to picturesque Tamarack

Lake, which is one of the fairest lakes of the wilderness. To locate the trail to the lake, start beside the camp on the *northwest* bank of Tamarack Lake creek. After you've gone up the creek about 100 yards you'll emerge from the lodgepole cover and enter a wide, sagebrush-covered alluvial fan. This has been constructed of successive layers of sediments, laid down in times of flood or snow avalanche which spread out as they exited from the mouth of the canyon. Starting up the alluvial fan, you should easily spot the trail, which diagonals to the right, across the fan.

Once on the gravelly trail, you should be able to follow it without problems. Climb into a viewless forest, level off, and reach a small, marshy meadow. The trail heads through it, but to keep your feet as dry as possible, you might instead walk along its southeast side about 45 yards to Tamarack Lake creek, where you should find the trail's resumption.

You're now at a high enough elevation that mountain hemlocks join the lodgepoles, western white pines and red firs. You make a curving, level traverse southward, which quickly yields to a steady, very steep uphill climb, which seems to—and indeed does— climb too high. Bedrock gets in the way, so instead of arriving at Tamarack Lake's outlet, we climb above it, parallel the lake's east shore, and then drop to its south shore. Skirt along it to a campsite under protective mountain hemlocks and whitebark pines above the **southwest corner of Tamarack Lake.** The

flat, spacious campsite is large enough to hold an entire Scout troop.

At about 9300 feet in elevation, Tamarack Lake is warm enough for swimming only in early and mid-August. Rock climbers will enjoy short, ragged, granitic cliffs that press in on the lake's north and west shores. From rocks near the base of these cliffs, one can dive into the lake's invigorating water. Tamarack Lake, seemingly perched at the brink of the world, will please some visitors still more with its tranquil, reflective, framed sunrises.

Anglers will be pleased with this 5-acre, 40-foot-deep lake. It contains abundant but small Lahontan cutthroats resulting from a single plant of fingerlings made by pack stock in 1988. Most reports indicate that 9-10 inch fish are easily caught on any bait or artificial lure. In addition some scarcer but larger Paiute cutthroat have been planted in recent years as part of the Recovery Plan for Paiute cutthroat in Silver King Creek. See page 136 for details on this plan.

If you also plan to visit Whitecliff Lake *and are in excellent shape,* you needn't descend all the way to Lower Fish Valley, hike upstream, and then ascend Bull Canyon. Rather, from the south shore of Tamarack Lake, strong-legged hikers can make a very steep, though safe, climb south up through a hemlock forest to a granitic saddle 600 feet above the lake. Leaving this saddle, you head one mile over to the glacial cirque holding Whitecliff Lake, contouring as best as the topography will allow.

Tamarack Lake

RF-5   Rodriguez Flat to Corral, Coyote and Upper Fish Valleys

Distances
2.3 miles to Corral Valley Creek
4.6 miles to Coyote Valley Creek
6.1 miles to Upper Fish Valley
6.3 miles to Connells Cow Camp
6.9 miles to Llewellyn Falls
7.5 miles to Commissioners Camp

Trailhead   Same as the Route RF-1 trailhead

Introduction   The eastern part of the wilderness is prime rangeland, and you'll encounter herds of cattle in Corral and Coyote valleys as well as in the Fish Valleys and other valleys of Silver King Creek. So why visit this area? Well, if you're on horseback, you'll be assured of ample grazing for your stock. Furthermore, this part of the wilderness is lightly used, at least by two-legged animals. So if you don't mind a mooing serenade and are careful where you step, you can find peace and respite from the stresses of urban life.

Description   Use the first three paragraphs of Route RF-1 to guide you 1.0 mile to a broad, scenic crest that has a junction with the Driveway Trail. Branching left, south, we stay on Snodgrass Canyon-Fish Valley Trail 1020 and enter the Paiute Trout Management Area. All the creeks you encounter along this route and along Routes RF-6 and RF-7 are closed to fishing except for Silver King Creek below Llewellyn Falls.

Our dusty, volcanic-soil trail reaches, after 330 yards, a gate in a northeast-trending stock fence and then descends moderately past sagebrush, bitterbrush and mule ears. We also skirt a major stand of aspen, which seems incongruous in this dry environment, then pass scattered junipers and lodgepoles before arriving at **Corral Valley Creek.** Since this valley is several ridges east from the Sierra crest, it lies in a considerable rain shadow and the creek is no more than a step-across creeklet. From this vicinity, as well as along the descent to it, you'll note Antelope Peak, which rises almost 2000 feet above the valley, 1½ miles to the southeast. The direct route to its summit would be an easy one for peak baggers were it not for an extensive, obstructing aspen forest. Peak baggers, read on.

Beyond the creek and a nearby well-used campsite, we enter forest and curve south-west. Our 500-foot climb up to a saddle is well-graded, virtually dust-free, and amply shaded by conifers. After 1.0 mile of effort, we arrive at the dry saddle. Peak baggers: to reach Antelope Peak, start east from the saddle. Don't tackle the steep crest head-on or tackle its brush-and-bedrock south slopes, but rather, stick to the shady north slopes, and make an ascending traverse to a conspicuous saddle. From it your climb eastward stays near the crest. Technical rock climbers will be fascinated by a soon-seen 400-foot-high outcrop ½ mile to the west, at the end of a rugged ridge.

Leaving the saddle and its stunning view southwest toward Whitecliff Peak, we negotiate short, fairly steep switchbacks as we start a 670-foot-drop to Coyote Valley. Fortunately, the deep, granitic gravel cushions our steps. Along this route down a gully you'll pass through a juniper woodland that contains some of the Sierra's larger specimens. Near the bottom of the gully, just before crossing a usually dry wash, you'll encounter an old trail, which seems to persist only because so many folks mistake it for the true route. This trail leading southwest dies out after just 100 yards.

Instead of taking the abandoned trail, we veer left, immediately cross the dry wash, and momentarily come to an enormous, two-trunked juniper. With a diameter of 12 feet and a girth of 36, this specimen is one of the largest junipers in the Sierra. Beyond it, the trail winds south down toward Coyote Valley, reaching its sagebrush-covered floor beside a 5-foot-diameter lodgepole pine, the key landmark to look for if you're hiking this route in the opposite direction. Since from a distance this tree is hard to distinguish from other pines, look for it, from the creek crossing, along a 345° bearing. Fortunately, the trail is usually quite obvious, though cattle may create misleading paths. Once on the valley floor, we walk a level ¼ mile south-southeast to an easy crossing of **Coyote Valley Creek.**

Across the creek we find ourselves beside a small lodgepole-shaded campsite, and then we diverge from the creek to begin a gentle climb south. This climb to a broad saddle is easy, for the distance and the elevation gain are little more than half those of the previous climb.

Now we make a 400-foot descent, passing a grove of large junipers and then negotiating short, steep switchbacks down to the east edge of sagebrush-covered, cattle-populated **Upper Fish Valley**. Here you can expect to find a signed trail junction near a tall snow-depth marker. To follow Silver King Trail 1017 (incorrectly signed as 1701 in 1986) up-canyon, consult Route RF-7. If **Connells Cow Camp** is your goal, head across Upper Fish Valley to the union of Bull Canyon creek with Silver King Creek. From the campsite here, Route RF-6 starts a climb up a primitive trail to Whitecliff Lake.

Most folks, however, either stay near the corrals of the camp, which is under the Forest Service, or else head down-canyon to Commissioners Camp. Heading north toward that goal, one goes about 350 yards to a meeting of three fences, each with its own gate. Go through the north gate and follow the path that parallels the west side of the north-northeast-heading fence. The trail soon starts to curve northwest, climbs over a low moraine left by a retreating glacier, and crosses bedrock slopes to get you to a sign—perhaps still standing when you get here. From the sign you can head 120 yards south to a chorusing, 20-foot-high cascade, **Llewellyn Falls.**

Llewellyn Falls is a barrier that trout cannot ascend (upstream trout occasionally go

Llewellyn Falls

over the falls unharmed). Perhaps as a giant glacier slowly retreated up Silver King canyon, perhaps about 140,000 years ago, cutthroat trout followed its path. They would have been able to swim into Upper Fish Valley and to higher valleys *if* they did so before Silver King Creek eroded away bedrock to form the falls. Once isolated, they evolved into a subspecies called Paiute cutthroat trout (*Salmo clarki seleniris*), or simply, Paiute trout. These trout became threatened by extinction through overfishing and also through introduction of Lahontan cutthroat and rainbow above Llewellyn Falls in the 1940s and '50s through human error. Paiute cutthroat readily cross bred with Lahontans and rainbows to form hybrids. This interbreeding was noted in 1963, and in 1964 Department of Fish and Game workers removed purebreds and treated Silver King Creek with rotenone to kill the hybrids. The purebreds were then reintroduced above the falls. Their population grew from about 150 in the late 1960s to about 600 in the early 1970s. However, some hybrids were missed, so a second rotenone treatment was done in 1976. This too failed to get all the hybrids.

In the early 1980s the U.S. Fish and Wildlife Service prepared a recovery plan for Paiute cutthroat of the Silver King Creek drainage. The plan, endorsed by the California Department of Fish and Game (CDFG) and by Toiyabe National Forest (TNF), had three elements: 1) salvage and replanting of hybrid trout in nearby waters for angling; 2) chemical treatment with the registered pesticide rotenone of all target waters above Llewellyn Falls; and 3) replanting with adult Paiute trout from identified streams not included in items 1 and 2. Work by CDFG, TNF and Trout Unlimited began in July 1991 with capture of about 1000 hybrids. The live trout were air lifted by helicopter and released in Tamarack and Poison lakes and in the East Carson River near Soda Springs Guard Station. Later, a far more intensive rotenone treatment was performed from Llewellyn Falls all the way up to the headwaters. This will be repeated in 1992 and '93, and later, if necessary, to remove hybrids arising from chemically unscathed eggs and missed adults.

Beyond the Llewellyn Falls gorge you enter fishing country as the trail descends briefly northwest to the south end of Lower Fish Valley. It then approaches Silver King Creek and reaches a white-bordered, carbonate spring just before leaving the creekside. Not far past the spring, the trail again approaches Silver King Creek and then parallels it for about 150 yards. Then, where the creek meanders west, you can walk along the north edge of the meander toward **Commissioners Camp,** which is located near the confluence of Tamarack Lake and Silver King creeks. Look for a packer's campsite. To take the fairly steep trail from it up to Tamarack Lake consult the last part of Route RF-4. To continue down-canyon along the Silver King Trail, follow Route RF-4 in reverse.

RF-6 Whitecliff Lake and Whitecliff Peak

Distances
2.7 miles (approx.) to Whitecliff Lake
3.6 miles (approx.) to Whitecliff Peak

Trailhead Same as the Route RF-1 trailhead

Introduction Whitecliff Lake, about 10 miles from Rodriguez Flat, certainly offers one of the most alpine and most isolated camps in the wilderness. But camping space around the lake is minimal, and the lake's glacial bowl certainly lacks the forage necessary for stock. It's doubtful that any equestrian would want to ride to the lake anyway, particularly since the massive 1986 avalanche, which made one stretch of trail virtually impassable to stock. Backpackers are also rare, for the lake lacks trout, and fishing is prohibited downstream. And the strenuous nature of the route discourages all but the most determined mountaineers. These individuals are the most likely souls to take this route, for the towering, intimidating east face of Whitecliff Peak offers countless Class 5 routes up to the summit. Undoubtedly, virtually everyone who's climbed to the summit has made a much easier ascent, which is described at the end of the route. As at virtually every peak in the wilderness or along its border, the summit views make up for the labor of the ascent.

Description After you've trekked 6.3 miles from Rodriguez Flat to Connells Cow Camp, you begin a hike upstream along the north bank of Bull Canyon creek. Within 100–200 yards you should be able to find an abandoned trail, and shortly thereafter the creek veers south. You continue in your same direction, southwest, soon climbing au a swale—a shallow, broad gully. The trail essentially disappears before the head of the swale, but by maintaining a steady course you should quickly find its resumption on slopes above Bull Canyon creek.

Now ½ mile up from the camp, the white firs have yielded to red firs, and lodgepole pines are joined by increasingly numerous Jeffrey pines. We also pass through fields of aromatic mule ears and then, ½ mile farther, skirt beneath a prominent granitic point (point 9191 on 7.5' topos). Now well within Bull Canyon, we see, dead ahead, an intimidating, precipitous ridge, which is the end of a cleaving ridge that separates the canyon from the Whitecliff Lake basin. For utter solitude, one can head cross-country up the lakeless canyon, and from a base camp perhaps climb somber, volcanic Peak 10,990. Easy ridgetop hiking south from it provides a variety of options to the imaginative mountaineer, including a descent from the headwaters of Silver King Creek down to Connells Cow Camp.

Soon our abandoned, deteriorating trail crosses a granitic bench, and from it we have a view down Bull Canyon. Then, 200 yards later and 1½ miles from the camp, we start to curve right, into a side canyon. The trail soon reaches a rocky, brushy area just within the side canyon proper, and from this vantage point one can survey the damage done by a 1986-vintage avalanche. Trees were strewn about the canyon floor like matchsticks. Before the avalanche, the hike northwest up through the short stretch of canyon was difficult enough, due to an extensive stand of willows near its head, and now the fallen timber compounds the problem.

The route is now cross-country. Traverse northwest across sagebrush slopes, then drop to the canyon's creek, crossing it on a convenient log, and continue up-canyon on bedrock slabs. Soon the canyon makes a right angle to lead southwest, and hiking becomes more convenient on the creek's northwest side. You'll see traces of tread as you climb steeply southwest. Then, after a few hundred exhausting yards, increasing vegetation will urge you to recross the creek. Now about ⅓ mile from your first goal, you make a final steep push past mountain hemlocks and whitebark pines to arrive at the southeast shore of **Whitecliff Lake.**

At about 9730 feet elevation, this lake is the highest one in the wilderness. In the area covered by this book, only Wolf Creek Lake, just outside the wilderness at the base of Sonora Peak, is higher, by about 370 feet. Whitecliff Lake lies in a deep cirque bordered by a granitic tapestry of the overpowering east face of Whitecliff Peak and its adjacent pair of sawtooth ridges.

Camping beside this emerald gem is restricted to some small sites. The thousands of yellow-legged frogs indicate that no trout are present. Starting in 1964 and continuing for several years, approximately 70 pure, adult Paiute cutthroat trout were laboriously packed to up this lake. Periodic sampling with gill nets in later years showed no survival, probably due in part to the severe winters at this high elevation. Furthermore, if Paiute cutthroat trout are as closely related to Lahontan cutthroat trout as is commonly believed, then they are only average in tenacity, certainly far less able to cope with extreme cold than brook trout.

Even if trout were present, you couldn't fish here due to the fishing ban on all lakes and streams above Llewellyn Falls. Thus the only water sport left is swimming, which is brisk. From late July to late August you can expect the lake's surface water to warm in the afternoon to about 60°.

The lake and the adjacent peak are named "whitecliff" for a very good reason—a broad, nearly vertical cliff, about 400 feet high, com-

posed of Topaz Lake granodiorite (or, according to other geologists, Topaz Lake quartz monzonite). If you've done technical rock climbing up faces in Yosemite National Park's high country, you'll know what to expect. Climbing the white cliff is like climbing the hard routes up Cathedral Peak or Matthes Crest. Literally dozens of routes exist, nearly all of them untried.

For the average mountaineer, the simplest route to the summit of Whitecliff Peak will suffice. To do it, start from the far end of the lake, climb up slabs and across talus to the base of the cliff, and then ascend a steep, narrow gully by the cliff's north end. The gully requires only a minimal use of hands (Class 2), and the rock is generally solid. From a notch at the top, head south, keeping just west of the ridgecrest sweeping up to the summit. After panting past wind-cropped whitebark pines of increasingly lower stature, you arrive at the base of the volcanic summit block and make a short, easy (Class 3) safe scramble to the top of **Whitecliff Peak.** Use the book's map to identify the major points of interest.

The ridge we ascended extends north for several miles, and by doing relatively easy cross-country, one can use it to drop down to either Tamarack or Poison Lake. Day hiking out from Rodriguez Flat, after climbing Whitecliff Peak, I took the route along the ridge, diagonalled northeast down to a saddle, and then made a steep descent to the south shore of Tamarack Lake—overall, an invigorating hike. The rest of the route—down to the Silver King Trail, north on it, and up the Driveway Trail—was a piece of cake.

Whitecliff Lake, from Whitecliff Peak

RF-7   Upper Silver King Canyon

Distance
4.7 miles (approx.) to saddle dividing the
Silver King Creek and Silver Creek
drainages

Trailhead   Same as the Route RF-1 trailhead

Introduction   No fishing allowed! With that
stated, many folks won't even consider this
route. And hardly anyone else will take it, for
it is essentially a utility trail used by cattlemen
who drive their herds in this area. Perhaps the
route's only recreational users are hunters,
who go up-canyon from Connells Cow Camp
just before the first major snow storms arrive,
usually in mid-October.

Description   Near the snowmarker in Upper
Fish Valley, 6.1 miles in from Rodriguez Flat,
there is a trail sign that identifies Silver King
Trail 1017, which in 1986 was incorrectly
signed as 1701. On it you head south through
the large valley, passing perhaps hundreds of
cows before you have to cross Silver King
Creek, which is often a wet ford. Just 50 yards
to the south is a prominent, white-carbonate
spring deposit, atop a 20-foot-high knoll.

The Silver King Trail follows its namesake
about 300 yards upstream to where you may
see a FOURMILE CANYON sign, but no trail.
This canyon provides access to Fish Valley,
Lost Cannon and Wells peaks, and a small
lake near the canyon's head, but all these features are more easily reached via Chapter 18's
Route PM-3. By far the canyon's commonest
visitors are cattle, and you'll see their
droppings all the way up-canyon to the small,
subalpine lake. That lake, which has both a
northwest and a northeast outlet, lacks an adequate campsite. However, one could camp
about 200 yards down from the lake, on a flat
just west of the northwest outlet creek.

From the sign opposite the mouth of
Fourmile Canyon you hike upstream about 90
yards to where, beside some rapids, a small,
fair-to-good campsite under lodgepoles can be
found. Beyond the campsite, the trail up-
canyon soon becomes ill-defined, due to
underuse by humans and overuse by cattle.
Still, as long as you stay on the west side of
Silver King Creek until the saddle above the
creek's headwaters is plainly in view, you
shouldn't have any problem.

Along the ½-mile-long, ill-defined stretch
above the campsite, you'll first approach a

A carbonate spring south of Upper Fish Valley

small, triangular pool immediately west of the
trail which is rich in carbonates. The trail then
almost dies out as it heads 130 yards southwest to the northernmost of three carbonate
springs. While looking for the trail here, also
watch for swallows, which feed on the abundant flying insects that inhabit this alkaline
microcosm. From the largest spring, or from a
granitic boulder near it, get your bearings.
You'll want to end up along the west side of an
aspen grove, which is located beyond the
snags at the far end of the springs' meadow. To
keep your feet dry, walk cross-country along
the meadow's west edge, passing some large
junipers on low, granitic outcrops about
midway to the aspen grove.

Along this traverse you may see a FLY
CANYON sign at the meadow's edge. This
glaciated canyon is easily missed. Labeled *Fly
Valley* on the map, this canyon probably holds
no more flies than any other canyon in the
Sierra. But since I didn't visit it, I can't verify
this. The canyon may make a good retreat for
those hermits who don't demand lakeside
campsites.

A saddle view north of the upper Silver King Creek drainage

Once at the west edge of the aspen grove, you should easily find the trail south. It climbs up a small gully, veers left over a granite ridge with erratic boulders resting on it, and proceeds south up along brisk, clear Silver King Creek. Above the creek's rapids we encounter a very large juniper, beyond which we keep left of a stand of willows and aspens. The trail climbs up across a slope dotted with sagebrush and mule ears, then curves east to a campsite at the beginning of a steep, taxing section of trail.

The trail changes from steep to moderate as we approach our second and last ford of Silver King Creek, which will probably be a wet one before August. About ½ mile below the saddle ahead, reclusive hikers can leave the trail and climb to either of two relatively flat-floored cirques. One is due west, the other is southwest. Both of these alpine cirques have granitic floors and volcanic walls. From a base camp in either, you could climb to the ridge and walk north along it to Whitecliff Peak (and beyond) or south along it to White Mountain (and beyond).

From the last ford of Silver King Creek, skilled climbers may want to proceed directly upstream. Others will cross the creek and attempt to follow the trail, which is now faint-to-nonexistent, but the route is marked by old blazes. We hike south 300 yards through a very open forest, arc southwest-to-south up a steeper, lodgepole-covered slope, and then climb 40 yards southeast up an open slope to more lodgepoles together with whitebark pines (look for more old blazes). About 40 yards past these trees, we curve south, then cross 20 yards of open slope to reach a switchback by some ducks perched beside leafy, aromatic mule ears that are growing near the edge of a willow cluster. Here we start northeast, then curve south up a narrow, evident, steep trail that passes just below a wide, seeping spring. Go up and around it or be prepared to sink at least ankle-deep in the volcanic muck beneath it.

About 100 yards south of the spring we encounter a short, very steep switchback leg, then huff and puff up the final, essentially trailless ¼ mile to the **saddle.** Here you can rest amid some wind-trimmed whitebark pines and enjoy the views north down the Silver King Creek drainage and southeast down the Silver Creek drainage. To head down Silver Creek, consult Chapter 18's Route PM-2, which is described in the opposite direction. To climb Wells or Lost Cannon Peak, consult Route PM-2, whose description begins at this saddle.

Chapter 14   The Dardanelles

TD-1   Wheats Meadow Trail to Wheats Meadow and Twin Meadows Lake

Distances

1.6 miles to junction with Dardanelles Creek Trail

3.1 miles to Burgson Lake

3.2 miles to junction with Trail 18E04

4.2 miles to junction with Twin Meadows Trail

5.5 miles (approx.) to Twin Meadows Lake

Trailhead   From the Highway 49/108 junction in downtown Sonora, drive about 30 miles east up 108 to the Summit Ranger Station, which is immediately past the Pinecrest Lake road. Get a wilderness permit here, if necessary, and continue 19 miles east on 108 to the Clark Fork Road junction. Branch left onto this road and follow it 0.7 mile down to a bridge over Middle Fork Stanislaus River, then 0.2 mile farther to a bridge over its cascading Clark Fork.

Immediately past it you branch left onto 6.3-mile-long Road 6N06. Just 0.3 mile up the road is a spur road right, which leads into nearby, primitive Fence Creek Campground. Get water at Fence Creek, immediately west of the spur-road junction. For Routes TD-1 and TD-2 you drive 3.5 miles past the spur-road junction up to a tight curve in Road 6N06, where it bends from west to east. Parking here is limited, with space for about 10 vehicles. For Routes TD-3 through TD-6 drive to road's end, which has parking for about 20 vehicles—though on some weekends even this space is not enough.

Introduction   Although this route to Twin Meadows Lake is about 1.3 miles longer and has a bit more climbing than the one from Spicer Meadows Reservoir, it is nevertheless an acceptable way to the lake. Furthermore, the route is more diverse, heading past cliffs suitable for climbing and meadows suitable for botanizing. However, you won't want to take this trail before late July at the earliest, for in early summer mosquitoes are very abundant along a number of trail stretches as well as at the lake. This route also offers a side trip to Burgson Lake, which due to a lack of prominent landmarks is a route recommended only for those experienced with map and compass.

Description   Because of the trailhead's low elevation, we see black oaks, incense-cedars and greenleaf manzanitas as well as the usual Jeffrey pines and white firs. In ¼ mile the switchbacking trail makes a moderate ascent to a saddle, where it enters Carson-Iceberg Wilderness, whose boundary here follows a low, granitic ridge. The trail descends momentarily west, then turns northwest past the east shore of a seasonal pond. (Late-summer travelers are likely to see only a grassy meadow with corn lilies and bracken ferns.)

We quickly cross and recross the pond's usually dry outlet creeklet, then make a short drop to a seasonal, south-flowing creek in a minor canyon. Due to the low elevation, cottonwoods and creek dogwoods grow along the creek's banks together with the more typical willows and aspens. Under forest shade one may also see trail plants and white hawk-weeds, two plain sunflowers that are also found in shady environs in California's coast ranges.

From the west bank we stroll about 250 yards up-canyon, noting some potentially enjoyable rock-climbing cliffs above and south of us, then execute a series of short switchbacks up glacier-polished slopes. We then enter a fairly shady forest and climb northwest past occasional glacial erratics to a ridge saddle, 1⅓ miles from the trailhead. Immediately west of and above us is a smooth granitic face, about 80 feet high, which is particularly suited for teaching basic rock-climbing skills. Advanced climbers can find a challenge just around the corner on a higher, mostly crackless face.

Our trail starts down along the base of the closest face, then turns south and makes a moderate ¼-mile descent, losing 200 feet before reaching a junction with the **Dardanelles Creek Trail.** Route TD-2 describes the easy 2.6 miles of trail north from here up to a junction with the County Line Trail. We follow Wheats Meadow Trail 16E06 first southwest over a slight ridge and then west down to a crossing of usually flowing Dardanelles Creek. About 200 yards downstream from the crossing, the creek plunges down some steep slopes, and climbers interested in remote, probably unscaled routes should check out the cliffs extending east from the creek there.

From the creek and a nearby campsite we climb moderately for about ¼ mile to our third significant ridge saddle, then drop about 120 feet into a shady, well-watered glen. Beneath cottonwoods and lodgepoles, we make an easy ¼-mile climb west across soil that is often damp, if not downright muddy, through much of July. However, it does support quite a lavish display of wildflowers, including tall, scarlet alpine lilies, which are never found in truly alpine places.

Burgson Lake

From anywhere along the muddy stretch, preferably from near its upper west end, one can start a ⅔-mile cross-country jaunt over to **Burgson Lake.** This is the wilderness' warmest swimming lake, its water warming in late afternoon to the mid-70s. The temperature, however, may be too high for trout; I failed to see any. The east shore has rocks high enough for diving into the 4.5-acre lake, while the west shore has a campsite. This hike is for *experienced* routefinders who want to escape from the crowd and who don't mind forgoing the chance of a trout dinner.

On the Wheats Meadow Trail you leave the mucky stretch where the grade steepens and the soil is better drained, and make a short climb to a low notch in a minor divide, immediately beyond which is a grassy pond that typically dries up late in the hiking season. From it you descend west for several minutes to a stock gate, which marks your official entrance to spacious Wheats Meadow. Heading west, you quickly reach the meadow's east edge, then on an indistinct tread bear 250° to a bend in Wheats Meadow Creek, where above its east bank you arrive at a junction with **Trail 18E04.** This indistinctly starting trail heads north along the east bank. The only discernible tread I found was a 70-yard path south from the bend in the creek over to Wheats Cow Camp, which has one cabin in good condition. The meadow will probably attract only equestrians; virtually all others will want to camp elsewhere.

In early season, Wheats Meadow plus Clover Meadow and Twin Meadows above it all have a superabundance of mosquitoes, which makes camping and hiking all the more unpleasant. In addition, Wheats Meadow—the driest of the three—does support rattlesnakes, which are most likely to be seen in early season, if at all.

Burgson Lake

Bound for Twin Meadows Lake, you leave the bend in Wheats Meadow Creek, staying close to the east bank as you head initially north, then northwest. Soon you parallel the creek between two low, granitic knolls, and immediately past them your creek curves to the right and is joined by a tributary from the west. Trail 18E04 is vague here, but you cross by this creek juncture. It appears to continue northeast, but this is in part due to folks looking upstream for a place to cross and in part because this is the south end of an abandoned trail. Don't try to follow it upstream.

Once you've crossed to the west bank of Wheats Meadow Creek, you start on a vague tread, bearing 340°, heading through Clover Meadow. At its north end the trail becomes clearer as it climbs over a low, granitic ridge

and reaches another nearby meadow. Here again the trail is vague as it diagonals northwest across the sloping, seasonally marshy meadow. Your trail parallels the meadow's north edge as it climbs northwest, and soon it parallels a tributary of Wheats Meadow Creek. About ¼ mile past the meadow both tributary and trail turn north and you climb a short, fairly steep stretch (two trail variations possible) up to dry slopes, where you'll find a junction with the **Twin Meadows Trail** immediately west of and above the tributary creek. Westward, Trail 18E04 heads over toward Spicer Meadows Reservoir. Very short Trail 18E06 north to Twin Meadows is described at the end of Chapter 7's Route SM-5, as is the cross-country route to **Twin Meadows Lake**, which is the source of Wheats Meadow Creek.

TD-2   Dardanelles Creek Trail to Sword and Lost Lakes

Distances
4.2 miles to junction with County Line Trail
4.7 miles to Sword Lake
5.0 miles to Lost Lake

Trailhead   See the Route TD-1 trailhead

Introduction   This trail, which provides an alternate route to Sword and Lost lakes, is 2.0 miles longer than the newer County Line Trail (Route TD-3). Being longer, it receives little use. However, it does have a redeeming attribute. When you head back to the trailhead, most of the trail is down along Dardanelles Creek, and when you leave the creek, you make two relatively short climbs, a 200-foot ascent to one saddle and a 100-foot ascent to a second saddle. Contrast that to the County Line's protracted 750-foot ascent, which can leave you hot and perspiring.

Description   Follow the first part of the previous route 1.6 miles to a junction with the Dardanelles Creek Trail. This Trail 19E05 begins by making a ¼-mile-long traverse northwest over to a small campsite just above Dardanelles Creek. You now stay close to the often unseen creek, following it north for about ½ mile, to where it veers briefly west. You wind northwest over to it, reaching it in several minutes. Here you cross Dardanelles Creek, which may be bone-dry by early August. You

then head about 200 yards north to a snowmelt creeklet that emanates from a small side canyon. This has the start of a visible, but abandoned, trail.

On the Dardanelles Creek Trail you continue about ⅓ mile northeast to a boulderhop crossing. Back on the east bank, you make a lazy ascent up-canyon for ⅓ mile to a crossing of a major tributary near the unnoticed Alpine-Tuolumne county line. This creek is the only sizable one you cross if you take the County Line Trail, which crosses it about ½ mile upstream above our trail crossing. This tributary is, in fact, larger than Dardanelles Creek proper, the latter often dry above where the two join. (This juncture, incidentally, is incorrectly located about ⅓ mile downstream on U.S. Geological Survey 7.5 and 15′ maps.)

With 0.8 mile remaining to the County Line Trail junction, you head north along the west base of a 300-foot-high granitic monolith, which can go unnoticed due to the forest cover. If the trail hasn't been maintained for a while, it can be quite indistinct, but you stay along the east bank until you are just past the monolith and see a low knoll to the northwest, just above the creek. Cross in this vicinity and quickly reach the mouth of a small side canyon. Now climb shortly north, then northnortheast up a minor gully, beyond which you immediately reach a junction with the more popular **County Line Trail.** Consulting the last part of Route TD-3, you follow a stretch of trail just 0.3 mile north to a junction with an equally short stretch of trail west to **Sword**

Lake. You'll find smaller, lesser used **Lost Lake** just west of it. These are probably the most heavily used lakes in the wilderness. See the Route TD-3 description for details.

TD-3   County Line Trail to Sword and Lost Lakes

Distances

0.8 mile to junction with Dardanelles Spur Trail
2.2 miles to junction with Dardanelles Creek Trail
2.5 miles to junction with Sword Lake Trail
2.7 miles to south shore of Sword Lake
3.0 miles to east shore of Lost Lake

Trailhead   See the Route TD-1 trailhead

Introduction   Lying barely an hour's walk from the trailhead, the corrugated bedrock bench holding Sword and Lost lakes is undoubtedly the most popular vicinity in the Carson-Iceberg Wilderness. Here, you're more likely to find wildness than wilderness, at least on summer weekends. Some degree of solitude reigns during the weekdays, and it is then that you can enjoy camping by the lakes. On weekends, try to dayhike to them in order to lessen impact, both real and perceived, on the area. After the new Spicer Meadow Reservoir becomes filled to capacity, perhaps in 1990, you'll be able to drop to it from Lost Lake, adding one more attraction to this route.

Description   Only 30 yards up from the road's end your broad trail splits. The lesser used McCormick Creek Trail forks right, climbing east-southeast, while your route, the County Line Trail, curves left, north. This former jeep road soon narrows to a trail and climbs briefly northeast before yielding to a very short, very steep climb north up rubbly volcanic soil. (Be careful on your return hike.) Next you then climb briefly west to the Carson-Iceberg Wilderness boundary at a viewpoint. About 20,000 years ago the 3½-mile gap between The Dardanelles and Whittakers Dardanelles was filled with a Highland Creek glacial overflow that spilled south to join the Middle Fork Stanislaus glacier.

From the viewpoint the County Line Trail climbs north for about 200 yards and then

starts a descent, crossing the unsigned Alpine-Tuolumne county line in about 100 yards. Continuing downward, we head through a field of mule ears and shortly reach a broad, open saddle. The County Line Trail could have been routed along a steady, moderately climbing grade to this saddle, but instead, expediency prevailed, resulting in your rollercoaster route from the old jeep road to the saddle. In a meadow by the north edge of the open saddle you'll find a junction with the **Dardanelles Spur Trail.** This rarely taken trail is described in the following route.

You now have about a 430-foot, unrelenting drop ¾ mile to a creek. First the meadow gives way to brush, and your rocky tread becomes fairly steep. Views of the massive, towering Dardanelles disappear, and then in a couple of minutes, just past a seasonally trickling creeklet, you pass a sloping granitic outcrop, on your left, which has a commendable view of the area.

Next you descend for several minutes through forest cover, and if you watch carefully, you may note a spur trail left. This goes but a few yards west to a viewpoint. Here, the rock you stand on is rhyolite—a volcanic equivalent to the granitic rocks that dominate the view. This rhyolite is a welded tuff, the solidified product from a tumultuous eruption of incandescent volcanic glass that occurred perhaps 20–25 million years ago. In the Sierra Nevada, a lot of volcanism, uplift and erosion have occurred since then, so rhyolite outcrops such as this one are quite scarce.

Only a few paces below this site the County Line Trail crosses a snowmelt creeklet, then descends north several hundred yards before angling sharply west down to a creek crossing. This usually dependable creek appears surprisingly large when one notes on the map just how short it is. This creek is receiving most of its sustenance in the form of ground water draining through porous sediments of The Dardanelles' west slopes. The creek has cut a steep-sided gully where you cross it, but for years folks have crossed on a massive, fallen tree trunk. I certainly prefer the trunk, fairly high above the creek bed, but most people get nervous at the exposure.

Once across this creek, which is the main arm of Dardanelles Creek, you parallel it momentarily downstream, then turn north and cross over a trivial gap. A ⅓-mile-long, 160-foot descent ensues, which ends with the crossing of a tributary and the adjacent "main" branch of Dardanelles Creek, both creeklets dry through most of the summer. We then climb almost ¼ mile north to a junction with the **Dardanelles Creek Trail.** Those taking Route TD-2 join us here.

On Dardanelles Creek Trail 19E05 we go 0.3 mile north, skirting the west edge of a brackish pond on the way to a junction with the **Sword Lake Trail.** The old, northbound section of the Dardanelles Creek Trail, which received little use in the '70s and '80s, should become more popular as hikers and equestrians discover it is a relatively easy way down to the upper part of the new Spicer Meadow Reservoir. Perhaps this reservoir's large "Gabbott Bay" will reduce pressure on overused Sword and Lost lakes. See Route TD-5 for details.

If you're bound for Sword or Lost Lake, as most folks are, you'll fork left and curve northwest to a small gully, head west up it, and then descend briefly but steeply northwest down to a fairly large campsite near the **south shore of Sword Lake.** From here you have a view up the lake toward a volcanic skyline butte, Bull Run Peak. Additional, more private campsites can be found on the granitic bench above the

lake's east shore. This bench is exceptional for high diving. After diving and swimming in the lake, which can warm to the low or mid-70s on a hot summer afternoon, you can bask on the bench's flat slabs.

Sword Lake has a small annual planting allotment of only 500 brook fingerlings. From 1969 through 1976 this 6.5-acre lake was planted with rainbow. Because of its small size and heavy use, Sword Lake offers only marginal fishing except immediately after ice-out in spring. Bullhead catfish are present, in common with most lakes in the area.

From the south shore of Sword Lake the trail splits into several use paths. The main path winds west, and if you're on the proper route, you'll pass above and just south of a brackish pond in about 250 yards. You'll then start a traverse across a sloping, glacier-polished slab. If you walk northwest up to the slab's brink, you'll be just above the south shore of Lost Lake. From your vantage point you'll easily be able to pick out a route over to the **east shore of Lost Lake.**

I prefer the harder-reached west shore. To reach it, descend southwest along the sloping slab to its base, cross a gully, and climb quite steeply up the bedrock mass ahead of you. Atop it, you walk past the southwest shore, then find a way down to a brushy area where, among shrubby huckleberry oaks, you could set up camp.

Lost Lake is smaller and has a shallower average depth than fairly deep Sword Lake, so it tends to be a few degrees warmer. Neither lake is fed by streams, but rather from snowmelt alone, so neither is a clear mountain lake. Indeed, by mid-August, shallower Lost Lake can become murky enough that

Sword Lake

you're lucky to see 10 feet down through the water.

Fishing, as at Sword Lake, is only fair during summer. The lake has an annual allotment of 1000 rainbow fingerlings. From 1956 through 1968 it was planted with brooks, then switched to rainbow to provide angling diversity in an area of few rainbow waters. Bullheads are present and compete with planted rainbows for food.

From about 1990 on, you'll be able to visit a third lake—a reservoir, actually. From the west shore of Lost Lake head west up to a low, open ridge (don't bother climbing to its high spot above the lake's north end). From this vantage spot, you will be about 350 feet above the new Spicer Meadow Reservoir, and you should be able to pick out a likely route down to an attractive stretch of shoreline. Along this middle part of the reservoir, which will be narrow enough to swim across, boats and rafts will be permitted, but only nonmotorized ones. You may find more peace and quiet here than at either Sword or Lost Lake.

TD-4   Dardanelles Spur Trail

Distance
2.2 miles from County Line Trail junction to campsite in glaciated bowl

Trailhead   See the Route TD-1 trailhead

Introduction   This is a seldom used trail that apparently was used through about the 1950s to connect a grazing area on slopes below The Dardanelles with the Gabbott Meadow grazing area. Today the trail, though signed and generally followable, offers very little recreation value except perhaps for hunters.

Description   The Dardanelles Spur Trail leaves the County Line Trail heading north through a lush, cow-grazed meadow. The trail contours for about 300 yards, then from just above a small stand of aspens it makes a diagonal ascent north-northeast across open slopes. The first several hundred yards can be vague in spots, but just keep bearing in the same direction, and you should do fine. Across open slopes you have views to the north and west of the angular, joint-controlled granitic landscape below you. Glaciers have smoothed this landscape and have removed much of the original soil, so that many of the granitic hills, domes and knolls are barren. Above to the east is the seemingly unclimbable, nearly vertical side of a massive lava flow that makes up the bulk of The Dardanelles.

About ⅔ mile from the County Line Trail, your route levels off, then even drops a bit as it leads ⅓ mile across gullied slopes to a trickling, alder-lined creeklet. Leaving this cow-frequented vicinity, you now take a more northern forested route for ¼ mile. Then you make a moderate climb ¼ mile northeast across avalanche chutes and near the end cross three adjacent alder-lined creeklets. Ahead, past a short, fairly open meadowy stretch, you climb moderately east for about 250 yards up an increasingly vague tread to a creeklet that drains a nearby glacier-carved bowl. Follow the creek, keeping to its south bank, and in about 150 yards you'll reach the floor of the bowl. Continuing a similar distance east, you'll reach a **campsite** beneath trees that are near the edge of a meadow of corn lilies. The meadow's water-loving vegetation is a response to abundant, near-surface water, which is dammed behind a low, rocky lateral moraine left by a retreating glacier.

If you cross the meadow and start up some slopes, you're likely to find one or more paths that join as they lead steeply east-southeast. This route climbs toward a ridge, then bends south-southwest over to a nearby saddle that separates The Dardanelles proper, to the southwest, from another set of Dardanelles, to the northeast. From the saddle, a ⅔-mile-long path leads down to the McCormick Creek Trail, but this path is hard to follow in places and other paths may lead you astray. The best way to the McCormick Creek Trail is to follow a path from the saddle southeast steeply down the east side of a gully, then veer east near the gully's bottom, where the path dies out at the meadow's edge. It reappears as a poor tread on the opposite side, to the east-southeast. You're better off heading along the meadow's west edge to the brink of a blocky lava flow and downclimbing it to the nearby trail.

TD-5 County Line and Dardanelles Creek Trails to upper Spicer Meadow Reservoir

Distances
3.7 miles to "neck" of new Spicer Meadow Reservoir
6.3 miles to junction with Highland Creek Trail

Trailhead See the Route TD-1 trailhead

Introduction Sword and Lost lakes can be too crowded on summer weekends. For more solitude, try camping near the middle and upper reaches of the new Spicer Meadow Reservoir. However, be aware that by late summer the reservoir can be quite low, and the upper mile or so may be an exposed, unsightly lake bottom. However, the "neck" should have water in late summer except perhaps during drought years.

Description First, follow Route TD-3 just 2.5 miles—most of it downhill after an initial, fairly steep climb—to a junction with a spur trail to Sword and Lost lakes. Routes TD-2 and TD-3 go west to those lakes, but you continue northeast along Trail 19E05, which is mostly level or downhill all the way to the Highland Creek Trail.

First you traverse a joint-fracture gully before making a short descent to two closely spaced seasonal creeks, the second one being 0.8 mile from the last trail junction. The two creeks join, and guide you northwest cross-country about 0.4 mile over to the **"neck" of the new Spicer Meadow Reservoir.** Campsites may be found in a number of secluded "nooks and crannies."

From the second creek Trail 19E05 climbs gently northeast, heads east over a minor gap, then continues northeast up a joint-fracture gully to a seasonal pond on a deep divide. Here climbers will immediately notice about a dozen Class 5 climbing routes up cracks in the steep, granitic cliff just above the divide's east side. Nonclimbers can scramble about 160 feet up to the top of a west-side knoll for views up and down the reservoir.

Onward, your trail moderately descends along a gully of the same fracture system. Just before the gradient eases and your trail crosses east across the gully, you can make a second cross-country trip. Basically just traverse west-northwest about 250 yards to a saddle, from

which you can either descend west about 180 yards to the reservoir or else climb and explore the hummocky, glacier-polished-and-striated knoll just north of the saddle. Look for isolated campsites on this knoll.

The original Trail 19E05 used to continue down the gully past a shallow pond to Gabbott Meadow. Now a newer segment, completed in about 1990, traverses around part of the reservoir, crossing a usually reliable alder-lined creeklet about midway to a gully from which the trail climbs briefly west. The trail then traverses 0.4 mile north-northeast across varied slopes, offering views of the reservoir's Gabbott Meadow section before reaching another gully. If the reservoir looks appealing, you can parallel this gully briefly westward to a small bay.

Onward, in 0.5 mile your trail climbs briefly northwest before climbing around northwest-facing slopes of a knoll and then winding down to Highland Creek. From the creek crossing, which may be a wild ford in early summer, a momentary climb will take you past campsites to a nearby junction with the **Highland Creek Trail.** The last part of Chapter 9's Route PG-3 describes a stretch of this trail from the Bull Run Creek Trail eastward past your junction up to the Jenkins Canyon Trail.

Spicer Meadow Reservoir

TD-6   McCormick Creek Trail to The Dardanelles, Dardanelles Butte and Dardanelles Cone

Distances

1.2 miles to start of cross-country route up to The Dardanelles

2.2 miles to The Dardanelles

2.2 miles to start of cross-country route up to Dardanelles Butte and Dardanelles Cone

2.8 miles to junction with connecting trail to Dardanelles Spur Trail

4.0 miles to Dardanelles Butte

5.0 miles to Dardanelles Cone

Trailhead   See the Route TD-1 trailhead

Introduction   The McCormick Creek Trail seems to be a fairly popular route for both equestrians and hunters. For me, it is a gateway to the more prominent summits of one of the best-known volcanic features in the Sierra Nevada: The Dardanelles. On this guidebook's topographic map, as on the U.S. Geological Survey 15′ topographic maps, "The Dardanelles" refers to the western volcanic palisade, which is readily visible from Highway 108's Donnells Vista Point. However, on the Survey's newer 7.5′ topographic maps, "The Dardanelles" also includes a central palisade plus the eastern one, which is capped by Dardanelles Cone. Just southwest of the cone is an outlier, a vertical-walled monolith I call Dardanelles Butte. Routes are described to the summits of the three main features: The Dardanelles proper, Dardanelles Cone and Dardanelles Butte. On each ascent you'll encounter some exposure and some loose rock, so good mountaineering sense and basic climbing skills are recommended prerequisites. The Dardanelles area is no place to have an accident.

Description   Only 30 yards up from the roadend, your broad trail splits. Take the lesser used McCormick Creek Trail, which forks right. Follow it briefly east-southeast to a low ridge, round it, and then parallel the ridgecrest north-northeast an equally brief distance. Your path, a former logging road, then circles around a small bowl, but a shortcut trail goes east-northeast 120 yards through it. After you hike another minute or two along the old road, it ends at the boundary between Sections 7 and 8. On a path you traverse northeast to a seasonal creek, about ½ mile

from the trailhead, then from it climb 150 yards east to a low ridge, which is part of the Carson-Iceberg Wilderness boundary. This spot of trail also happens to be very close to the Alpine-Tuolumne county line.

Next you traverse ¼ mile east-northeast, crossing several snowmelt creeklets, and then climb a similar distance to the west bank of a minor creek. A more substantial though still seasonal creek lies just east of it. You walk about 150 yards north up the minor creek, then cross it and quickly reach the upper edge of a sloping meadow. This is a signal for an upcoming decision point. From the edge you climb about 180 yards north to where the trail turns abruptly northeast. This is the **start of a cross-country route up to The Dardanelles.**

The Dardanelles

Your route to a saddle is quite obvious—just follow a gully north-northwest up to it. You'll do some bushwhacking on the lower 600 feet of the climb, where vegetation grows on volcanic soils, but the steeper, upper 600 feet is rather sparse in vegetation. As you approach the saddle, you can veer left from the gully and traverse beneath the south summit block, then climb gentler slopes northeast to its top. However, since the middle summit block is higher, most mountaineers will head for it. From the saddle you take a winding path of least resistance up easy slopes to what is the highest point of **The Dardanelles.**

This broad summit area is steep to overhanging on three sides, and since it's composed of rubbly latite lava, you should venture close to the brink with great caution. To the north you see an ascending ridge, which culminates in the north summit of The Dardanelles. All three summits are remnants of an extremely long lava flow known as the Dardanelles formation. This flow oozed down an ancestral Stanislaus River canyon about 9¼ million years ago, just after a larger lava flow, taking the same path, had congealed. This larger flow, which you crossed on the upper half of the climb to the saddle, is known as the Table Mountain latite, and you drove past its western part on Highway 108 just after you passed the Highway 120 turnoff to Yosemite National Park.

The best summit view, however, is not to the north but to the west. A low, granitic landscape lies below, much of it stripped of soil by a glacier that scoured the area until about 10–12,000 years ago. The pattern on the land you see was determined by the existence of master joints. A master joint is a large, long, straight crack in the granitic rock. Rocks bordering a joint were more easily removed by glaciers, so that a linear gully was formed along a joint. Sediments left by the last retreating glacier accumulated in many such gullies, and soils developed there. Today the joints are readily recognized, from your vantage point as well as on aerial photographs, by lines of trees.

You'll also see a pair of lakes—Sword and Lost, which are close enough that if you have sharp vision, you can actually see people at them. But from about 1990 on, perhaps the most striking feature will be the new Spicer Meadow Reservoir, whose 6½-mile length you'll be able to trace from the 240-foot-high dam to the far end, a bay that will flood former Gabbott Meadow.

From the start of The Dardanelles' cross-country route, the McCormick Creek Trail heads northeast, up-canyon. Soon you come to within 35 yards of a seasonal, willow-lined creek, which is the same creek you may have noted by the base of the sloping meadow. You then walk around the edge of a willow patch and momentarily cross the creek at a low, granitic outcrop. Across open, granitic terrain the trail first climbs north, offering fine views of The Dardanelles, then traverses northeast. You soon pass a seasonal creeklet, and the trail then takes on a more northern trend.

You now parallel at a distance your trail's namesake, McCormick Creek. From where

you enter a field of corn lilies you can leave the trail and head 110 yards east to where the creek is grinding a course through the granitic bedrock. You'll find a spacious campsite here, by several large boulders and scattered lodgepole pines. About 200 yards farther up the trail, you're even closer to the creek, and can find two campsites between the trail and the west bank. These mark the **start of a cross-country route up to Dardanelles Butte and Dardanelles Cone.** Before heading up it, be aware that you could also set up a base camp about 0.2 mile farther up the trail. There, you'll pass your last creekside campsites, first a fairly large one among red firs and lodgepole pines, then a small one just past it.

Dardanelles Butte and Dardanelles Cone

From the two centrally located camps, cross the creek and proceed due east directly up granitic slopes and minor benches. After about ⅔ mile of climbing, you'll reach a gully and along its west slopes climb northeast up to a granitic ridge. This is a good spot to rest and assess a steep-walled volcanic butte, which I call Dardanelles Butte. From your spot it looks impossible to climb short of forging difficult Class 5 ascents up its corrugated walls. But a hidden, easy way lies on its southeast side.

If you decide to skip the 9070′ butte, then the shortest way to the route up Dardanelles Cone is to make an ascending traverse east across some fairly steep slopes below the northwest and northeast faces of the butte. Along this variation to a saddle immediately east of the butte you may encounter snow patches through late July. You'll also see some pretty intimidating routes up the butte. Generally, the routes get easier as you progress east, and just 100 yards before the saddle

The Dardanelles and McCormick Creek canyon, from Dardanelles Butte

you'll see a 10-foot-wide chimney. This can be ascended unroped, but having done it, I don't recommend it. It is, in essence, an avalanche chute.

If you decide to climb the butte, you should make an ascending traverse across slopes below its southwest and southeast faces. Along the southeast face, about 200 yards before the aforementioned saddle, you'll find a 25-foot-wide cleft. Walk just a few paces up it to where it splits. You can continue straight ahead, if you want, climbing Class 3 up a 15-foot-wide chimney, which tops out at the top of the other side's 10-foot-wide chimney. From there you scramble up a short headwall to the top. However, the easier way is to branch left at the split and follow a steep, Class 2 gully to the flat top of **Dardanelles Butte**. This route is not exposed, and it requires minimum use of hands.

Your summit views are limited, since The Dardanelles to the west, the unnamed Dardanelles ridge to the north and Dardanelles Cone to the northeast all block much scenery. However, several notable summits are seen: Mokelumne Peak, northwest above the saddle north of the Dardanelles; Bull Run Peak, north above the unnamed Dardanelles ridge; and The Three Chimneys, south-southeast above the chasm of Middle Fork Stanislaus River.

To reach the summit of Dardanelles Cone, first get to the saddle immediately northeast of Dardanelles Butte, and then contour northeast below a lava ridge, preferably along forested slopes just north of it. You'll then reach a second saddle, where some of the folks starting along the Arnot Creek Trail, Chapter 15's Route CF-1, join us. Here, at the southwest corner of Dardanelles Cone, you first traverse 50 yards north, to where you are below two Class 3 chutes. I ascended one and descended the other and found them equally difficult. Neither is all that steep, difficult or exposed, but both have loose rock, so watch your step, particularly on your descent. Easier climbing lies above, and you scramble up safe, somewhat brushy slopes to a gently sloping summit area. Along this ascent, be sure to

look back often, for if you're not paying attention, you could have a hard time locating your route. Once on gentle slopes, you head north, skirting just east of a secondary summit, then climbing to the nearby top of **Dardanelles Cone**. Although you have a 360° panorama, your summit views are definitely inferior to those from Sierra-crest summits. With map and compass in hand, you should be able to identify the surrounding features.

From the last two McCormick Creek campsites, the McCormick Creek Trail climbs north-northeast. Just ¼ mile past the campsites the trail, now curving east-northeast, crosses a willow-lined creeklet at the base of a blocky lava flow. If you want to climb to the saddle just northeast of The Dardanelles, it's quicker to leave the trail here, scramble up past junipers growing on the low lava flow, cross the west edge of a flat, often wet meadow, and then climb up a steep gully, keeping to its east side. You'll find a path here which goes all the way to the saddle. Avoid other, less steep paths. On the McCormick Creek Trail, you'll find the start of this path, a **connecting trail to the Dardanelles Spur Trail** (Route TD-4), just 140 yards east of the creeklet. This junction is obscure, for the trail is rarely used. It first climbs northeast over to a gully, then west up it and over a nearly flat ridge, with a campsite, to the meadow's east edge. There the trail dies out, but it reappears to the west-northwest, near the base of the steep gully up to the saddle.

From the obscure junction, the McCormick Creek Trail continues east about 300 yards to a crossing of a McCormick Creek tributary in an open area. Ahead, the trail goes only about 200 yards, if that, before dying out. By heading south toward McCormick Creek, you might find suitable camping in this vicinity. You can reach the saddle by the southwest corner of Dardanelles Cone by crossing the creek and then maintaining an eastern course up forested slopes. This route is not inspiring, though from Dardanelles Cone it does provide the fastest way back to your trailhead.

Chapter 15 Clark Fork

CF-1 Arnot Creek, Woods Gulch and Jenkins Canyon Trails to Highland Creek Trail

Distances
1.6 miles to junction with Woods Gulch Trail
4.7 miles to saddle between Woods Gulch and Jenkins Canyon
6.2 miles (approx.) to Dardanelles Cone
7.1 miles to junction with Highland Creek Trail

Trailhead From the Highway 49/108 junction in downtown Sonora, drive about 30 miles east up 108 to the Summit Ranger Station, which is immediately past the Pinecrest Lake turnoff. Get a wilderness permit here, if necessary, and then continue 19 miles east on 108 to the Clark Fork Road junction. Branch left onto the road and follow it 5.6 miles up the Clark Fork Stanislaus River canyon to a junction with Road 7N13, on your left, which is just 230 yards before the Clark Fork Campground entrance road. On ½-mile-long Road 7N13, you quickly meet a road left to Camp Liahona. Your road bends right here, then winds to a roadend parking loop.

Introduction This route is a fairly heavily traveled part of the quasi-official Tahoe-Yosemite Trail. The traffic isn't due so much to TYT trekkers as to children from summer camps near the trailhead. The route offers more exercise than views, though one can leave it at its high point for a cross-country climb to the top of Dardanelles Cone. Two climbs are mentioned, both requiring the use of hands but not ropes, and both up somewhat loose rock. Only careful mountaineers should try either route.

Description On the Arnot Creek Trail we start north from the end of the parking loop, quickly pass through a gate, and soon come alongside Arnot Creek. From here to the next trail junction you'll find campsites, which are useful if you're making an overnight trek through this part of the Sierra. The creek is a good stream for rainbow and brown trout. Its upper portions have naturally produced fish, while the lower end receives catchable trout in summer. The brown trout move upstream from Clark Fork, which is also planted in summer with catchable rainbow trout.

We parallel the creek, generally at a short distance, for about ⅓ mile to the Carson-Iceberg Wilderness boundary, then we quickly come beside the creek once again. Along this stretch, the Woods Gulch creek joins Arnot Creek, and we cross the former either on boulders or on a fallen log. Now we go 110 yards northwest to a junction with the **Woods Gulch Trail**.

From the trail junction you could continue north along the Arnot Creek Trail. See Chapter 10's Route HL-6, which describes this 5.6-mile stretch in the opposite direction. Then you could head 6.4 miles down the Disaster Creek Trail, first following part of Route HL-7, then following in reverse the first part of Route CF-2. A 4.0-mile car shuttle would be needed to get you back to your trailhead.

Route CF-1, however, turns west, as does the Tahoe-Yosemite Trail. Passing creekside willows and aspens, we go just over ⅓ mile before we come to a boulderhop or log crossing of Woods Gulch creek. The splashing creek drowns out the sound of a nearby waterfall, whose base you can reach by following the north bank about 300 yards upstream. Once across to the creek's south bank you'll find a small campsite.

Southward, the Woods Gulch Trail makes a series of short, steep switchbacks, and then a short, steep climb to a minor ridge. Along the upper part of this 450-foot elevation gain, you can look north across the canyon and see, as well as hear, the waterfall mentioned earlier. Views disappear as you briefly climb a moderate-to-steep grade southwest to the bank of a creek in a shallow canyon. This usually reliable creek parallels Woods Gulch creek, the two separated by a low ridge. These two linear creeks are cutting down along a set of parallel fractures in the granitic bedrock. You hike along the first creek for ¼ mile, then leave it for a slightly shorter, steeper climb to the low ridge. Follow it west for several minutes, then angle right to begin a traverse along shady north-facing slopes.

Woods Gulch creek is now about 80 yards from you, and you parallel it at a distance for 0.6 mile before finally reaching it. Frolicking Woods Gulch creek, bordered here by large cottonwoods, is so inviting that you may want to camp on the flat land in this vicinity. Westward, the route becomes increasingly open as you climb the variably graded trail 0.9 mile up to a **saddle between Woods Gulch and Jenkins Canyon.** The last part of this climb is across dry, volcanic slopes that support a rich range of sagebrush and mule ears with a smattering of junipers.

Dardanelles Cone

The saddle marks the start of the Jenkins Canyon Trail and the start of a cross-country route to the top of Dardanelles Cone. On this latter route you head southwest to a nearly flat area and continue until you reach the foot of a steep bowl that lies below the *northeast* face of the summit. About one mile from the saddle, you now scramble up this bowl until you are stopped by steep headwalls. Ahead of you will be a deep, vertical chimney, which is fortunately not your route. Rather, climb right (west) up an exposed slope to the top of a vertical cliff that makes up the west side of bowl. From the top, continue westward, climbing up and then exiting from a short, vertical chimney. From it scramble up to the northwest ridge, then walk up it to the top of **Dardanelles Cone.** This Class 3, loose-rock route is not recommended for the faint-hearted or the inexperienced.

An easier but longer route to the top of Dardanelles Cone is to continue your traverse across gentle terrain all the way to the broad crest about ½ mile northwest of the summit, then traverse ¾ mile south across moderately steep slopes to a saddle beside the southwest corner of Dardanelles Cone. From here you begin a shorter Class 3 route, which is also up loose rock. See the last part of Chapter 14's Route TD-5 for details.

The Jenkins Canyon Trail starts by descending quite steeply west through a small grove of red firs. Crossing and recrossing the infant Jenkins Canyon creek, the trail turns northwest and descends through a lengthy

Dardanelles Butte and The Dardanelles, from Dardanelles Cone

meadow. About ¾ mile from the saddle we leave the meadow and, paralleling the seasonal creek at a distance, make a descent past red firs, lodgepole pines and western white pines. The gradient is first moderate, but then we round a ridge and make a moderate-to-steep descent southwest toward a creek in a side canyon. Now on a moderate grade, we briefly parallel this creek at a distance, then curve right to a nearby crossing of the main creek.

Now we head straight down Jenkins Canyon, but after ½ mile the trail contours for some distance, veering away from the creek. Only a few yards before Highland Creek a use trail starts downstream, going 40 yards to a relatively small camp. If you went another 40 yards, you'd reach Jenkins Canyon creek.

From late July onward, the Highland Creek crossing is usually a 5-yard-wide boulderhop, but earlier it can be a 20-yard-wide ford. Once on the northwest bank you take the Jenkins

Canyon Trail 50 yards west to its end at a junction with the **Highland Creek Trail.** Between Highland Creek and this junction you'll find a well-used camp. Chapter 9's Route PG-4 describes the Weiser Trail and part of the Highland Creek Trail down-canyon to this junction, while the first 1⅓ miles below this junction are described, in an up-canyon direction, in the last paragraph of Route PG-3. What you should know is that along the first 0.2 mile of trail west from the junction you'll find two adjacent, creekside campsites, and these lie about 200 yards upstream from the start of a string of trout pools.

Highland Creek is a noted producer of brook trout throughout its course from Upper Highland Lake to Spicer Meadow Reservoir. All tributaries of any consequence, such as the one in Jenkins Canyon, are assumed to have brook trout also if they are still flowing in mid- or late summer.

CF-2   Disaster Creek Trail to Arnot Peak and Upper Gardner Meadow

Distances
2.9 miles to junction with Paradise Valley Trail
5.0 miles to low gap separating the Arnot Creek and Disaster Creek drainages
6.4 miles to junction with Arnot Creek Trail in south corner of Upper Gardner Meadow
6.8 miles (approx.) to Arnot Peak

Trailhead   From the Highway 49/108 junction in downtown Sonora, drive about 30 miles east up 108 to the Summit Ranger Station, which is immediately past the Pinecrest Lake turnoff. Get a wilderness permit here, if necessary, and then continue 19 miles east on 108 to the Clark Fork Road junction. Branch left onto the road and follow it up the Clark Fork Stanislaus River canyon, passing the Clark Fork and Sand Flat campgrounds at roughly miles 5.7 and 6.6, then continue toward road's end, 9.2 miles from Highway 108. Routes CF-2 and CF-3 follow the Disaster Creek Trail, which begins from the north side of the road just 0.1 mile before the road's end at the edge of Iceberg Meadow. Routes CF-4 and CF-5 follow the Clark Fork Trail, which begins from the south side of the road by its end.

Introduction   If you're staying in the Clark Fork area, you can climb two peaks of nearly equal height. The first is Arnot Peak, and one of several ways to it, mostly along the Disaster Creek Trail, is described in this route. The second is Disaster Peak, the first 2.9 miles toward it being described in this route, and the rest of the distance plus summit views being described in the next route. That route offers an even shorter way to the summit of Arnot Peak plus a cross-country Sierra crest route that allows you to also visit Disaster Peak—all in one long day. Check that route's description to see if it is more appealing.

Botanists will find the first 2 miles of this route particularly rewarding in midsummer, when there are dozens of flowering species to identify.

Finally, those who like to just hike up and down canyons can ascend the Disaster Creek Trail and descend the Arnot Creek Trail. This is a fairly lengthy route, but except for an initial, fairly steep 15-minute climb, the route up the first canyon is mostly a gentle ascent. The first canyon offers wildflowers and meadows; the second offers some fairly impressive canyon scenery. This route is a

13.6-mile hike (plus a 4.0-mile car shuttle or hike), though one can take a shortcut that shaves 2.0 miles off the distance.

Description   Our northbound Disaster Creek Trail quickly leaves forest cover behind as it makes short, generally moderate switchbacks to get us 300 feet higher. Now ½ mile up from the trailhead and just within the Carson-Iceberg Wilderness, we start a diagonalling traverse up the lower slopes below a granitic monolith, The Iceberg. This feature would probably attract many technical rock climbers were it not for the dense, virtually impenetrable brush of huckleberry oak, greenleaf manzanita and snow bush that covers the slopes.

As you enter the *hanging canyon* of Disaster Creek, you draw near to the creek and re-enter forest cover. After you climb moderately for ½ mile to a brink that is just above cascading Disaster Creek, your path up-canyon is mostly a gently ascending one. The creek is apparently barren above the cascades. Some attempts have been made to introduce Lahontan cutthroat, but apparently haven't succeeded. Several creeklets soon cross our trail, and each in midsummer flaunts a lavish display of wildflowers. This botanical mecca lasts for over a mile, and along this stretch you'll see evidence of recent landslides in the form of decapitated and broken aspens.

The trail's course now is a northwestern one, and for ½ mile we hike under forest shade before breaking into a fairly large, open valley. We traverse across its eastside sagebrush slopes, then past a creeklet we round the head of the valley. Here we enter forest cover again, and over the next ½ mile climb northwest to a low, flat ridge, then north across it to a meadow's edge. We follow the edge momentarily northeast, then from a bend go 40 yards north to a sometimes obscure junction with the **Paradise Valley Trail.** See the next route if you want to hike up this fairly strenuous trail, either to climb Arnot or Disaster Peaks or to reach the Pacific Crest and Golden Canyon trails.

While the Paradise Valley Trail is perfectly obvious, the next section of the Disaster Creek Trail isn't. It begins along the edge of a meadow that can be saturated with water through mid or late July. During early season you start by making a short, soggy traverse north-northwest along the meadow's east edge, then turn west to skirt its north edge. Along this short stretch is a crossing of 40-yard-wide

Paradise Valley creek. Though the creek is very shallow, you'll have a hard time keeping your boots dry. This is quite a contrast to what late-season hikers encounter: a dry meadow, a discernible path, and a barely flowing creek.

Lightning Mountain

From this vicinity one can make a straightforward climb west-southwest up a side canyon to this ridge's obvious saddle. On the lower part of this climb, keep north of the canyon's creek. From the saddle head north to high point 9328, the apex of a knife-edge (though relatively safe) ridge. Views are better than one would expect, given the higher peaks surrounding this ridge. You can make a lengthy though uneventful descent north along Lightning Mountain ridge to its end and then make the ascent of Arnot Peak.

Bound for Upper Gardner Meadow and the northeast Highland Lake, the west branch of the Disaster Creek Trail becomes quite obvious after it curves north just beyond the crossing of Paradise Valley creek. In this vicinity you are directly across from the 9328-foot summit of Lightning Mountain, which is little more than a long, high ridge. To climb to the summit, you can leave the trail here, at about 7750 feet in elevation. However, the farther you hike up the Disaster Creek Trail, the lower the ridge becomes, which makes access all the easier.

On the trail you parallel Disaster Creek up-canyon, always at a distance, though you do cross several tributaries that supply water at least through midsummer. The first of these you meet almost ½ mile past the trail junction, and you walk beside it for a spell before leaving it to reach and cross a second, nearby creek. The trail now leads northwest and in ⅓ mile you pass a family of mature junipers.

About ½ mile past the junipers you step across a creeklet that flows southwest into a prominent meadow with corn lilies. About 280 yards farther, you cross a slightly larger, willow-lined creeklet—a jump across in early season. These two streams alert you to an upcoming, important, easily missed point: a **low gap separating the Arnot Creek and Disaster Creek drainages.** This is about ¼ mile past the second creeklet and about 320 yards before the trail crosses the first Arnot Creek tributary. A 1.8-mile-long cross-country route to the summit of **Arnot Peak** begins from the low gap, and this route is described at the end of Chapter 10's Route HL-7.

Upper Gardner Meadow, viewed from its south corner

From the low gap you have a couple of other alternatives. The first is to continue 1.4 miles up the nearly level Disaster Creek Trail to a junction with the **Arnot Creek Trail in the south corner of Upper Gardner Meadow.** For this, you also follow part of Route HL-7, though in the reverse direction. Along this stretch, you reach the south end of a linear, soggy meadow just 0.6 mile past the low gap. The trail up through the meadow is indistinct in places, so if you have problems, you can continue north to the meadow's end, jump across Arnot Creek, and climb west over a nearby low ridge to find your trail on its other side.

To start the second alternative, leave the Disaster Creek Trail only a few yards beyond the low gap, descend about 200 yards northwest to Arnot Creek, and climb about 100 yards up to the Arnot Creek Trail. Take this trail 4.8 miles down to a junction with the Woods Gulch Trail, then continue 1.6 miles past it to the Arnot Creek Trail's trailhead. This part of an 11.6-mile route, plus a 4.0-mile walk along roads back to your trailhead, is described in the last part of Route HL-6.

CF-3   Disaster Creek Trail to Arnot Peak, Disaster Peak, and the Pacific Crest and Golden Canyon Trails

Distances
4.6 miles to west edge of Paradise Valley
5.9 miles (approx.) to Arnot Peak
5.9 miles to 9425' saddle on Sierra crest
6.2 miles to junction with Pacific Crest and Golden Canyon trails
6.7 miles (approx.) to Disaster Peak
10.0 miles to junction with East Carson River Trail
11.3 miles to saddle above Boulder Lake canyon

Trailhead   See the Route CF-2 trailhead

Introduction   No desirable feature along this route is easily attained. On the map, it may look like a quick way in to the heart of the East Fork Carson River canyon, but you'll have to first climb about 3000 feet to the Sierra crest and then drop about 2300 feet to the canyon floor, which can be quite an effort with a backpack. Disaster Peak, done as a day hike, involves a minimum of 3600 feet of climbing. You can also make a 16.4-mile semiloop trip, part of it cross-country, which visits both Arnot and Disaster peaks and the stretch of crest between them. This strenuous day hike requires a minimum of 4200 feet of climbing. Finally, there's a 17.0-mile loop trip—the loop most taken—which climbs up to the Sierra crest, briefly descends to the Pacific Crest Trail, goes southwest along it, then takes the Boulder Creek Trail down past Boulder Lake to the Clark Fork Trail, on which you return to Iceberg Meadow. If you add a side trip to Disaster Peak, the trip is 18.6 miles long—quite a hefty day hike.

These last two trips seem to be done in the opposite direction, starting up the Clark Fork Trail, which is certainly the better-graded direction. However, there are several advantages to going in the described direction. First, if you plan to climb Disaster Peak, you're more likely to actually do it. Hiking the other way, you'd have to do 13.2 miles of mostly uphill climbing *before* you started the side trip to the peak, and you probably wouldn't be very motivated. Second, you might arrive at the summit late in the afternoon, when shadows lengthen and the sky becomes hazy—

not good for photographs. By climbing the peak first (and not climbing Arnot also) you get all of the major climbing out of the way probably before noon, and then can casually take a lengthy, easy route back toward the trailhead. And you can stop for a midafternoon refreshing swim in Boulder Lake, about 4 miles uphill from the trailhead.

Description First, follow the previous route 2.9 miles up to a sometimes obscure junction with the Paradise Valley Trail. Leaving the east edge of a seasonally wet meadow, you continue north, and in 320 yards you cross a creek from Paradise Valley. After an initial climb north, you turn east to climb toward that feature. The first mile from the junction is generally at a moderate grade, but then the trail turns north for a steep, ⅓-mile-long, 300-foot elevation gain. You cross an alder-lined creeklet part way up, then end by turning northeast just above a gushing spring. Now you climb a moderate-to-steep stretch ¼ mile up to a second spring, which like the previous one is emanating from the base of the volcanic strata. A brief, forested traverse completes your climb to the **west edge of Paradise Valley.**

Arnot Peak

From the forest's edge, you can make a direct climb northwest up a ridge to the summit of **Arnot Peak.** This route has the following advantages over the cross-country ascent mentioned in the previous route: overall, the distance from the trailhead is 0.9 mile shorter, one way, and the cross-country part is 0.4 mile shorter and has 400 feet less elevation gain. See Chapter 10's Route HL-7 for summit views. Rather than down-climbing, follow the scenic Sierra crest for about 3.0 miles over to the saddle crossed by the Paradise Valley Trail.

If you keep to the trail, you'll immediately enter Paradise Valley, which is probably paradise only to the cows and to the myriad mosquitoes that pollinate the wildflowers through midsummer. Only adequately protected wildflower lovers will likely enjoy this seasonally soggy stretch. Before August, part of the trail can be wet; consequently, hikers don't always stick to the route, so it can at times be quite vague. Basically you climb 0.2 mile northeast up through this sloping valley, the tread becoming very obvious at the far end. This is not true westbound, and you may have to hunt for the trail just within the forest. Not finding it could result in a miserable, somewhat brushy descent along Paradise Valley's creek.

Beyond the meadow you climb ¼ mile east to a tributary of Paradise Valley's creek, then after another ¼ mile farther southeast, up steeper terrain, you reach the main creek. The trail now climbs steeply but briefly south—up a snowbank through midsummer—to a nearly flat area. Over the next ½ mile you descend a bit south to a nearby meadow, curve southeast across mostly open, marshy terrain, then reach drier ground as you approach and reach a **9425' saddle on the Sierra crest.**

Disaster Peak

If you can handle an additional 600-foot gain, don't pass up Disaster Peak. Its summit views are far superior to the view of eastern lands you get from the saddle. The first ½ mile is easy: a walk south along the Sierra crest. You hike through a forest of lodgepoles, whitebark pines and mountain hemlocks—the domain of raucous Clark's nutcrackers—then the gradient increases as the crest runs southwest toward the nearby summit.

The U.S. Government did a number of geographic surveys of its western lands in the

Corn lilies in Paradise Valley

Stanislaus Peak, from Disaster Peak

1870s, one of these—the Wheeler Survey—covering, in part, the Sierra Nevada. Most of the Sierra Nevada work was led by Lieutenant M. M. Macomb, who covered a lot of ground during the summers of 1876, '77 and '78. On September 6, 1877, his party climbed to the summit of what back then was called King's Peak. Writes Lieutenant Macomb: "We had finished a very successful day's work, and were completing our labors by putting up the usual [triangulation] monument, experiencing considerable difficulty in finding suitable material, the peak being composed of large fragments of heavy magnetic rock [andesite lava]. In attempting to detach a small piece, Mr. Cowles [the party's topographer] loosened a heavy mass, which, slipping from its bearings, precipitated him some fifteen feet upon the jagged rocks below, passing over his legs as it rolled on." With a lot of effort, the party got Cowles down to a much lower elevation and summoned a doctor from Genoa, about 55 miles away. Despite a compound fracture in each leg, William A. Cowles luckily made a complete recovery, partly because his high boots had given him some protection from abrasion.

There are two relatively easy though potentially dangerous routes to the summit. If there's a spreading snowfield below the north face, you may find it convenient to traverse across it beneath the summit and then carefully make a short climb up *loose,* blocky lava

to a minor notch immediately west of the summit. When the steep north-slope snowfield is icy, you could take a speedy slide down it onto some dangerous, blocky talus.

Alternatively, you can start southwest up the crest toward the nearby summit, then veer left when the going gets steep and stay close to the crest until you are just south of the summit. The summit area, composed of loose, volcanic lava, is virtually lifeless, though I found three readily recognized alpine species along the summit ascent: Sierra primrose, alpine sorrel and alpine gold.

Quite likely you probably didn't climb to the top of 10,047' **Disaster Peak** to study plants or rocks, but rather to "bag" a peak and absorb the summit views. Straddling a spot on the Sierra crest midway through the wilderness, the summit provides fine views. You'll undoubtedly recognize Arnot Peak's summit block, which is officially only seven feet higher than Disaster's. The highest peak just above and to the right of it is 10,935' Highland Peak, 6½ miles away, which reigns over Highway 4's Ebbetts Pass region.

Clockwise, we scan from Highland Peak and its several summits past the unseen floor of Wolf Creek canyon to a secondary ridge of unnamed summits. Fairly shallow, hanging Murray Canyon lies immediately east of this ridge, and one more ridge over lies the Sierra's largest eastside canyon, that of East Fork Carson River. Unfortunately, you can't see the entire stretch of this winding canyon nor can you see its floor, though you can guess where it originates—at a saddle at the upper end. Lofty, 11,233' Stanislaus Peak, to the right on the Sierra crest, soars above it, completely obscuring slightly higher, 11,459' Sonora Peak, the highest summit between Highways 4 and 108. To its right lies a snowy, volcanic ridge that has as its high point 11,569' Leavitt Peak, which lies on the Sierra crest as well as the Emigrant Wilderness boundary.

Neither 10,009' Red Peak nor 9,715' Bald Peak, a few miles away in the south, is impressive—they are merely high points along a volcanic ridgecrest. Nor is 9,524' Dardanelles Cone, the highest point of the Dardanelles ridgecrest 8 miles to the west-southwest, very impressive. What is impressive is the 3,500' deep chasm between them—the canyon of Clark Fork Stanislaus River. You've climbed a long way! You complete your scan with a view of 9,781' Iceberg and 9,942' Airola peaks, this pair separated by a deep cleft from isolated 9,795' Hiram Peak.

From the Sierra crest saddle separating Paradise Valley canyon and Golden Canyon, the Paradise Valley Trail concludes by making a short, fairly steep descent northeast to the base of a minor ridge, where the trail's tread essentially disappears. Continue eastward about 100 yards across fairly gentle, open terrain and find a junction with the **Pacific Crest and Golden Canyon trails.** You certainly won't miss the "PCT," but you may end up a little north or south of its junction with the Golden Canyon Trail. If you've arrived at this junction via another route and want to start up the Paradise Valley Trail but can't find it, your best bet is to go about 100 yards due west up toward the base of the minor ridge. If you want to head 3.8 miles down Golden Canyon to a junction with the **East Carson Trail,** consult the last part of Chapter 10's Route HL-10.

Route CF-3 proper follows a scenic 5.1-mile stretch of the Pacific Crest Trail. You first contour 0.1 mile south-southwest to a small, fair campsite by the north bank of a willow-lined creek, then tack south-southeast, traversing in just over ½ mile to a side canyon with an alder-lined, jump-across creek. Heading toward this creek, you're bound to notice a conspicuous dark, volcanic hill, about a mile east, which your route will pass.

First, you continue your fairly open traverse. Cross an often wet meadow, then curve east, one mile from the last junction, to cross the outlet creek of Golden Lake. Here, early-season hikers may cross a large snowbank, and perhaps not see the creek, while late-season hikers may cross a dry creek bed. The "lake" lies on a flat bench, just above the trail and out of sight. Golden Lake is so small and shallow that it typically dries up in September.

Under forest cover we hike a couple of minutes southeast to a "buttercup bog," which lies just below a minor gap along an unimpressive part of the Sierra Nevada crest. A trail continues southeast to that gap, passes through a stock fence, and then quickly dies out near the edge of a spacious meadow. The Pacific Crest Trail turns northeast, and in about two minutes we cross a similar crest gap. From it we briefly arc northeast along a low crest and just above the meadow, then we pass through a stock gate and climb east to a minor ridge just below a splendid viewpoint.

Now you descend ¼ mile northeast, crossing terrain that can be snowy through late July, then arrive at the edge of a generally marshy meadow. The trail skirts its north end, and then passes the base of a dome of blocky, andesite lava, point 9501 on the topographic map. This dome rests on a low, gently sloped part of the Sierra crest that was periodically covered by glaciers advancing east from the east slopes of Disaster Peak, one mile to the west. However, since the last glacier retreated perhaps about 13,500 years ago, the dome's blocky lava has been so intensely fractured by repeated freezing and thawing of water that no sign of glaciation remains.

On a low, granitic ridge by the south edge of the dome, you have fine mountain views in three directions. Here, about 2.1 miles past the Disaster Creek/Golden Canyon trails junction and 3.0 miles before the Boulder Creek Trail junction, you begin a 1½-mile-long, 700-foot descent. First you ramble ⅔ mile, on a general course east-northeast, dropping only 200 feet to a minor Sierra crest saddle. You then turn south and soon parallel a Boulder Creek tributary. Just past a meadow with lots of willows and corn lilies, the trail curves around the south end of a granitic ridge, leaving the tributary by its union with Boulder Creek. On a moderate grade, you hike about ⅓ mile, first east, then south, down to a second tributary.

With the descent behind us, we now hike about 300 yards south to a bend, where the trail starts east up a side canyon. For nice camping, go about 100 yards downslope toward the confluence of the east canyon's wildflower-lined creeklet with Boulder Creek. A cross-country route heads down the short, steep, somewhat brushy canyon, and where you see a hanging side canyon coming in on the left, you contour over to its mouth and find the Boulder Creek Trail. On it, Boulder Lake is just a two-minute walk to the east. From the bend in the Pacific Crest Trail, this downhill route to the lake is just under a mile long. Along the PCT and then the Boulder Creek Trail, the route to the lake is 2.8 miles long, and the first ½ mile is a moderate climb.

On the PCT, climbing east up the side canyon, you quickly leave scattered lodgepoles for open slopes of sagebrush, lupine and coyote mint. Stay north of the creek, whose upper half generally runs dry by early August, then make a final climb up its snowmelt headwaters gully to a major saddle. It seems that from here a fair number of people make a ⅓-mile-long, 500-foot climb to the top of 9393′ Boulder Peak. Be forewarned: trees obscure the views.

East Carson canyon, from Boulder Peak

Now you leave a grazing area by first traversing south across the east slopes of a volcanic summit to a saddle, then make a minor climb southeast up to the top of a low granitic ridge with views to both the north and the south. Then the trail descends fairly steeply south, and you leave the last whitebark pines behind as the short descent ends at a **saddle above Boulder Lake canyon.** If you want to continue 3.1 miles along the Pacific Crest Trail down into the upper part of the East Fork Carson River canyon, consult the last part of the next route. To descend along the Boulder Creek Trail and then along the Clark Fork Trail, see the first part of the next route, which is described in the opposite direction. In brief, you make a scenic 1½-mile descent to shallow Boulder Lake, whose east end offers some pleasant swimming, and then descend fairly steeply another 1½ miles to the Clark Fork Trail. Take this mostly gently descending trail 2.7 miles west along Clark Fork Stanislaus River to its trailhead at Iceberg Meadow. Your starting trailhead, also beside Iceberg Meadow, is just 0.1 mile west along the road.

CF-4   Clark Fork and Boulder Creek Trails to Boulder Lake, Pacific Crest Trail and upper East Fork Carson River Canyon

Distances
2.7 miles to junction with Boulder Creek Trail
4.2 miles to Boulder Lake
5.7 miles to junction with Pacific Crest Trail
8.8 miles to junction with East Carson Trail

Trailhead   See the Route CF-2 trailhead

Introduction   The first 2.7 miles coincide with a small part of the Tahoe-Yosemite Trail, which continues up the Clark Fork Canyon to Saint Marys Pass and beyond. Many folks, however, prefer to branch off this route and hike up to Boulder Lake, which is an ideal day hike and not a bad overnight hike. Strong hikers can continue to the Pacific Crest Trail, hike north on it, and then follow the Paradise Valley and Disaster Creek trails back to Iceberg Meadow, perhaps taking in a side trip to Disaster Peak along the way. This loop trip is best done in the reverse direction, as explained in the introduction of the previous route. Route CF-4 offers a suitable way in to the upper part of the East Carson canyon, though if you're not in good shape, you'll want to spend your first night at Boulder Lake. Although the lake is less than halfway to that canyon, it nevertheless is beyond the great bulk of your climbing.

Description   The Clark Fork Trail begins from the south side of the roadend, and it touches the north bank of Clark Fork Stanislaus River as it curves around the south edge of fenced-in Iceberg Meadow. Just beyond the meadow we reach an immense Jeffrey pine beside the bank of an alder-lined creek. Jump across this creek, jumping into the Carson-Iceberg Wilderness as you do so, and then you make a short, steep climb up to a minor granitic ridge. From it you have a tree-framed view northwest of The Iceberg, which would be climbers' heaven were it not for the essentially impenetrable brush that lies between this cliff and Iceberg Meadow.

After a few minutes you reach the Clark Fork's bank a second time, and then in a couple of minutes, just past some aspens and bracken ferns, reach the bank again. Next we walk along the base of a relatively small cliff and enter a short stretch of trail that is a joy to wildflower lovers—in season. Here among the tall cow parsnips, alpine knotweeds, Brewer's angelica, California cone flower and common mullein, you'll find dozens of smaller, water-loving species.

For almost 2 miles, now, to Boulder Creek, our route is mostly within sight or sound of alder- and willow-lined Clark Fork. The under-footing is alternately sand and duff, and we are shaded by moderate-to-dense red and white firs and Jeffrey pine. There are several good campsites along this stretch, and the wet banks of the tributaries host columbine, monkey flower and many other moisture-loving flowers.

The Clark Fork Stanislaus River is a renowned rainbow-trout producer. Brook trout are also found throughout its length. Whether it is the best fishing stream in the wilderness is arguable in comparison to the East Carson River, the other main contender.

Just above the union of Boulder Creek and Clark Fork, we climb moderately up to a junction with the **Boulder Creek Trail.** If you plan to continue up the Clark Fork Trail, go to the right here and immediately boulderhop Boulder Creek. See the next route for trail description up the 5.0-mile stretch to the northwest edge of Clark Fork Meadow.

On the Boulder Creek Trail we climb moderately northeast for about 300 yards along the creek bank to a gate in a stock fence, then continue a similar distance before climbing a steeper stretch. Then behind a glacier-polished outcrop cut by a 5-foot-wide feldspar dike, the creek is placid, and we have an easy hike through a meadowland to a crossing of the alder-lined creek. Before early July this crossing could be a wade.

From the east bank we head northeast, soon cross a seasonal creeklet, and then climb north over a low ridge to a more substantial creek. This creek drains the Boulder Lake canyon, but not Boulder Lake itself. Heading for the lake, we confront the only real sustained climb of this route: a 370-foot grind more or less straight up south-facing, brushy slopes of huckleberry oak and snow bush. In about a ¼ hour you top out at a juniper flat, and then, feeling relieved, traverse briefly northeast to the seasonal outlet creek of Boulder Lake. The trail crosses the creek and continues 70 yards north before turning abruptly northeast.

Boulder Lake

Here you could be misled, for the trail appears to continue north. That tread, however, quickly dies out. For a shortcut, one could continue north and make a grueling 400-foot climb up Boulder Creek canyon to some easier upland terrain. There you could continue along the creek past isolated campsites before reaching the Pacific Crest Trail at one of several possible points. Such a route would shave about 2 miles off your hiking distance if you are bound for northern points along the Pacific Crest Trail.

Keeping to the Boulder Creek Trail, you climb northeast just a minute or two, cross a low ridge and quickly make a minor drop to the north shore of **Boulder Lake.** One could easily wade across the west part of the lake, but the east part is deep enough for enjoyable swimming and for overwintering trout. Because of its shallow 10-foot depth, it is at best a marginal lake for trout. Still, despite its small, 2.5-acre size and its shallow depth, the lake is planted annually with 500 brook fingerlings, and it produces some nice catches at times.

Photogenic granitic outcrops

This lake is about as far as most people will want to go, but the trail does continue 1.5 miles up-canyon to a Sierra-crest junction with the Pacific Crest Trail. From the lake you hike east across a sagebrush slope to a soon-reached crossing of a snowmelt creeklet, which together with early-season snow on adjacent slopes is the only source of inflow for the lake.

After several minutes we enter a pleasant valley and briefly come alongside the canyon's seasonal creek. Then in ⅓ mile, near the valley's upper end, we make a moderate climb into a narrow part of the canyon. Photogenic granitic cliffs, attractive to rock climbers, stand out from the canyon's north slopes. Beyond these, we're in another picturesque valley, and have an easy, enjoyable hike up-canyon for ¼ mile, to where we tackle the canyon's headwall, and in a few minutes arrive at a saddle and a junction with the **Pacific Crest Trail.** Some 20,000 years ago, this spot was beneath over 500 feet of glacial ice.

From the saddle, the Pacific Crest Trail climbs very steeply in either direction, but the Sierra crest is too narrow and rocky to offer much choice of routes. In the southbound direction, which initially keeps just west of the crest, you finally top out at a minor gap in the crest about 280 feet above the saddle. You then descend briefly southwest, curve around a meadow east of you, and then traverse over to a second minor gap, this one well off of the Sierra crest. Immediately past it you reach a seasonal creek that drains a meadow just west of you.

We now head southeast over to what is essentially the brink of an inner gorge of the East Fork Carson River canyon. Past a splashing creek, turn north for a fairly long, fairly steep descent on a switchback leg. The remaining ½ mile of route is better graded, and it crosses a tributary just before a junction with the **East Carson Trail.** North, this trail first goes 150 yards to a crossing of the East Fork Carson River. The stretch of trail down-canyon is described in Chapter 12's Route WC-5 in the up-canyon direction. *Be aware that the 5.5-mile stretch down to the Golden Canyon Trail junction is an unmaintained trail that will increasingly become more like cross-country over time.* For the adventuresome types, I suggest you take this trail down to Murray Canyon, climb up that canyon to a saddle with a trail junction, traverse south 1.9 miles up to the PCT, then take it south to the Paradise Valley Trail (Route CF-3). Take that trail up to a nearby saddle and then down to the Disaster Creek Trail (Route CF-2), which you follow back down to Iceberg Meadow. On the other hand, if you want to take the Pacific Crest Trail up-canyon or as far south as Sonora Pass, consult Chapter 17's Route SP-4, which is described in the northward direction.

CF-5   Clark Fork Trail to
Clark Fork Meadow

Distance
7.7 miles to northwest edge of Clark Fork
Meadow

Trailhead   See the Route CF-2 trailhead

Introduction   Like part of the preceding
route, this one is a part of the Tahoe-Yosemite
Trail. Perhaps most of the trail users are hikers
passing through on the TYT route, for Clark
Fork Meadow, by itself, is not a very attractive goal. Being a subalpine meadow, it may
hold some charm, but perhaps in August only,
after most of the mosquitoes have gone and
before the late-summer storms hit.

Description   First follow the previous route
2.7 miles up the Clark Fork Trail to its junction with the Boulder Creek Trail. Keeping to
the Clark Fork Trail, you use any of the giant
boulders in Boulder Creek to make a crossing,
then start east-southeast straight up a moderate slope. The trail quickly curves south-
southeast and makes a short, moderate-to-
steep climb up to a granitic brink along a
miniature gorge. From it you can peer down at
cascading Clark Fork Stanislaus River as well
as admire the view down the deep Clark
Fork canyon. The stretch of river flowing
through this gorge probably has good fishing.
Many years ago, pack stock brought in rainbow and brook fingerlings for planting upstream. However, since there was already an
established trout population, the planted
fingerlings didn't survive long enough to produce a fishery.

Beyond the brink and its massive junipers,
the trail crosses two alder-lined seeps. You
then climb a bit and quickly arrive at a nice
two-tent campsite beside the upper end of the
Clark Fork's cascades. Beyond it you traverse
through a fairly dry meadow, then enter forest
cover.

Ahead, you parallel the Clark Fork, usually
at a distance, not crossing it until close to
Clark Fork Meadow. Along this stretch you

Clark Fork Meadow

cross about a half dozen tributaries, and the
lodgepole-shaded campsites you find along
here are better than those at Clark Fork
Meadow, for there are fewer mosquitoes.
About a mile past the brink, after the canyon's orientation has definitely become north-
south, you start a mile-long climb south-southeast, gaining about 500 feet by the time you
top a granitic flat. Now the grade is considerably easier, and you traverse ½ mile
south to rejoin the Clark Fork, which now will
stay within earshot all the way to Clark Fork
Meadow.

Over the next 1½ miles, look for campsites
both along the trail and on flats just away from
it. You may also see remnants of an old trail or
two, though the main trail should be obvious;
you just keep to the east side of the Clark Fork
until you approach a steep wall, above which
lies the long-sought meadow. Before reaching
the wall, the trail first crosses to the west
bank, then parallels the infant river some
yards upstream. You then climb steeply for ¼
mile before making a short traverse over to the
brink of the wall. Here you recross the Clark
Fork and find yourself among campsites by
the **northwest edge of Clark Fork Meadow.**
To continue 2.4 miles up to Saint Marys Pass,
then 1.3 miles down to a trailhead on Highway
108, consult Chapter 17's Route SP-1. This is
described in the reverse direction, which is
certainly the easiest way in to the meadow.

Chapter 16   Eureka Valley

EV-1   Columns of the Giants

Distance
0.3 mile to Columns of the Giants

Trailhead   At the Pigeon Flat Picnic Area. Along Highway 108 you reach the entrance to this picnic area by either driving 4.4 miles east from the Clark Fork Road junction or 3.4 miles west from the Kennedy Meadow road junction. The entrance road immediately forks, the longer branch going left, up the river to nearby Pigeon Flat Walk-in Campground, the shorter branch going right, into the adjacent picnic area.

Introduction   If you're staying at any of the Middle Fork Stanislaus River's seven campgrounds (five along Highway 108, two along the Kennedy Meadow road), you might take the time to follow this short nature trail to the base of an impressive lava flow, the Columns of the Giants.

Description   From the picnic area you descend to an adjacent bridge across Middle Fork Stanislaus River. Wildflower lovers will find the river banks in this vicinity a very good site for botanizing. Once across the bridge, you follow a winding trail across the east edge of Pigeon Flat, reaching trail's end in several minutes near the base of the **Columns of the Giants.** Here, at trail's end, the Forest Service has constructed a geologic exhibit, which is not entirely accurate, but may be sufficient for laymen.

I believe this basalt flow, which is over 400 feet thick at its maximum, was erupted locally about 120,000 years ago, and future eruptions are likely. Since that time, glaciers have appreciably widened the canyon. You can see signs of their former existence by climbing to the top of the massive Columns of the Giants flow. Cautiously climb a steep gully just to the left of the main face. Atop the flow you'll see where glaciers have polished and striated the lava and have left stray boulders, known as *erratics,* strewn about.

EV-2   Seven Pines Trail

Distance
2.7 miles to juniper-shaded campsite
3.6 miles to second campsite
5.6 miles to saddle along Carson-Iceberg
   Wilderness boundary

Trailhead   Drive to the West Douglas Summer Home Tract road, in the middle of the Middle Fork Stanislaus River canyon's Eureka Valley. Along Highway 108, the tract-road junction is 6.0 miles east of the Clark Fork Road junction and 1.8 miles west of the Kennedy Meadow road junction. (With five Highway 108 campgrounds between the two junctions and two more along the short Kennedy Meadow road, this is a popular area for campers, particularly fishermen.) The hopefully signed tract road is between Eureka Valley Campground, 0.8 mile to the west, and a major bridge across the Stanislaus River, 0.2 mile to the east. On the tract road, drive about 200 yards northeast to a fork and park by it. In the past, parking up by the summer homes along the left fork has caused problems, so walk along this fork. You'll quickly reach Douglas Creek, which can usually be crossed without wetting your feet. Then hike about 250 yards farther, passing several summer homes between the creek and the obvious trailhead.

Introduction Climbing about 3600 feet in elevation, steeply at times, up south-facing slopes that can be very hot in midsummer, this trail to essentially nowhere would not be included in this book but for the fact that it is still used. This trail offers a strenuous workout. At trail's end, on a high-ridge saddle, you do have some views, but much better ones could be had from many other, more easily attained high points. Peak baggers can go on to climb Bald and Red peaks, though only the latter has views to justify the workout. Perhaps the trail is best in late season, when temperatures are cooler. Then, deer hunters—on *horseback*—will be the most likely users.

Description Starting from one of this guidebook's lowest trailheads, we are within the realm of incense-cedars and black oaks. We ascend moderately northwest for ½ mile, then make a climb of 500 vertical feet via short, steep switchbacks. Shady trees may protect one somewhat from the sun, and seeping springs can create muddy spots on the trail. All the black oaks disappear before we leave the forest and climb east up brushy slopes. On this ½-mile brushy traverse, one can look southwest down the deeply glaciated Middle Fork Stanislaus River canyon and see a dark lava flow resting on the canyon bottom—the previous route's Columns of the Giants basalt flow.

From the end of our traverse the trail turns directly upslope to a viewful ridge. Now, looking up Douglas Creek canyon, we see a crest composed of horizontal volcanic flows— flows that buried an ancient granitic landscape over a period perhaps from about 10 to 6 million years ago. Leaving the ridge the Seven Pines Trail undulates 0.6 mile northeast to a trickling creek, then climbs steeply up to and across a slope covered by aromatic snow bushes and mule ears. About ½ mile above these slopes our now creekside trail passes an easily missed **juniper-shaded**

campsite that is beside Douglas Creek. Look for brook trout here.

Should anyone wish to climb to Bald Peak, whose views don't really justify the effort, he should leave the trail here and climb more or less up an obvious side canyon to a saddle just east of the peak.

Between some clumps of trees, sagebrush predominates as the trail parallels the creek for ⅔ mile up-canyon to a **second campsite,** actually several, which are found under red firs and lodgepole pines. Beyond them we leave the creek and climb about ½ mile up sagebrush slopes to a ridge. We follow Douglas Creek, on our right, ¼ mile upstream before both creek and trail bend right and we have a view up-canyon.

From here you can head northwest up a minor gully, cross the top of the granitic ridge, and then climb ⅓ mile up to a saddle by the east base of Red Peak. At 10,009 feet elevation, the volcanic peak provides better summit views than Bald Peak, which is about 300 feet lower, but the better views aren't due so much to the added elevation as to the peak's location. Bald Peak offers views down into the lower Clark Fork canyon plus views of the western, lower part of the wilderness. Red Peak also offers these views, plus a view east of the upper Clark Fork canyon, Stanislaus Peak and Sonora Peak, and a view north straight up the Disaster Creek canyon and beyond to the Ebbetts Pass environs.

With 1.2 miles remaining to a crest saddle, the Seven Pines Trail bends east, quickly reaches a large sedge meadow, and dies out. We parallel its northwest edge, then beyond it climb northeast steeply ⅓ mile to slopes decorated with willows and corn lilies. Our cross-country route now climbs east-southeast, up to an evident saddle along the **Carson-Iceberg Wilderness boundary.** Beyond the fairly open saddle and its scattered whitebark pines, those wanting to continue down to the Clark Fork can start a descending arc east across a wide, open bowl. In times past, a trail descended to the Clark Fork, but this is certainly a very strenuous way to reach it.

Chapter 17   Sonora Pass

SP-1   Highway 108 to Saint Marys Pass and Clark Fork Meadow via Tahoe-Yosemite Trail

Distances
1.3 miles to Saint Marys Pass
3.7 miles to northwest edge of Clark Fork
   Meadow

Trailhead   From Sonora Pass drive 0.85 mile northwest down Highway 108 to a blocked-off, hopefully signed, former jeep road with parking for about 10 vehicles. If you drive past it 0.5 mile, you'll reach the beginning of an increasingly steep descent beside Deadman Creek.

Introduction   This route provides the shortest and certainly the most scenic way to subalpine, fairly isolated Clark Fork Meadow. Only the first mile is an actual path, the rest being cross-country or on a faint use trail. This route is a short part of the Tahoe-Yosemite Trail, and most folks visiting Clark Fork Meadow plan to do some or all of this quasi-official route, which begins at Tahoe's Meeks Bay and ends at Yosemite's Tuolumne Meadows. The descent to Clark Fork Meadow described below is only one of at least three possible routes. Thomas Winnett, the author of the *Tahoe-Yosemite Trail* guidebook, prefers another route—one that makes a lot of sense if you're hiking in the opposite direction—up the Clark Fork canyon. Regardless of how you reach Clark Fork meadow or how you leave it, you can't get lost; at all times either you're hiking up or down the canyon or ascending from or descending to Highway 108.

Description   This jeep road, or at least a path close to it, was part of the first trail across the Sonora Pass area. From that pass the trail descended close to our trailhead, then climbed to Saint Marys Pass. This trail to the

Clark Fork Stanislaus River was opened to pack animals in September 1862, but it was to be short-lived. When the William H. Brewer party passed through here in July of the following year, a wagon road was already being constructed down Deadman Creek—the route of today's Highway 108. Such a road was deemed necessary in order to connect Bodie, Aurora and other mining towns east of the Sierra crest with Sonora, Jamestown and other mining towns in the Sierra foothills.

Starting through this historic area, we ascend the jeep road about ½ mile to a level area, which was about as far as passenger cars got before this road was closed to motor vehicles around 1980. Now about 9650 feet in elevation, the visitor will find this near-timberline landscape ablaze in midsummer with acres of tall mountain helenium. Early- and late-season hikers will see mostly sagebrush and lodgepole and whitebark pines. If you smell these yellow sunflowers, you'll discover that unfortunately they're members of the sneezeweed genus. Higher up, you may be treated to a more endearing species, the delicate Drummond's anemone, which grows in soil saturated with water from adjacent melting snow patches. Like many members of the buttercup family, this species lacks petals, the flowers composed instead of five-to-eight whitish petal-like sepals.

You now climb up a steeper part of the old road, and then it drops a bit and quickly dies out. Find an obvious trail that skirts above the road over to a close-by gully. The trail climbs steeply up this gully to a minor saddle on a ridgecrest, which has been called **Saint Marys Pass.** The next route (SP-2) climbs to this

Stanislaus Peak and upper Clark Fork drainage, from Saint Marys Pass

minor gap, which is on the Carson-Iceberg Wilderness boundary. During glacial times, an ice cap in the upper Clark Fork drainage overflowed south across this ridge.

Bound for Clark Fork Meadow, however, we choose not to make this climb, but rather start a cross-country route by traversing ⅓ mile west-southwest to a shallow saddle on a fairly broad part of the ridgecrest. From this saddle we cross a low granitic knoll and a low volcanic one, immediately beyond which is another shallow saddle. Here, at the county line, you may see a metal stake. Our cross-country route leaves the scenic crest, with its views of Sonora and Leavitt peaks, and starts a descent north toward dominating, pyramid-shaped Stanislaus Peak. You go about 200 yards north, and if on my route, you'll reach a straight, narrow gully. From its lower, north

end you should be able to locate a ducked route and a faint, discontinuous tread, which descends steeply north before veering northwest on a more reasonable grade toward Clark Fork Meadow. The route to this marshy meadow can be vague, but you always stay south of the infant Clark Fork.

Once in the meadow, cross Clark Fork anywhere you like and proceed to campsites by the **northwest edge of Clark Fork Meadow.** Until about early August, you can expect quite a horde of mosquitoes, so if you plan to camp here before then, bring a tent. Just past the campsites the cross-country route recrosses the creek before it cascades into a scenic gorge. A 7.7-mile-long official trail begins from here, and it is described in an up-canyon direction, starting from a trailhead at Iceberg Meadow, in Chapter 15's Route CF-5.

SP-2 Highway 108 to Sonora Peak and Stanislaus Peak

Distances
2.2 miles to Sonora Peak
3.7 miles to saddle at base of Stanislaus Peak
4.2 miles to Stanislaus Peak

Trailhead   Same as the Route SP-1 trailhead

Introduction   Exactly which peak between Highways 4 and 108 offers the best experience is probably a matter of subjective opinion, but Sonora Peak has got to be among the top contenders. It is not only the highest peak in the area, it is also one of the most easily reached. And while the Sierra Nevada boasts of two officially named Triple Divide Peaks, Sonora Peak can be touted as Quintuple Divide Peak. Its summit feeds the headwaters of five drainages: East Fork Carson

River, Clark Fork Stanislaus River, Deadman Creek, Sardine Creek and Wolf Creek. Stanislaus Peak, only 226 feet lower, pales by comparison: it divides only two drainages. Still, this technically more difficult summit will attract peak baggers, who can top it after only a two-hour hike from the trailhead.

Description   First, follow the first three paragraphs of the preceding route for the 1.3-mile climb to Saint Marys Pass. This is just above 10,400 feet and just over 1,000 feet lower than Sonora Peak. If you're bound for that peak, you now more or less follow the Carson-Iceberg Wilderness boundary along a ridgecrest east toward the peak. Initially, this alpine cross-country route is fairly steep, though it is certainly safe. Quickly the grade abates, and soon you traverse a flat to the base of the actual peak. The summit, about 700 feet above you, is almost due east, but you probably won't want to tackle it head on. I preferred to diagonal northeast up the steep slopes to a minor saddle about on the Sierra Nevada crest. From there, about halfway between the flat and the summit in elevation, I followed the steep though easy crest southeast directly to the top of **Sonora Peak**. Actually, I stayed just a few yards left of the crest, since on that day chilly winds were gusting to 50+ miles an hour (I was almost blown off Stanislaus Peak). Usually, the winds are minimal and one doesn't have to worry about a subfreezing windchill factor. Use the book's topographic map to identify most of the features. It is, however, insufficient for distant ones, such as Tower Peak, about 15 miles to the south-southeast, and Mt. Lyell beyond it, about 46 miles from your summit.

Leaving the top, you have a choice of three routes. First, you could return the way you came, which is the fastest route down. Second, you could descend east across fairly snowy slopes, reach the Pacific Crest Trail, and follow it about 3.6 miles back to its trailhead near Sonora Pass—see Route SP-3. Finally, you could retrace your route only to the flat at the base of Sonora Peak, and then proceed to Stanislaus Peak. Leaving the flat, you parallel the crest for about ⅔ mile, the gentle slopes evolving into a well-defined gully. This gully curves west, and you make a brief, steep descent through it to a meeting with a conspicuous trail.

Starting from Saint Marys Pass, hikers meet this obvious gully in about ¾ mile. This route is a trail that traverses across mostly open terrain, and the only possible problem you could encounter is a snowfield on the north side of the pass. Generally through late July you'll have to slide or kick-step down it to reach the trail.

About ½ mile beyond the obvious gully the trail traverses past some dense clusters of whitebark pines, then leaves them and provides an impressive view of Stanislaus Peak. If you want to avoid the direct route up it, which has some loose rock and is definitely Class 3 in difficulty (use of hands required), then you'll want to take an easier route (marginal Class 3) up the peak's south slopes. Do this by first leaving the trail and then dropping to and climbing up from an open nearby, flat-floored basin.

Those bent on the direct route take the trail to its end by a **saddle at the base of Stanislaus Peak**. From the granitic outcrops around the saddle you get a fine view down into the East Fork Carson River canyon. Views from the peak aren't substantially better, but if you're still determined to reach it, follow the ascending Sierra Nevada crest, keeping just to the left of it. The route is obvious, and you're bound to see signs of former travel. From the summit of **Stanislaus Peak** you don't see the miles of scenery to the south and east that are seen from Sonora Peak, but you do have an unobstructed view north-northwest straight down the ridge—the Sierra Nevada crest—separating the East Fork and Clark Fork canyons.

Sonora Peak, distant Tower Peak, and Leavitt Peak, from Stanislaus Peak

SP-3   Sonora Pass to Sonora Peak, White Mountain and Wolf Creek Lake via Pacific Crest Trail

Distances
2.7 miles to 10,500' saddle
3.6 miles to granitic ramp
4.0 miles to saddle above Wolf Creek Lake
4.4 miles (approx.) to Sonora Peak
4.5 miles to Wolf Creek Lake
5.9 miles (approx.) to White Mountain

Trailhead   From Sonora Pass, drive about 0.15 mile down Highway 108 to where it bends west. From the bend a short paved road climbs southeast to a trailhead parking area atop a usually windy crest.

Introduction   Compared to Chapter 18's Route PM-1, this route certainly provides the more scenic way to Sonora Peak, White Mountain and Wolf Creek Lake. It also starts about 1000 feet higher, so even though the distances to features are longer than along Route PM-1, the energy required, except for the stretch to Wolf Creek Lake, will be less. However, this route, along the Pacific Crest Trail, has one definite disadvantage: the trail cuts across steep, potentially treacherous slopes, some with long-lasting snowbanks. Snow across the trail on steep slopes will absolutely stop horses and can be a major obstacle to backpackers. So, in a typical year, don't take this trail before late July *at the earliest*.

You might also ask the Forest Service about the trail's condition. In 1986 a heavy snowpack had apparently dealt a severe blow to a very short stretch of trail just before the 10,500' saddle. Although I'm a fairly accomplished mountaineer, I found the lack of tread at this spot very intimidating—and I was only carrying a day pack. Carrying a backpack across this spot would have been a frightening experience. Indeed, there were ample tracks indicating that hikers had abandoned the trail and headed straight down toward Sonora Pass. The trail will probably be in good shape when you hike it, but it wouldn't hurt to check first.

Description   The Pacific Crest Trail crosses the trailhead's road about 70 yards up from Highway 108. South, the "PCT" heads 0.2 mile to Sonora Pass, from which it makes a switchbacking climb to a 2-plus-mile-high ridge. This stretch of trail is beyond the scope of this book, but if you want to take it, be aware that it is probably even more treacherous than the northbound stretch if you attempt it before late July. However, from then until the snow falls, it is quite scenic, and it provides relatively easy access to the 11,569' summit of Leavitt Peak. It also provides a long, highly scenic entrance to Yosemite National Park. See my *Yosemite National Park* guidebook for details.

Camouflaged marines at 10,500' saddle

Wolf Creek Lake and the West Walker River canyon

Northbound on the PCT, one leaves the parking area for a one-mile traverse in and out of many gullies, which are typical of this high country's eroded volcanic landscape. Finally the trail turns northwest to begin a real ascent. At this point you can look northeast and see at least two obvious windows in large, loose pinnacles, near whose tops the trail will pass. On the 0.6-mile-long northwest ascent over sagebrush-covered terrain, we veer in and out of more gullies before reaching a switchback on a low ridge.

The trail, now climbing east across steeper slopes, provides ever-improving views of the volcanic terrain and of several peaks in Emigrant Wilderness and Yosemite National Park. Halfway to a ragged crest, our eastbound segment crosses a saddle that sits right on the Alpine-Mono county line. Immediately south of it are the tops of the conspicuous group of pinnacles seen earlier. A 30-yard scramble up to one of their most accessible summits provides you with a sweeping panorama.

Leaving the pinnacles on a well-graded trail, we duck in and out of stark, steep gullies, then top out at a **10,500′ saddle** on a ragged crest. There's a small chance that you'll encounter a platoon of marines dug in here. In the field for two or three days anywhere from January through October, marine recruits operating out of Pickel Meadow's Mountain Warfare Training Center stage war games in and around Wolf Creek and Silver Creek canyons.

Now we traverse across steep slopes well above the floor of Wolf Creek canyon. Iced-over snow patches can be a real hazard in at least one spot, so be prepared if you're passing through before late July. In about ¼ mile these slopes give way to gentler ones, across which we make a safer, more relaxing traverse. Along this stretch, notice how the whitebark pines have been reduced to shrub height by winter's freezing winds. As recently as about 15,000 years ago there would have been no vegetation at all, just a thick river of ice slowly flowing east down Wolf Creek canyon to meet an enormous river of ice flowing down the West Walker River canyon.

The Pacific Crest Trail continues to traverse north along the bleak, volcanic lower slopes of Sonora Peak, and below us we soon see Wolf Creek Lake, on a bench. Well into August this sometimes soggy part of the PCT can be obscured by snow, hiding the spot where the trail bends right and quickly reaches a **granitic ramp.** This bend is located near two creeklets found immediately beyond a cluster of wind-cropped willows. Hikers who want exceptional summit views can leave the trail here for a stiff but technically easy 1000-foot climb west to the summit of **Sonora Peak,** the highest peak between Highways 4 and 108.

Keeping to the PCT, we descend the often snowbound, steep granitic ramp, which is bordered by a granitic cliff on its west side. At the ramp's base we enter a field of granitic blocks, then wind among them to a junction atop a windblown **saddle above Wolf Creek Lake.** Here you enter Carson-Iceberg Wilderness, if you're continuing northward, and you follow the next route. To climb from the saddle up a wilderness-boundary ridge to **White**

Mountain, consult the last part of Chapter 18's Route PM-1. If you're just day hiking, you may want to drop to nearby **Wolf Creek Lake,** the route to it being quite obvious. Bordered on the east by a steep, bouldery ridge and on the west by a seasonally boggy sedge meadow, the shallow 5-acre lake has essentially nothing to offer to campers, fishermen or swimmers. Perhaps what this lake, with its photogenic backdrop, offers most is serenity—unless the Marine Corps' war games are in progress nearby.

SP-4 Sonora Pass to upper East Fork Carson River Canyon via Pacific Crest Trail

Distance
5.2 miles to junction with East Carson Trail

Trailhead   Same as the Route SP-3 trailhead

Introduction   If you plan to hike the entire stretch of Pacific Crest Trail between Sonora and Ebbetts passes, you'll have to include this subalpine, virtually campless stretch. Heading down-canyon, the route is certainly easy enough, which permits you to appreciate the splendors of the deep, glaciated East Carson canyon. The only drawback is reaching the start of this segment of the Pacific Crest Trail. See the introduction of the previous route for cautions along the segment of "PCT" north from Sonora Pass, and see the trailhead and description in Chapter 18's Route PM-1 up Wolf Creek canyon for its problems. The latter route, though not as scenic, is easily the safer of the two ways to the saddle at the head of the East Carson canyon.

Description   After you've hiked either 4.0 miles along the previous route's Pacific Crest Trail or 3.8 miles along Chapter 18's Route PM-1 up Wolf Creek canyon, you deserve a rest at the 10,250-foot-high saddle just north of Wolf Creek Lake. Here you enter Carson-Iceberg Wilderness as you start a descent north into the headwaters of the scenic East Fork Carson River canyon. The Pacific Crest Trail first makes several switchbacks, descending steeply past sharp, ice-shattered boulders, lingering snow patches and windswept whitebark pines. From about where views of the saddle disappear, the trail's gradient decreases considerably, and you soon cross a permanent stream.

Granitic point near Stanislaus Peak

Continuing down the East Carson canyon, we see fresh evidence of glaciation. Here, erratics were left behind as a glacier melted back some 13,500 years ago. Down-canyon, you'll see that the rock is quite weathered. This canyon's bedrock is part of a large granitic body called the Topaz Lake pluton, and like Yosemite's better known Cathedral Peak pluton, it is characterized by large feldspar crystals existing among various smaller crystals. Because they are more resistant to weathering, these large crystals stand out above the bedrock surface.

We now exit from a forest of lodgepole pines and cross the path of an old avalanche. By noting the size and therefore age of the lodgepole pines that have sprouted since the avalanche, one can guess it probably occurred in the 1940s. Debris from this and other avalanches you may see can wreck trails and can temporarily dam the river, leading to floods that ruin the trout-spawning gravels.

In ½ mile we cross the path of a smaller, more recent avalanche, which built up so much force on its descent of the west slope that it swept all the way across the East Carson river and knocked down trees on the east slope. Hiking north for one mile takes us past mountain hemlocks and other conifers to a small flat, with fair camping, where we find a junction with the **East Carson Trail.** This trail is unmaintained from here down to the Golden Canyon Trail junction.

To continue down-canyon, follow Chapter 12's Route WC-5, which is described in the opposite, up-canyon direction from the Soda Springs Guard Station. From your junction the Pacific Crest Trail makes about an 800-foot climb to the rim of the East Carson canyon's inner gorge. Consult the last part of Chapter 15's Route CF-4 for a 3.1-mile climb to a junction with the Boulder Creek Trail. Route CF-4, described in the opposite direction, begins at Iceberg Meadow, 8.6 miles from the East Carson Trail junction.

SP-5   Sardine Falls

Distance
0.9 mile to Sardine Falls

Trailhead   From Sonora Pass, drive 2.6 miles east down Highway 108 to Sardine Meadow and park on the roadside. If you're coming from Highway 395, drive 12.5 miles west up Highway 108 to this meadow, from which the distant falls will be quite visible.

Introduction   From when Highway 108 first opens until often as late as early August, Sardine Falls is crashing with such volume that it can be heard all the way from the highway. By September, however, the falls barely splash enough to be seen from Sardine Meadow. When you stop at the meadow, you'll be able to judge for yourself whether a hike to the falls will be worth the minor effort. The hike is best done in the morning, when the falls are well lit and at their most photogenic.

Description   Your route at first is an old jeep road, which heads west-southwest across Sardine Meadow for about 100 yards to reach Sardine Creek. Until mid-July you're likely to get your feet wet fording this creek. It probably has brook trout, but no fish information on the creek is available. Once across, hike southwest through the sagebrush and past clusters of lodgepoles. Soon the old road arrives at the north bank of McKay Creek and ascends beside it to the base of a low knoll. From here onward your route is a trail, which first tops the knoll. Just past it a use trail forks left over to the creek while the main trail joins the creek about 100 yards farther and paral-

Sardine Falls in late summer

lels it about ⅓ mile up to the base of **Sardine Falls.** Just below the falls is a fairly large, shady campsite beside the verdant, wild-flowered south bank of McKay Creek, though being so close to the highway, this vicinity is better visited on a day hike.

SP-6   Leavitt Falls

Distance
100 yards to Leavitt Falls viewpoint

Trailhead   From Sonora Pass, drive 6.1 miles east down Highway 108 to an easily missed spur road, on the right. You'll reach this junction about ¼ mile after you leave Leavitt Creek canyon and get your first views of giant West Walker River canyon. If you miss the junction, you'll make a tight switchback 0.5 mile beyond. If you're coming from Highway 395, drive 8.5 miles west up Highway 108 to this switchback, which is about 1.2 miles past Leavitt Meadow Campground. The spur road goes south only about 120 yards before ending.

Introduction   This hike is almost too short to be included, but I feel one should never pass up the opportunity to view a waterfall, particularly when it is so easily reached. From the viewpoint you also get a commanding view up and down one of the largest canyons of the east side of the Sierra Nevada.

Description   You take a use trail, dropping to a small, flat-topped granite ledge—the **Leavitt Falls viewpoint,** which is at the brink of the steep-sided Leavitt Creek gorge. Watch your footing here: attempts to get a better view of the falls could be dangerous. From the brink, you're about 600 feet above spacious, 7200-foot-high Leavitt Meadow, which spreads out directly below you on the floor of the West Walker River canyon. Yet this 600 feet is not even half the thickness of each of a number of glaciers that advanced down and later retreated up this canyon.

In this vicinity, the most recent glacier was at least 1500 feet thick, and almost filled Leavitt Creek canyon to the rim. This glacier

originated at the head of the West Walker River canyon, which is about 13 miles south of your viewpoint, seen to the left of the highest visible peak—11,755' Tower Peak. From your spot this glacier continued northeast to a mile or so beyond the Highways 108/395 junction. An ancient glacier, 32 miles long, continued north about 12 miles farther, almost to the town of Walker.

Leavitt Falls

Chapter 18   Pickel Meadow

PM-1   Wolf Creek Canyon to Wolf Creek Lake, Pacific Crest Trail, Sonora Peak and White Mountain

Distances
3.3 miles to Wolf Creek Lake
3.8 miles to Pacific Crest Trail
5.0 miles (approx.) to Sonora Peak
5.7 miles (approx.) to White Mountain

Trailhead   There are two approaches to the trailhead: a longer one, described first, which is hard on your vehicle's transmission and suspension; and a shorter one, which will tax your brakes as well. These are the two worst roads to any Carson-Iceberg Wilderness trailhead. Both are certainly drivable, at least after early July, though each can test your nerves.

The first begins closest to Sonora Pass, starting from a junction with Road 062, which is located just 1⅓ miles east down narrow, winding, paved Highway 108. This vicinity is a *de facto* camping area. Road 062 goes 6.5 miles to a junction with Road 042, which goes up Wolf Creek canyon. The first 3.0 miles east on Road 062 are relatively uneventful, but then from a saddle junction you curve left and plunge down to nearby Little Wolf Creek. Avoid spur roads as you rollercoaster about 3 more miles to Road 042.

The second route joins the first one here. This is the better of the two routes, and it begins by leaving Highway 108 from a junction 11.2 miles east of Sonora Pass and 4.0 miles west of Highway 395. This junction, signed SILVER CREEK ROAD—PUBLIC ACCESS, lies ⅓ mile east of the main entrance to the U.S. Marine Corps' Mountain Warfare Training Center, located along the edge of Pickel Meadow. From this junction you have two Highway 108 camping possibilities: Sonora Bridge Campground, 2.5 miles east of the junction, and Leavitt Meadow Campground, 3.3 miles west of the junction.

Starting up along the west bank of Silver Creek, Silver Creek Road heads through the Marines' camp, then makes a switchbacking ascent, quite steeply at times, giving rise to spur roads along the way. About 3.0 miles from Highway 108 and near Silver Creek, your Road 059 meets Road 062. Turn left onto Road 062 and drive almost 1.5 easy miles to the junction with Road 042 which was mentioned in the second paragraph. Take Road 042 1.6 miles up lower Wolf Creek canyon to its end, immediately above the far end of a long meadow.

Introduction   This rugged, partly cross-country route seems to get more equestrians than backpackers, although I wonder why anyone would want to camp at shallow, cool, fishless Wolf Creek Lake. On occasion from January through October, U.S. Marine Corps units also use the canyon for their war games, which can be unnerving. Hence, this is not the kind of hike one would recommend to friends. What it does offer, however, is the quickest way in to the head of the eastern Sierra's largest canyon, that of the East Fork Carson River. Starting at about 8650 feet you climb to the 10,250-foot saddle at the head of the canyon, then take a dramatic, mostly downhill or level hike all the way along the East Carson Trail to Wolf Creek Meadows. Be aware, however, that a 5½ mile stretch of former trail is now abandoned and in places could be hard to follow. If you take this route, you'll need a car shuttle, and you will want to take at least three days to do this memorable excursion. Route PM-1 also offers the most direct way to White Mountain as well as a good route to Sonora Peak, the two highest summits between Highways 4 and 108.

Description The first mile of the route is along a former jeep road, and its first ¼ mile is quite steep. A series of water-diversion bars crosses this stretch to check erosion that was initiated when a major 1986 avalanche, 0.7 mile wide, diverted a creek down the road. A very heavy snowpack built up atop deep, loose gravel and, becoming unstable, it slid *en masse*. This was not a rock avalanche from the canyon's cliffs, but rather a snow avalanche from slopes below them.

Where the road gets steep, a use trail branching from it avoids the road's unnecessary climb and descent. However, at least in 1990 the trail died out, so you had to do some climbing back up to the road. From the very end of the road you head about 210° cross-country through a large, seasonally wet meadow to a crossing of Wolf Creek, where you may see a blaze on a lodgepole pine. Over the first ½ mile along the south bank of the creek, the route west-southwest is marked with blazes, rock "ducks" and PCT posts. The latter are present because before the current route of the Pacific Crest Trail was constructed, the temporary route ran up this canyon.

Where you encounter a low, creekside ridge of large granitic blocks, you go just south of them and then start to curve west-northwest. Soon you cross a broad avalanche and just past it, after about one mile of walking close to the south bank of Wolf Creek, you turn southwest, away from it. Your route first climbs through a meadow, then up a ridge of granitic blocks, willows and lodgepoles. You head southwest toward a glaciated bowl, crossing a usually flowing creek just below it, and from there climb west about 300 yards steeply up bouldery slopes. If you take the wrong route, you'll have to make an uphill fight through dense clusters of willows. The largely cross-country route ends by traversing north-north-west ⅓ mile among boulders and willows, staying just below the base of steep slopes all the way to the outlet of **Wolf Creek Lake.**

Bordered on the east by a steep, bouldery ridge and on the west by a seasonally boggy meadow, shallow, subalpine Wolf Creek Lake has essentially nothing to offer to campers, fishermen or swimmers. However, desperate long-distance hikers on the Pacific Crest Trail do camp here, as they do at other minimal "PCT" sites. This 10,090-foot-high lake—the highest one between Highways 4 and 108—

does have a photogenic backdrop, and the lake usually offers serenity. The environs can get noisy or crowded when the Marine Corps' war games are in progress, which they are for 2 or 3 days out of each 30-day training period.

From the lake's north end you have just over a ¼-mile climb to the Carson-Iceberg Wilderness boundary at a prominent, nearly alpine saddle that is crossed by the **Pacific Crest Trail.** To descend north into the upper reaches of the mammoth East Fork Carson River canyon, take this trail, following Chapter 17's Route SP-4.

From the nearly alpine saddle you can climb into clearly alpine domains with an ascent to either Sonora Peak or White Mountain. Sonora Peak is more easily reached along Chapter 17's Route SP-2, but starting from the saddle above Wolf Creek Lake, you have the opportunity of bagging two 11,000+' peaks. Bound for Sonora Peak, you start south on the Pacific Crest Trail, winding through a field of granitic blocks to the base of a steep ramp. Your trail ascends this ramp. From the top of the often snowbound ramp, the trail starts a traverse south across wet, willow-clad slopes. You, however, leave the trail for a straightforward, 1,000-foot-climb up largely snowy slopes to the top of volcanic **Sonora Peak.** Descending back to the saddle is clearly more fun than ascending from it, since for most of the summer there is sufficient snow for sliding or "skiing" part way down.

To climb to White Mountain, start from the saddle and climb northeast up a broad, granitic ridge, gaining about 650 feet in elevation before its gradient abates. You then follow it a bit more to where the gradient increases. If you can't tarry to "bag" Peak 11,324, continue straight ahead. Otherwise, start an ascending traverse north, pass beneath the summit of Peak 11,345, and reach the 11,240' saddle just north of it. Now keeping to the crest, you make a short, final ascent to your long, granitic ridge's high point, 11,398' **White Mountain.** If you've traversed a considerable distance along the crest, you should have spotted several possible descents from it east into Silver Creek canyon, which offers an interesting alternative to retracing your steps. With proper navigation, you can reach Chango Lake—due east of the White Mountain summit—and go for a refreshing swim in the south part of this mostly shallow lake before heading out to the Silver Creek trailhead.

PM-2   Silver Creek Canyon, Chango Lake and White Mountain

Distances
1.7 miles (approx.) to Chango Lake
3.5 miles (approx.) to saddle along Carson-Iceberg Wilderness boundary
6.0 miles (approx.) to White Mounttain

Trailhead Leave Highway 108 at a junction 11.2 miles east of Sonora Pass and 4.0 miles west of Highway 395. This junction, signed SILVER CREEK ROAD—PUBLIC ACCESS, lies ⅓ mile east of the main entrance to the U.S. Marine Corps' Mountain Warfare Training Center, located along the edge of Pickel Meadow. From this junction you have two Highway 108 camping possibilities: Sonora Bridge Campground, 2.5 miles east of the junction, and Leavitt Meadow Campground, 3.3 miles west of the junction.

Starting up along the west bank of Silver Creek, Silver Creek Road heads through the Marines' camp, then makes a switchbacking ascent, quite steeply at times, giving rise to spur roads along the way. About 3.0 miles from Highway 108 and near Silver Creek, your Road 059 meets Road 060. This road, heading west, provides access to Wolf Creek canyon. Continue straight ahead on Silver Creek Road, reaching a fork in ¾ mile. The fork right is signed SUMMIT MEADOWS, and if you take Route PM-3's optional way back from Lost Cannon Peak, you'll end your cross-country trek about ⅔ mile up this road. To start along Route PM-2 and PM-3, fork left and drive 1.0 mile to the roadend.

Introduction This route provides a way in to Chango Lake, which, being shallow, fairly high in elevation, and probably fishless, won't attract too many folks. The route also offers a number of suggestions for getting to the summit of White Mountain. And those who want a maximum of seclusion can take the route to its end at a saddle dividing Silver Creek and Silver King Creek canyons, then enter the latter and camp in any of three alpine cirques below a main crest or camp down in Fly Valley. With rugged, generally lakeless country and a soggy, hard-to-follow trail, Silver Creek canyon is usually devoid of people except when the marines stage some war games, which they do a couple of days each month.

Description From the roadend we start west-southwest on a closed jeep road and after 250 yards reach a small cabin. In the past it was used by Basque sheepherders, though in July 1986 I saw not a trace of man or sheep. The jeep tracks continue a bit farther to the north edge of a meadow, where they die out. However, if you can spot blazes on lodgepoles by the meadow's west edge, you'll find the tracks' resumption.

Looking west across this meadow, approximately in the direction of travel, you'll see the steep, glaciated east face of White Mountain. If you want to climb to the summit, you have several options, the first one beginning here. Head south across the meadow and adjacent Silver Creek, then climb due south 400 feet in elevation to a conspicuous saddle. From it, ascend an undulating ridge 2 miles west to Peak 11,324—also seen from the meadow—then traverse one mile north along a high ridgecrest to White Mountain.

Once beyond the meadow, the jeep tracks gradually transform into a trail, following blazed lodgepoles across somewhat soggy terrain. Along this stretch the trail bends from west-southwest to west-northwest, and just ½ mile from the last meadow we enter another one. Continue up-canyon through the meadow, reaching its northwest edge beside placid Silver Creek. This creek has a good population of naturally produced brook trout, and it provides good fishing along its gentle-gradient stretches.

Above the meadow the creek's gradient increases, and the trail becomes hard to follow. In the past there have been as much as several poor treads of varying degrees of continuity, so you are free to go up whatever side of the creek you choose. Both sides have their soggy parts.

Chango Lake

If you're bound for this lake, you'll definitely want to be on the creek's south bank. Within the first 150 yards beyond the meadow, leave the bank and start climbing west, directly up fairly steep slopes. With luck you may see a rudimentary trail, which stays just north of a shallow gully. On or off the trail, follow this gully up to a bench, about 600 feet above the start of your side trip, and here you'll find lackluster **Chango Lake.** If you want to camp near the 2-acre lake, try just above the north shore. Most of the lake is too shallow for swimming, except for the southern part. Temperatures should reach the low or mid 60s on afternoons from late July through mid-August. The lake has been planted in the past with brook trout, but at present is considered barren. I saw no trout, though there were plenty of yellow-legged frogs.

From the north shore one can head up to White Mountain by any of a number of variations. All start by first traversing northwest across a bouldery granitic ridge to a nearby marshy meadow. From its far side, start climbing west up a low ridge. If you're skilled, you can continue climbing up to a cirque just below the mountain, then tackle its east face or climb north onto its descending east ridge and follow it to the top. An easier way is to climb around the base of the east ridge to a shallow cirque and head southwest up it to the top.

Those adhering to Silver Creek will climb northwest ⅓ fairly soggy mile to a meadow that occasionally receives debris from late-spring avalanches. About ⅓ mile beyond this meadow, you come to a really wet one, beyond which you should get onto the north bank of Silver Creek, if you haven't done so already. Soon the gradient increases, and at last we're on fairly well drained soils. About ¾ mile past the wet meadow, the canyon splits. To the northwest, the conspicuous saddle at the head

of the main canyon stands at nearly 10,000 feet elevation, about 600 feet above you.

White Mountain

To the west lies an obvious side canyon, and a hike starting up it provides the safest albeit the longest route to White Mountain's summit. There are several possible variations up it, but I suggest that you curve southwest, climbing about 800 feet in elevation to a flat-floored cirque. From it several routes are possible, the easiest one climbing north to a nearby small point, then ½ mile northwest to a broad, nearly flat erosion surface. A spur ridge, with a dropoff at its end, branches northeast—avoid it. The main ridge leads northwest, offering very easy, view-packed, high-elevation trekking. To reach **White Mountain,** follow the main ridge over one mile south, skirting past five minor summits before reaching the apex.

If you're bound for Wells or Lost Cannon Peak or for upper Silver King Creek canyon, stay on your virtually nonexistent path, which is part of Silver King Trail 1017. After a considerable amount of exertion up the steep grade, you come to an open, windswept **saddle along the Carson-Iceberg Wilderness boundary.** To follow your sometimes visible trail onward, consult Chapter 13's Route RF-7, which is described in a southward direction up to your saddle. Be aware that fishing is prohibited in the Silver King Creek drainage. To continue up to Wells Peak and beyond, see the following route.

PM-3 Wells Peak, Hidden Lake and Lost Cannon Peak

Distances
5.3 miles (approx.) to Wells Peak
6.9 miles (approx.) to Hidden Lake
7.9 miles (approx.) to Lost Cannon Peak
11.8 miles (approx.) for loop trip (without Hidden Lake side trip) back to trailhead along alternate return route and roads

Trailhead   Same as the Route PM-2 trailhead

Introduction   In my opinion, the best parts of the Silver Creek country are the high ridges and summits to the north, standing well above the creek. Wells and Lost Cannon peaks are

easily reached, though the highest pinnacle on the latter's broad summit area is for technical climbers only. Both peaks and the gentle ridge between them are part of a relatively uneroded landscape that has largely escaped glaciation. By climbing either peak, you can view this high, gentle landscape, which has changed very little in the last few million years, when the Sierra Nevada began its latest major uplift.

Description   The previous route describes the first 3.5 miles up to a saddle along the Carson-Iceberg Wilderness boundary. The rest of the route is quite straightforward: start northeast along or just east of the ridgecrest boundary. There are no streams along the route, so unless you make a side trip to what is locally called Hidden Lake, you had better carry water. This caveat doesn't apply to those hiking before August, since then there should be reliable snowfields both at Wells Peak and at Lost Cannon Peak.

The steepest part of your hike is the initial part up from the saddle, which you'll find isn't all that bad. Staying close to the actual ridgecrest, you gain about 350 feet in elevation before the grade abates. Since you're above 10,000 feet, you'll probably want to stop a number of times to catch your breath, and the ever-improving views of the magnificent scenery are worth stopping for anyway. About 450 feet above the saddle, the cross-country route bends east-southeast and skirts the base of a minor crest summit, then arrives at a saddle immediately east of it.

Now, a relaxing route lies ahead. You start along the crest, which quickly broadens to a small plateau. Go between its north and south outliers as you start a minor dip to a broad saddle. Here you're at the west toe of linear Wells Peak, which is little more than a giant pile of volcanic rocks. The alpine vegetation in this general area is prostrate, indicating that icy winter winds really whip across the surface. Carefully, pick your footing up toward the summit, preferably staying just north of the actual crest. Regain the crest when the summit appears in view.

From the top of **Wells Peak,** where the wilderness boundary turns from east to north, you'll see a slightly lower summit about 100 yards to the east. That vantage point offers better views down Silver Creek canyon, for the slopes are quite precipitous beyond that point. There, you'll also find a windbreak, though it would be of little use in stormy weather. The peak is named for John C. Wells, who was a supervisor of Mono National Forest.

The most dominating feature seen from the summit area is a ridge to the southwest which has White Mountain as its central high point.

In the east-northeast is broad, pinnacle-studded Lost Cannon Peak, and you can see all of the straightforward cross-country route to the peak's summit. Familiarize yourself with the route before leaving Wells Peak.

The first part of your short northeast descent down a bouldery slope is fairly steep, but is nevertheless quite safe if you *carefully* pick your way down; this is no place to turn an ankle. The unstable talus slope quickly gives way to a stable slope supporting brushy whitebark pines, which in turn yields to a broad saddle.

Hidden Lake

If you want to visit this relatively small lake, descend about ⅓ mile north from the saddle, following a very shallow gully to the brink of a steep slope. From here you can decide whether the 500-foot descent to the lake is worth it. I couldn't find a sign of either campsites or fish (and anyway fishing is prohibited in this and other waters of the Silver King Creek drainage).

If you do want to drop to the lake, do so from slopes just west of the gully. A snowfield, often lasting to August, helps make the initially steep descent enjoyable, provided it's not iced over. Next, barren ground yields to an open stand of lodgepoles and whitebark pines before you reach **Hidden Lake.** The lake, just under 2 acres in size, has no surrounding campsites, but it offers brisk swimming—up to the low 60s at best. You'll probably have this oversized frog pond to yourself.

From the broad saddle where the side trip to the lake begins, we go east-northeast, ascending a broad, fairly easy ridge, which requires little switchbacking. The ridge seems to be hardly more than an oversized volcanic dirt pile, and if there were a trail up it, the route would be quite dusty. Lupines, wallflowers, pussy paws and other herbs hold the soil in place, as do clusters of whitebark pines.

About ⅔ mile from the saddle, the ridge becomes narrow and rocky, and you veer to

Fourmile Canyon holds Hidden Lake

Lost Cannon Peak's east-ridge summit pinnacles

the right from it, curving east on a traverse across a bowl. You slog up the gravelly, barren east wall of the bowl, your boots sinking deep into the sterile, decomposed granite, or *grus*. You'll find a few species of alpine plants growing in it, including a pungent sunflower, alpine gold. This plant's distribution is too sparse for pollination to be left to the wind, so it apparently uses a strong scent to attract suitable insects to do the job.

Now you climb northeast up a ridge to a close-by summit, the westernmost one on Lost Cannon Peak. Skirt along its base, then slog east across the broad summit plateau. Head toward the north end of a string of summit pinnacles, crossing a veneer of volcanic rocks and soil just before reaching them. A few of the pinnacles, including the highest one, require a rope and climbing equipment for safety, but if you're not up to towing that along, you can nevertheless get excellent summit views from a lone summit north of the volcanic field. This summit block is only a Class 3 scramble. From it you see for dozens of miles to the north-northwest, to 10,881' Freel Peak, about 36 miles away, and through the spreading Carson Valley, to the right of it. To the east stand the pale-colored Sweetwater Mountains, which are topped by 11,673' Mount Patterson and 11,664' Wheeler Peak, both about 14 miles away.

To the northeast, you'll see Summit Meadow, from which Lost Cannon Creek flows northward. Supposedly, John C. Fremont's party abandoned a cannon by the creek, though this just might be myth. From at least as early as 1877 the creek was identified as Lost Cañon Creek, but during the 1950s, with the production of this area's 7.5 and 15' topos, someone added an *n* to the creek's and peak's names.

If you've brought along about a half-dozen climbing nuts for cracks from ½–3 inches wide, and at least 25 meters of rope, you can tackle the highest pinnacle on **Lost Cannon Peak**. In tennis shoes, I got halfway up a moderate Class 5 route when, being alone, I decided that to continue wasn't a good idea. I look forward to returning with equipment and at least one climbing partner to climb this pinnacle and at least a half dozen other Class 5 pinnacles. Don't expect to do a first ascent; marines from the Mountain Warfare Training Center down at Pickel Meadow have probably beaten you to it.

Rather than backtrack your entire route, you can take a shortcut route by backtracking only about ¼ mile west from the pinnacles, to gentle slopes just west of the dark veneer of volcanic rocks and soil. Start south down increasingly steep slopes, keeping to the left of a ridge that lies about 500 feet below the summit plateau. Descending a gully immediately east of the ridge, you'll negotiate even steeper slopes, but fortunately the grus underfoot cushions the descent.

About a mile from and 1200 feet below the summit area, you reach a snowmelt creeklet, briefly follow it east, and then quickly turn south for a very steep drop. Very early on this descent, get over to the creeklet's east bank. The vegetation is now somewhat dense, and mountain mahogany can be a minor obstacle. After about a 600-foot drop, you'll reach a couple of springs, seasonally painted yellow with monkey flowers. Among aspens and willows, you now start a gradually easing descent southeast, and in a few minutes arrive at a road climbing north toward Summit Meadow. Take it ⅔ mile down to a fork, turn right, and head 1.0 mile back to your trailhead at the roadend.

Recommended Reading and Source Materials

Hiking and Mountaineering

Darvill, Fred T., Jr., M.D. 1985. *Mountaineering Medicine*. Berkeley: Wilderness Press, 68 p.

Graydon, Don, ed. 1992. *Mountaineering: The Freedom of the Hills*. Seattle: The Mountaineers, 447 p.

Schaffer, Jeffrey P., and others. 1989. *The Pacific Crest Trail, Volume 1: California.* Berkeley: Wilderness Press, 475 p.

Winnett, Thomas, with Melanie Findling. 1988. *Back-packing Basics*. Berkeley: Wilderness Press, 133 p.

History

Beck, Warren A., and Ynez D. Haase. 1974. *Historical Atlas of California*. Norman: University of Oklahoma Press, 240 p.

Brewer, William H. 1960. *Up and Down California in 1860–1864*. Berkeley: University of California Press, 583 p.

Browning, Peter. 1986. *Place Names of the Sierra Nevada*. Berkeley: Wilderness Press, 253 p.

Clark, William B. 1970. *Gold Districts of California*. Sacramento: California Division of Mines and Geology Bulletin 193, 186 p.

Long, Ileen P., and others. 1964. *Alpine Heritage; One Hundred Years of History, Recreation and Lore in Alpine County, California, 1864–1964*. South Lake Tahoe: Anchor Printing, 72 p.

Egenhoff, Elisabeth L., ed. 1949. *The Elephant as They Saw It*. Sacramento: California Division of Mines and Geology, 128 p.

Farquhar, Francis P. 1965. *History of the Sierra Nevada*. Berkeley: University of California Press, 262 p.

Jenkins, Olaf P., ed. 1948. *Geologic Guidebook along Highway 49—Sierran Gold Belt*. Sacramento: California Division of Mines and Geology, 164 p.

Reid, Robert L., ed. 1983. *A Treasury of the Sierra Nevada*. Berkeley: Wilderness Press, 363 p.

Geology

Armin, Richard A., and others. 1984. *Geologic Map of the Markleeville 15-Minute Quadrangle, Alpine County, California*. Washington: U.S. Geological Survey Map I-1474.

Bateman, Paul C., and Clyde Wahrhaftig. 1966. "Geology of the Sierra Nevada." In *Geology of Northern California* (Edgar H. Bailey, ed.). Sacramento: California Division of Mines and Geology Bulletin 190, p. 107–72.

Clark, Malcolm M. 1967. *Pleistocene Glaciation of the Drainage of the West Walker River, Sierra Nevada, California* [Ph.D. thesis]. Palo Alto: Stanford University, 130 p.

Clark, William B. 1977. *Mines and Mineral Resources of Alpine County, California*. Sacramento: California Division of Mines and Geology County Report 8, 48 p.

Clark, William B., and Philip A. Lydon. 1962. *Mines and Mineral Resources of Calaveras County, California*. Sacramento: California Division of Mines and Geology County Report 2, 217 p.

Curtis, Garniss H. 1954. "Mode of Origin of Pyroclastic Debris in the Mehrten Formation of the Sierra Nevada." *University of California Publications in Geological Sciences*, v. 29, p. 453–501.

Evernden, Jack F., and Ronald W. Kistler. 1970. *Chronology of Emplacement of Mesozoic Batholithic Complexes in California and Western Nevada*. Washington: U.S. Geological Survey Professional Paper 623, 42 p.

Giusso, James R. 1981. *Preliminary Geologic Map of the Sonora Pass 15 Minute Quadrangle, California*. Washington: U.S. Geological Survey Open-File Report 81-1170.

Huber, N. King. 1983. *Preliminary Geologic Map of the Dardanelles Cone Quadrangle, Central Sierra Nevada, California*. Washington: U.S. Geological Survey Map MF-1436.

John, David A., and others. 1981. *Reconnaissance Geologic Map of the Topaz Lake 15 Minute Quadrangle, California and Nevada*. Washington: U.S. Geological Survey Open-File Report 81-273.

Keith, William J., and others. 1982. *Geologic Map of the Carson-Iceberg and Leavitt Lake Roadless Areas, Central Sierra Nevada, California*. Washington: U.S. Geological Survey Map 1416-A.

Keith, William J., and others. 1983. *Mineral Resource Potential map of the Carson-Iceberg Roadless Areas, Central Sierra Nevada, California*. Washington: U.S. Geological Survey Map 1416-B.

Lindgren, Waldemar. 1911. *The Tertiary Gravels of the Sierra Nevada of California*. Washington: U.S. Geological Survey Professional Paper 73, 226 p.

Ransome, F. Leslie. 1898. *Some Lava Flows of the Western Slope of the Sierra Nevada, California*. Washington: U.S. Geological Survey Bulletin 89, 74 p.

Schaffer, Jeffrey P. 1992. *The Glacial History of the Stanislaus River Drainage, Sierra Nevada, California*. Unpublished Ph.D. research, University of California, Berkeley.

Slemmons, David B. "Cenozoic volcanism of the central Sierra Nevada, California." In *Geology of Northern California* (Edgar H. Bailey, ed.). Sacramento: California Division of Mines and Geology Bulletin 190, p. 199–208.

Wilshire, Howard G. 1957. "Propylitization of Tertiary Volcanic Rocks near Ebbetts Pass, Alpine County, California." *University of California Publications in Geological Sciences*, v. 32, p. 243–72.

Biology

Austin, Oliver L., Jr., and Arthur Singer. 1985. *Families of Birds*. New York: Golden Press, 200 p.

Beedy, Edward C., and Stephen L. Granholm. 1985. *Discovering Sierra Birds*. Yosemite: Yosemite Association, 229 p.

Critchfield, William B. 1971. *Profiles of California Vegetation* (Research Paper PSW-76/1971). Berkeley: Pacific Southwest Forest and Range Experiment Station, Forest Service, U.S. Department of Agriculture, 54 p.

Cutter, Ralph. 1991. *Sierra Trout Guide*. Portland: Frank Amato Publications (also distributed by Wilderness Press), 112 p.

Gaines, David. 1977. *Birds of the Yosemite Sierra*. Oakland: Cal-Syl Press, 153 p.

Grater, Russell K., and Tom A. Blaue. 1978. *Discovering Sierra Mammals*. Yosemite: Yosemite Association, 174 p.

Griffin, James R., and William B. Critchfield. *The Distribution of Forest Trees in California* (Research Paper PSW-82/1972). Berkeley: Pacific Southwest Forest and Range Experiment Station, Forest Service, U.S. Department of Agriculture, 118 p.

Grillos, Steve J., and Rita Whitmore. 1966. *Ferns and Fern Allies of California* (California Natural History Guide 16). Berkeley: University of California Press, 104 p.

Hickman, James C., ed. 1993. *The Jepson Manual: Vascular Plants of California*. Berkeley: University of California Press, 1600 p.

Horn, Elizabeth L., and Kirk Horn. 1976. *Wildflowers 3: The Sierra Nevada*. Beaverton, OR: The Touchstone Press, 128 p.

Keator, Glenn, and Jeanne C. Koelling. 1978. *Pacific Coast Berry Finder*. Berkeley: Nature Study Guild (also distributed by Wilderness Press), 62 p.

Keator, Glenn, Ruth M. Heady and Valerie R. Vinemiller. 1981. *Pacific Coast Fern Finder*. Berkeley: Nature Study Guild (also distributed by Wilderness Press), 62 p.

Keator, Glenn, and Valerie R. Winemiller. 1980. *Sierra Flower Finder*. Berkeley: Nature Study Guild (also distributed by Wilderness Press), 126 p.

Klauber, Laurence M. 1982. *Rattlesnakes, Their Habits, Life Histories, and Influence on Mankind* (abridged edition). Berkeley: University of California Press, 350 p.

Munz, Philip A. 1963. *California Mountain Wildflowers*. Berkeley: University of California Press, 122 p.

Murie, Olas J. 1975. *A Field Guide to Animal Tracks*. Boston: Houghton Mifflin, 375 p.

National Geographic Society. 1983. *Field Guide to the Birds of North America*. Washington: National Geographic Society, 464 p.

Niehaus, Theodore F., and Charles L. Ripper. 1976. *A Field Guide to Pacific States Wildflowers*. Boston: Houghton Mifflin, 432 p.

Peterson, P. Victor, and P. Victor Peterson, Jr. 1975. *Native Trees of the Sierra Nevada* (California Natural History Guide 36). Berkeley: University of California Press, 147 p.

Peterson, Roger Tory. 1990. *A Field Guide to Western Birds*. Boston: Houghton Mifflin, 432 p.

Powell, Jerry A., and Charles L. Hogue. 1979. *California Insects* (California Natural History Guide 44). Berkeley: University of California Press, 388 p.

Ratliff, Raymond D. 1985. *Meadows in the Sierra Nevada of California: state of knowledge* (General Technical Report PSW-84). Berkeley: Pacific Southwest Forest and Range Experiment Station, Forest Service, U.S. Department of Agriculture, 52 p.

Smith, Gladys L. 1973. "A Flora of the Tahoe Basin and Neighboring Areas." *The Wasmann Journal of Biology*, v. 31, no. 1, p. 1–231.

Smith, Gladys L. 1983. "Supplement to A Flora of the Tahoe Basin and Neighboring Areas." *The Wasmann Journal of Biology*, v. 41, no. 1–2, p. 1–46.

Stebbins, Cyril A., and Robert C. Stebbins. 1974. *Birds of Yosemite National Park*. Yosemite: Yosemite Association, 80 p.

Stebbins, Robert C. 1972. *Amphibians and Reptiles of California* (California Natural History Guide 31). Berkeley: University of California Press, 152 p.

Storer, Tracy I., and Robert L. Usinger. 1964. *Sierra Nevada Natural History*. Berkeley: University of California Press, 374 p.

Thomas, John Hunter, and Dennis R. Parnell. 1974. *Native Shrubs of the Sierra Nevada* (California Natural History Guide 34). Berkeley: University of California Press, 127 p.

Verner, Jared, and Allan S. Boss and others. 1980. *California Wildlife and Their Habitats: Western Sierra Nevada* (General Technical Report PSW-37). Berkeley: Pacific Southwest Forest and Range Experiment Station, Forest Service, U.S. Department of Agriculture, 439 p.

Watts, Tom. 1973. *Pacific Coast Tree Finder*. Berkeley: Nature Study Guild (also distributed by Wilderness Press), 62 p.

Weeden, Norman F. 1986. *A Sierra Nevada Flora*. Berkeley: Wilderness Press, 406 p.

Whitney, Stephen. 1979. *A Sierra Club Naturalist's Guide to the Sierra Nevada*. San Francisco: Sierra Club, 526 p.

Index